CHOOSING FREEDOM

GUIDES TO THE GOOD LIFE

Stephen Grimm, series editor

Seeing Clearly: A Buddhist Guide to Life
Nicolas Bommarito

On Being and Becoming: An Existentialist Approach to Life
Jennifer Anna Gosetti-Ferencei

Choosing Freedom: A Kantian Guide to Life
Karen Stohr

CHOOSING FREEDOM

A Kantian Guide to Life

Karen Stohr

OXFORD
UNIVERSITY PRESS

OXFORD
UNIVERSITY PRESS

Oxford University Press is a department of the University of Oxford. It furthers
the University's objective of excellence in research, scholarship, and education
by publishing worldwide. Oxford is a registered trade mark of Oxford University
Press in the UK and certain other countries.

Published in the United States of America by Oxford University Press
198 Madison Avenue, New York, NY 10016, United States of America.

© Oxford University Press 2022

CIP data is on file at the Library of Congress
ISBN 978–0–19–753781–7

DOI: 10.1093/oso/9780197537817.001.0001

1 3 5 7 9 8 6 4 2

Printed by Sheridan Books, Inc., United States of America

*For Julia and Kate, who make me laugh and
give me hope for the future*

TABLE OF CONTENTS

Part II: Moral Assessment

Part III: Vices

Part IV: Life Goals

SERIES EDITOR'S FOREWORD

Several ancient philosophers held that the point of studying ethics was not just to learn about ethics—as one might learn about chemistry, astronomy, or history—but to become a better human being. They also recognized that this was not easy to do. In order for thinking about ethics to make a difference in our lives, our habits and inclinations needed to be educated right alongside our minds. They therefore claimed that what mattered to living well was not just *what* we thought but *how* we thought, and not just how we thought but how we emotionally responded to the world and to other people.

The books in this series highlight some of the transformative ideas that philosophers have had about these topics—about the good life, and the practices and ways of life that help us to pursue it. They tell us what various philosophers and traditions have taken to be most important in life, and what they have taken to be less important. They offer philosophical guidance about how to approach broad questions, such as how to structure our days, how to train our attention, and how to die with dignity. They also offer guidance about how to deal with the sort of everyday questions that are often neglected by scholars, but that make up the texture of our lives, such as how to deal with relationships gone wrong, family disruptions, unexpected success, persistent anxiety, and an environment at risk.

Because the books are written by philosophers, they draw attention to the reasons and arguments that underlie these various claims—the particular visions of the world and of human nature that are at the root of these stances. The claims made in these books can therefore be contested, argued with, and found to be more or less plausible. While some answers will clearly compete with one another, other views will likely appear complementary. Thus a Confucian might well find that a particular practice or insight of, say, Nietzsche's helps to shed light on his or her way of living in the world, and vice versa. On the whole, the idea is that these great philosophers and traditions all have something to teach us about how to be more fully human, and more fully happy.

Above all, the series is dedicated to the idea that philosophy can be more than just an academic discipline—that it can be, as it was for hundreds of years in the ancient world, a way of life. The hope is also that philosophy can enhance the ways of life we already feel pulled toward, and help us to engage with them more authentically and fully.

Stephen R. Grimm
Professor of Philosophy
Fordham University

PREFACE

Presumably you picked up this book because something sparked your interest in Immanuel Kant. Perhaps you studied him in a philosophy class years ago. Perhaps you're in college studying him now. Or perhaps you're a fan of *The Good Place* and are wondering why Chidi gets so excited whenever he talks about Kant. Or maybe you've only vaguely heard of Kant, but you're interested in what he said about how to live well. You may know that he is a philosophical giant of Western history. If you've ever encountered Kant's work, you will be aware that he wrote extremely complicated books about highly abstract topics. In any case, you may be at least a little bit skeptical about whether Kant has anything to teach you about how to live your life.

My aim in this book is to show you that Kant's ethical outlook is as relevant and useful as it was in the eighteenth century. Maybe even more so. Kant's arguments for the value of living in accordance with rational principles have appealed to many people over the past several hundred years. To others, however, Kant's theory has seemed overly abstract and perhaps even cold in its emphasis on rationality rather than emotion. This concern is understandable. It's also based on a mischaracterization of Kant, one that has been sadly common even among philosophers. In this book, I will be seeking to remedy that mischaracterization and introduce you to a different Kant, one you may not have met before.

Kant was a systematic philosopher, arguably the greatest systematic philosopher in Western philosophical history. By calling him a systematic philosopher I mean that he aimed at developing a comprehensive, coherent system of philosophical thought, one that would link together ideas about reality, knowledge, religion, art, politics, and of course, ethics. Whether or not Kant succeeded in this project is a matter of considerable debate, but even his most fervent critics acknowledge that Kant's attempts at systematic philosophy are the work of a genius.

This image of Kant as a genius, toiling quietly but brilliantly away in his little house in Konigsberg, is not wrong. But it also fails to reflect the full picture of the man, both as a philosopher and as a human being. You probably know the expression, "You can't see the forest for the trees." Usually when someone says this, they mean that we should stop focusing on the trees because that will prevent us from seeing the (more important) forest. At the same time, however, focusing entirely on the forest can mean that we miss out on some really interesting trees. The "forests" of Kant's thought are so impressive and so challenging to work through that one could spend a lifetime just trying to make them out. But we should also attend to the "trees" that make up that Kantian forest, particularly when it comes to his ethics.

The chapters in this book reflect a wide variety of concrete, practical ethical concerns. Kant had something to say about every single one of them. This often surprises people because it can be hard to believe that this philosophical giant would have bothered to write about dinner parties and gossip. But he did. He actually took such matters quite seriously, and what he has to say about them is fascinating. Kant's remarks on specific ethical topics, like lying, gratitude, sympathy, and friendship, are worth reading in their own right for the insights they contain. They also shed some light on his larger ethical theory. It turns out that the dense, abstract forest of Kant's moral system becomes clearer when we stop to look at some of the individual trees.

This book will begin with a trip to Kant's forest, by which I mean his systematic ethical theory. There's no real way to understand Kant without it. I will, however, keep our sojourn to the forest relatively short so that we have time to examine the trees. After many years of studying and teaching Kant's ethics, I've come to think that his highly formal ethical framework makes the most sense when you can also see how he meant it to work in practice. Kant did not regard ethics as a philosophical parlor game. His theory is supposed to help us figure out how to live our lives and become better people.

I suspect that the reason Kant is so often misunderstood is that people standardly learn about him through his most famous book on ethics, the *Groundwork for the Metaphysics of Morals*. In the *Groundwork* (as we will call it for short), Kant deliberately abstracts away from the actual conditions of human life, focusing entirely on our rational natures. He does this so that we can fully appreciate the basis of morality in rationality itself. Unfortunately, many people treat the *Groundwork* as if it represents all that Kant had to say about ethics. This could not be further from the truth.

In fact, twelve years after the *Groundwork*, Kant published another major book on ethics, *The Metaphysics of Morals*. Based on the titles alone, we might guess that he saw the *Groundwork* as laying the foundations for his later work. The *Metaphysics of Morals* is intended to show us what Kant's ethical framework looks like when it is applied to actual human beings. Unlike the *Groundwork*, the *Metaphysics of Morals* incorporates Kant's ideas about human nature. He identifies vices to which we tend to fall victim and tells us how we should cultivate the virtue necessary to fight those vices. He lays out specific duties that we owe to ourselves and to other people. He talks about friendship and social life, and he emphasizes the fact that we live in communities with other people. In the *Metaphysics of Morals*, we see hints of Kant's personal struggles and failings, as well as his sensitivity to nuance and social context.

You won't see this Kant if you read only the *Groundwork*. But this Kant shows up in lots of places, not just the *Metaphysics of Morals*. He shows up in the *Lectures on Ethics* (compilations of lecture notes taken by his students, but standardly taken to be accurate representations of his ideas). He also shows up in the *Anthropology from a Pragmatic Point of View* and the *Religion within the Limits of Reason Alone*. Because my aim is to introduce you to the wider picture of Kant's ethical thought, you'll find these and other, less familiar works mentioned throughout this book.

One especially interesting thing about Kant is that while he has a fairly pessimistic view about human nature, he is also deeply optimistic about our moral possibilities. In so many ways, humanity is a hot mess. As individuals, we are prone to all kinds of moral flaws and failings, compounded by our propensities toward rationalization and self-deception. Our political and social communities are often ugly, divisive, and violent. Kant acknowledged all of this. Crucially, though, he also believed we are capable of a great deal more. It is within our power, as individuals and as communities, to choose a better way of life. That better way is a life in which we are guided by reason. True to his Enlightenment roots, Kant had great hope in the power of reason to move us forward into a brighter future, one that represents freedom and progress. This is a message that still has profound appeal in the contemporary world.

Kant did not set out to write a moral handbook or become an ethical guru. Even if he had, it's not clear that he would have been a good one. He was not especially adept at giving moral advice and sometimes failed miserably. Kant also held some deeply objectionable views, particularly concerning gender and race. Indeed, despite the fact that his own theory provides a straightforward and powerful argument against slavery, Kant himself did not appear to see the moral problem with it until toward the end of his life. Suffice to say that Kant's theoretical brilliance surpassed his personal ethical capacities.

I mention all this because I want to emphasize that the goal of this book is not to help you become more like Kant. It is not even to help you adopt a "What would Kant say?" approach to leading your life. (As you'll learn in Chapter 11, Kant himself would have disapproved of this method of self-improvement.) Rather, the goal here is to use Kant's insights to illuminate dimensions of our moral life that can otherwise be difficult to see. This is not a guide for living by Kant's standards. It is a Kantian guide for living by your own.

A Kantian way of life is both realistic about human nature and hopeful about our capacities and possibilities. It offers us freedom, even as it requires us to exercise constraints on our behaviors, inclinations, and desires. It demands that we see ourselves and others as profoundly and equally valuable, and to organize our individual relationships and our moral and political communities around that fact. A Kantian way of life is a challenging one, perhaps now more than ever. And yet Kant believed that it represents our best hope for the future, both for us as individuals and for humanity as a whole. If you are feeling gloomy about the state of the world and are looking for ray of optimism, Kant may just well be the philosopher you need.

ACKNOWLEDGMENTS

Kant calls gratitude a sacred duty. That adds to the pressure of writing acknowledgments, especially because the list of people from whom I have learned important things about Kant is very long. I have been fortunate enough to participate in some wonderful workshops and conferences that have deepened my knowledge of Kant and shaped my ideas. I am indebted to fellow participants and audience members at those conferences, as well as the audiences at lectures that I've given over the years. This is a partial list of the people to whom I owe gratitude for helping me work through various themes in this book: Anne Margaret Baxley, Macalester Bell, Cheshire Calhoun, Erin Cline, Brad Cokelet, David Cummiskey, Adam Cureton, Richard Dean, Kyla Ebels-Duggan, Jon Garthoff, Rafeeq Hasan, Sarah Holtman, Tom Hill, Violetta Igneski, Jennifer Lockhart, Huaping Lu-Adler, Michelle Mason, Todd May, Corinna Mieth, Amy Olberding, Terry Pinkard, Karen Rice, Ryan Preston-Roedder, Carol Rovane, Nanette Ryan, Paul Schofield, Oliver Sensen, Cindy Stark, Charles Starkey, Martin Sticker, Krista Thomason, Helga Varden, Alice Pinheiro Walla, Garrath Williams, and Ariel Zylberman.

I am especially grateful to Krista and Huaping for their comments on draft chapters of this book, and to Helga and Kyla for their comments on the proposal (and in Kyla's case, the whole darned manuscript!) as reviewers for Oxford University Press. All four of them take seriously Kant's belief that one should correct mistakes without demolishing the self-respect of the one making the mistakes. This book is much better for their assistance. Needless to say, the remaining errors are all my own. I am also permanently in the debt of Tom Hill for instilling in me both a sound appreciation for Kant and the tools with which to study him. My gratitude for his mentorship, his wisdom, and his friendship runs very deep indeed.

I have truly wonderful colleagues at Georgetown. In so many ways, my department resembles a Kantian kingdom of ends. Every academic should be so lucky. I am also grateful for my university's financial and moral support for my research. The Ryan Family chair, which I am fortunate to hold, has made a crucial difference in this book getting finished more or less on time during a pandemic. I am particularly grateful to my graduate research assistant, Emma Nagler. Emma's nuanced appreciation of Kant and helpful philosophical insights improved this book in many ways, as did her sharp eye for small details.

My students here at Georgetown have served as my real and imaginary audience for this book. Years of teaching introductory ethics to undergraduates has encouraged me to think creatively about how to make Kant engaging and relevant to their lives. Graduate students have pushed me to deepen my understanding of the text and defend my interpretations. I could not have written this book without first having tried to teach it over and over. So, students, thank you for sitting through many first drafts. Your questions, puzzles, and challenges have improved every inch of text in this book.

Few things are as important to writing as a good editorial team. I have now been lucky enough to collaborate with Lucy Randall and Hannah Doyle on multiple projects, and I know how much my work benefits from their own. I am grateful for everything they do behind the scenes. It has been especially fun for me to work with Stephen Grimm on this book and on the Guides to the Good Life series as a whole. It would not have occurred to me to write this book if he had not suggested it. I'm indebted to him both for the opportunity and for many helpful comments, suggestions, and insights along the way.

Writing books is hard on authors, but it is probably even harder on their families. I am beyond grateful to my husband, Bob Nonnenkamp, for his untiring support, both emotional and practical. Whether it's driving kids around, keeping a couple of energetic dogs occupied, serving as instant technical support, or making dinner magically appear, he has it under cheerful control. His endless patience is both a marvel and mystery to me. I am so very lucky to have been married to him for twenty-four years and counting.

This book is dedicated to my daughters, Julia and Kate Nonnenkamp. Over the years they have perfected the skill of appearing interested while their mother goes off on some long tangent about Kant. In spite of the many unbidden philosophy lectures they have endured at dinner or in the car, they bring fresh perspective, Gen Z humor, Spotify playlists, technical expertise, and delicious baked goods into my life. Girls, the two of you light up my world. I love you more than I know how to say.

Part 1

Kantian Basics

GETTING TO KNOW KANT

If you're looking for a model for how to live your life, the eighteenth-century Prussian philosopher Immanuel Kant may not seem like an obvious choice. He lived his entire seventy-nine years quietly and uneventfully in the university town of Konigsberg. The son of a harness maker, Kant worked his way up to the intellectual heights of a professorship. His days were spent reading, giving lectures, engaging in (mostly) friendly philosophical discussions, and writing what is often nearly impenetrable prose. And yet this seemingly ordinary man shook up the Western philosophical world in ways that few others have managed to do. With exceptional intelligence and creativity, Kant built a strikingly original philosophical system. Central to that system is his understanding of what it means to live a morally good life.

For Kant, a morally good life is a life lived according to reason. On his view, such a life is difficult to achieve, but it is a profoundly worthwhile undertaking. To live according to reason is, for Kant, to live in accordance with our fundamental natures as free, rational beings. Kant's emphasis on rationality is both essential to his theory and distinctive of it. Other moral theorists writing at the time believed that morality had its source in our feelings, or in what was often thought of as our innate moral sense. Kant is skeptical that our natural feelings, emotions, and intuitions could ever serve as a firm enough foundation for morality. His own theory reflects both that skepticism and his confidence that reason should be our ultimate guide when we're seeking to lead a good life.

Although Kant has tremendous faith in human rationality, he is not under the illusion that our rational powers are limitless. Reason, however powerful it might be, cannot tell us everything we might want or need to know. For instance, Kant does not believe that we can know whether we have free will, or whether there's a God. (He does, however, argue that we can rationally act as though we have free will, and that we can have rational hope in God's existence. More on that later.) He also realizes that human beings do not always do what reason directs us to do. We waste hours on social media, we eat more sugar than is good for us, we buy things we can't afford, we get irritated at inanimate objects. We do all kinds of irrational things on a regular basis.

And yet, we're capable of something more. Often, it's perfectly obvious to me that I'm spending too much time on Instagram or eating too much sugar. I *know* that what I'm doing is bad for me, and that a more rational, self-controlled version of myself would be settling down to work with a bowl of edamame, not scrolling through Instagram eating Cap'n Crunch. It's true that I'm not being that more disciplined person right now, but for Kant, the key point is that it's in my power to be that person. We are always able to do what our reason tells us to do, even when we're choosing to ignore its voice.

It's crucial to Kant's theory that the voice of morality comes from within us, and not from outside forces, like society or religion. Kant is not interested in preaching to people about morality.

He does not see morality as a matter of coming up with a bunch of rules, and his ethical works are not reference books for looking up answers to moral dilemmas. In fact, Kant is adamant that we do not need outside guides that will tell us how to live. (He might even have been skeptical about your decision to buy this book.) Not only are we each capable of understanding morality for ourselves but basing our moral decisions on someone else's set of rules would be a major mistake. Morality is something we have to determine for ourselves, much as Dorothy in the Wizard of Oz had to figure out for herself how to get home to Kansas.

Now this does *not* mean that Kant is a moral relativist, or someone who thinks that there is nothing more to morality than each person's opinion. He is actually about as far from a moral relativist as you can get. Not only does he believe in moral truths, but he believes that moral principles are principles of rationality, and that they are objective, universal, and unchanging. On Kant's view, denying that killing innocent people is wrong is not all that different from denying that $2+2 = 4$.[1] If someone were to insist that $2+2 = 5$, we'd regard them as irrational and perhaps in need of some medical help. As we'll see, Kant holds that all rational beings, thinking rationally, will converge on the same fundamental moral principle. That principle serves as the basis for all of morality. This is an ambitious position to take, and possibly a surprising one, given that it flies in the face of our ordinary experience. People have very deep moral disagreements on a variety of topics, and it doesn't seem that we can easily settle them by way of appealing to a single moral principle.

Kant recognizes that working out moral disagreements is much more challenging than working out disagreements about obvious mathematical claims like $2+2 = 4$. Of course, most mathematical claims aren't that obvious, but that doesn't mean the rest of math is just a matter of opinion. Math is based in reason, although the rationality of a given theorem may not be evident to the untrained eye. For Kant, morality is also based in reason. We don't need to spend years in school to understand it, but we do have to be willing to stop and engage in rational reflection about what morality is and what it requires of us. If we do, then we can use reason to figure out how to be a good person, just as we can use it to calculate the area of a triangle.

So, a good life in Kantian terms will be a life lived in accordance with rational moral principles. There's a catch, though. To say that a reason-driven life is a good life doesn't necessarily mean that it will be a happy life in the usual sense. As we all know, some deeply immoral people seem to do pretty well for themselves, particularly if they can avoid getting caught. Kant is not suggesting that being a good person will get you everything that you want. He does, however, think that being a good person will make you *deserving* of happiness. That may not seem very satisfying to anyone hoping that moral virtue might come with material rewards. Shouldn't being a good person also get you a good life?

It would certainly be nice if virtue always paid off in terms of helping us achieve our life goals. Kant is just skeptical that this actually happens. We can see from our own experience that being a good person sometimes means you have to sacrifice things you want, and that bad people sometimes get away with murder—literally and figuratively. As far as Kant is concerned, the only one in a position to fix this mess is God, which is why we have reason to hope that God exists. On our own, we have no way of ensuring that virtue is rewarded with happiness. The best we can do is to try to make ourselves worthy of whatever happiness might come our way.

As Kant sees things, guiding your life according to rational moral principles isn't going to make you rich or famous. But there are other kinds of reasons why we might want to try out a Kantian way of life and why we might find it worthwhile. When we act on rational moral principles, we are *choosing* how to live. We are not simply allowing ourselves to be dragged around by things like Instagram's algorithms. Kant sees tremendous value in living according to principles that we have chosen, rather than just going along with what other people are doing or permitting ourselves to be ruled by outside forces. Now you may be thinking, "Well, don't we sometimes choose bad principles for ourselves?" That is certainly true, and we'll be returning to this issue later. The key point here is that if my life is going to go well in Kantian terms, I have to be behind the wheel, directing my own actions and choices and taking ownership of them. And I will chart a smoother course for myself if I use my reason as my GPS.

This emphasis on the importance of rationality and individual freedom is one of the hallmarks of the Enlightenment, the name given to the intellectual period in seventeenth- and eighteenth-century Europe during which Kant lived and wrote. Indeed, Kant is one of the central philosophical figures of the Enlightenment, and his work has had a profound impact (both positive and negative) on the course of European and American history. This is quite a legacy for the son of a harness maker in a small Prussian town. To see how Kant's ideas took shape, let's take a brief look at his own story. No one writes in a vacuum, not even a brilliant philosopher like Kant. If we're going to understand him, we must know something about the place and time in which he lived, and the forces and ideas that shaped his philosophical outlook.

***

Kant was born on April 22, 1724, into what we probably would now describe as a working-class family. His parents and grandparents were tradespeople, not scholars, and likely never expected a world-famous philosopher to emerge from their ranks. But they believed in education and Kant benefited from their efforts to ensure that he had access to a good one. As members of a guild, his parents were never truly poor. They did, however, face financial struggles. Kant's mother died when he was thirteen, and his father when he was twenty-two, leaving behind Kant and four siblings. As the oldest son, Kant took on great deal of responsibility for helping support his brother and sisters. He also received help from others, most notably an uncle who contributed financially to his education. As we'll see in later chapters, Kant has some subtle points to make about the moral complexities of beneficence and gratitude. He may well have been speaking from his own experiences as someone who was both a giver of charitable aid and a recipient of it.

Kant was devoted to his parents, especially his mother, and he clearly had tremendous respect for their commitment to hard work and their principled moral behavior. He saw his parents as having lived honorably and done their very best for their children, despite the hardships they faced. No doubt Kant's parents were very much in his mind as he developed his view of morality, particularly his conviction that each of us has it within us to be a good person. He believed strongly that no one needs a fancy education to know what's right. His own parents, with their limited opportunity for formal schooling, served as his proof. Good moral principles are available to anyone who cares enough to think through what morality requires from us.

Kant's upbringing was also profoundly influenced by the religious atmosphere in which it took place. His parents were devout adherents of Pietism, a movement within Lutheranism that focused on personal faith and a lived commitment to Christian principles. Kant spent a large part of his youth in a very strict Pietist school. Although Kant fully appreciated the positive effects that religious devotion can have on a person's moral character, he was also keenly aware of its darker, more pernicious elements. Kant did not care for the methods of religious education he experienced at school, believing them to be at odds with the essential task of cultivating individual rationality. Eventually, he largely rejected the Pietist tenets of his youth, but the existence and nature of his own religious commitments are not easy to sort out. No one would describe Kant as a religious man, and yet it isn't quite right to regard him as an atheist or agnostic either. Let's just say that his relationship with religion is complicated. In that sense, he fits right in with many of us in the twenty-first century.

After he finished school, Kant earned his keep mostly through tutoring and giving lectures at the university, for which he was paid on a by-the-student basis. Because he most definitely didn't have a trust fund, it was lucky for Kant that he proved to be an immensely popular lecturer. On top of his other duties, he lectured up to twenty-two hours a week on a range of different subjects.

Although he probably found the schedule exhausting, he was never short on students, who lined up early just to get a seat in his classroom. Despite his growing philosophical reputation, it wasn't until 1770 that he received a full professorship in philosophy at the university where he had spent his entire academic life. From then on, Kant was able to lead a relatively comfortable life, one that enabled him to produce his most famous works.

Kant is often portrayed as a bit of a curmudgeon, particularly for his habit of keeping to an extremely strict schedule. This isn't false, but it's a more accurate representation of the older man, worried about his health and rather set in his ways. The younger Kant was a sought-after dinner guest and companion, known for his conversational skill and his facility with a wide range of subjects. He never married and discussions of his romantic life do not rise much above the level of rumor. He did, however, have many friends and admirers, and he certainly had the respect of his colleagues and students. Kant didn't shy away from conflict or controversy, but he understood the importance of being a good citizen of his university and his city. He was also a dutiful brother and uncle, continuing to provide financial support to his sisters and their families throughout his life. And by the time he died in 1804, at the age of seventy-nine, he had solidified his place as one of the greatest intellects that Western Europe had ever produced.

Of course, Kant was far from perfect. He could be rather caustic in his criticisms of other scholars, and occasionally behaved unpardonably toward people who deserved better from him. (Here's one example: Kant conducted a philosophical correspondence with an intelligent and perceptive young woman named Maria von Herbert, who wrote to ask his advice on whether she needed to reveal her past relationships to her current suitor. Although Kant started out the correspondence well enough, he seems to have been unable to cope with her pointed challenges to his philosophical worldview. Eventually, he stopped responding to her and instead started using her letters as a warning to other young women about the moral dangers of romantic entanglements.) Kant did appear to hold a number of women in relatively high regard and he generally saw women as rational beings. He did not, however, use his considerable skill and influence to improve their situation or argue for women's political rights. Although it's possible to derive plenty of feminist conclusions from Kant's ethical theory, Kant himself failed to see them and indeed, said quite a few things that conflict with them.

Perhaps even more troubling are Kant's repugnant views about race, views that unfortunately outlived him by many decades. Here especially, Kant's own methods failed him. When it came to understanding people of different races, he relied too heavily on bad sources and engaged in lousy reasoning. The moral theory he developed so carefully over the years clearly points to the wrongness of slavery, and yet Kant himself condoned it until the very end of his life. By his own lights, he should have been open-minded and optimistic about the rational capacities of people of other races, and he should also have seen their oppression and enslavement as a violation of their most basic dignity. Unfortunately, he did not. That a person as smart as Kant was subject to such a profound moral error tells us something about the power of racism and the difficulty of disentangling ourselves from convenient and self-serving world views. As I hope we'll see, Kant's work can help us avoid making at least some of the mistakes that Kant himself made.

For a man who led a fairly ordinary life, Kant managed to have an extraordinary influence on Western philosophy. His analytical prowess, combined with his (usually!) insightful observations of human nature and social life, make him a figure of nearly unparalleled importance in the history of ethics. But Kant's importance is not merely historical. The ethical insights of this eighteenth-century Prussian philosophy professor remain useful for us today. Although it has been more than two hundred years since his death, Immanuel Kant still has something to teach us about how to live.

2 | FREEDOM

To understand Kant's ethical project, it's important to know at least a little bit about how he thought about human beings and our capacities. In this chapter, we're going to take a quick tour of Kant's ideas about human nature, rationality, and the possibility of freedom. Unfortunately, Kant's views on these topics are really complicated and we will be just scratching the surface of some of his most important big ideas. If you find yourself intrigued by what you learn about Kant in this chapter and want to dig deeper, you'll find recommendations for further reading at the end of the book.

Here is the very short version of how Kant sees us: as flawed, vulnerable beings, beset by various natural and social impulses and desires, who are nevertheless free to choose the principles on which we act. There's a lot to unpack there, and in many ways, this entire book is an attempt to explain what that very short description means. We'll start with the big picture and then work our way into the details. In this chapter, we'll focus on the ways in which we are free to choose our principles of action. In the next chapter, we'll focus on ways in which our natural human traits and tendencies affect that freedom. That will set the stage for introducing Kant's moral theory.

Kant is often perceived as a philosopher with his head entirely in the clouds. Much of his best-known work is highly abstract, barely touching on what most people would think of as practical ethical concerns. But it would be a mistake to think that Kant isn't interested in the details of how ordinary human beings should live. In fact, he wrote quite a lot about our everyday ethical experiences. For whatever reason, this side of Kant tends not to get much airtime in philosophy courses and textbooks. It's a shame, not only because Kant's lesser-known works are interesting in their own right, but also because reading them helps us make sense of the abstract ethical ideas and concepts that show up in his more formal writings. In this book, we'll be moving back and forth between Kant's formal ethical theory and the ways in which he saw that theory operating in practice.

In various works, Kant argues for something that is often referred to as a "two standpoint" theory about human beings. In Kant's technical language, the two standpoints are called the noumenal and phenomenal. Very broadly, we might say that the standpoint of the phenomenal is the world as it appears to us and the standpoint of the noumenal is the world as it is in itself. Kant thinks that we are limited in our ability to access the noumenal standpoint. There are many things that we simply cannot know for certain. One of the things we cannot know with any certainty is whether we are free. This might seem to pose a rather large problem for anyone trying to develop an ethical system. Doesn't the very idea of morality presuppose that we are free to make choices and that we can be held responsible for those choices?

Kant has a pretty creative solution to this problem, although it has generated a lot of controversy among philosophers. In a nutshell, his solution is to argue while we can't know that we are free, it is rational for us to act as though we are. That's because when we are deliberating about what to do and acting on those deliberations, we have to think of ourselves as being free. To make this a bit clearer, I'll use an example drawn from an influential contemporary Kantian ethicist, Christine Korsgaard.

Imagine that you are watching someone sitting in a chair, wondering whether he will get up. You are observing him and trying to predict his behavior. (Maybe you'll get it right and maybe you won't.) You can make your prediction without presupposing anything about whether he is making that choice freely. All you have to do is watch him. But now suppose that you are the one sitting in the chair and you are wondering whether you will get up. You can't really take that same "observer" stance toward yourself. This is because you're going to have to *decide* whether to get up. As Korsgaard puts it, you can't just sit there watching yourself, waiting to see what you will do. If you remain in the chair, that will mean that you have chosen to stay there. If you get up, you will also have chosen that. This perspective is what we might call a deliberative perspective, a perspective from which we regard ourselves as free to get up or free to stay in the chair. Kant's view is that we cannot help but take up this kind of deliberative perspective when making decisions about how to act. We have to see ourselves as capable of choosing to do one thing rather than another.

When we are deciding what to do, we are generally considering what reasons we have for choosing one option or another. We have the ability to ask ourselves, "Should I stay in this chair, or should I get up?" and to answer that question by way of assessing what reasons we have for doing either thing. Maybe a bomb will go off if I get up; if so, that's an excellent reason to stay seated. Or perhaps by standing up I'll be able to intimidate you into doing what I want. That's not such a great reason to stand up, but it can still serve as a reason from the deliberative perspective.

Kant thinks that I have to understand myself as free to choose courses of action. I must take up the deliberative perspective when I act, and from within that perspective, I cannot see myself as being subject to causal forces beyond my control. Kant describes this as freedom in a negative sense. It is essentially a rejection of determinism for practical purposes. We cannot know that determinism is false, that we have freedom of the will, but the deliberative perspective requires that we take that freedom for granted. To say that I have negative freedom is simply to say my actions are not determined.

But there's another sense in which, for Kant, we are free. This is the freedom that we exercise when we make choices in accordance with rational principles. Kant calls this positive freedom, and he thinks that we must also understand ourselves as being free in this positive sense. To have positive freedom is to be capable of acting for specifically moral reasons. I can choose between watching from my chair as someone drowns or getting out of the chair and saving them. Moreover, I can choose to save the person for the reason that it's the right thing to do. This, for Kant, is what positive freedom looks like when it's fully effective. It is the exercise of a choice to act for certain reasons rather than others. More specifically, it is the exercise of a choice to guide my life by rational moral principles instead of allowing my impulses and desires to boss me around.

Now the fact that I am capable of guiding my life by rational moral principles doesn't mean that I *will* actually guide my life that way. We can put it this way: while I'm always free, I don't always act like it. Human beings are not purely rational; we are also embodied. This means that we find ourselves pulled in two quite different directions. As embodied beings, we have desires, inclinations, and drives, all of which can exert a powerful pull over us. We find ourselves wanting to do things like eat vending machine Doritos for lunch, rather than the quinoa salad we packed ahead of time. As rational beings, however, we know it would be better for us to choose the quinoa salad. Alas, this means that we can expect to spend a lot of our lives in conflict with ourselves. Living a good Kantian life is about resolving this conflict in ways that enact our freedom in the positive sense.

In his most famous work, the *Republic*, Plato argues that a life of justice is the best life, on the grounds that the just person has a kind of harmony in their soul. Plato pictures the soul as having three parts—reason, appetites, and spirit. Justice consists in reason ruling the appetites with the help of spirit. In the just person, the appetites are not simply overpowered. Rather, the just person transforms their appetites through the use of reason. This is how the soul becomes harmonized. If you manage to achieve this harmony, you won't be constantly fighting with yourself to turn off Netflix when you have a project due in a few hours. You'll have become the kind of person who doesn't even think to turn on Netflix when a project is due.

This may sound hopelessly idealistic, but Plato was nothing if not an idealist. Kant is also an idealist in many ways. He did, however, seem to have more doubts about whether we can ever achieve the kind of harmony that Plato describes. The Doritos are just too tasty; the Netflix shows just too enticing. Still, the ideal represented in Plato's just soul, an ideal in which we control ourselves through reason, is very much Kant's ideal as well. It is in choosing to guide myself by reason, rather than letting my desires and inclinations push me around, that I act freely.

When we consider the alternative, the life in which our desires and inclinations are in charge, it becomes clearer why the rational life is the better, freer life. Plato describes the person ruled by their appetites as a kind of slave to themselves. If you think about someone experiencing a powerful addiction to opioids, it makes some sense to think of them as enslaved by their desire for the drug. You can't be free if you are unable to extricate yourself from your desires and appetites. Plato takes this a step further, arguing that the worst possible situation is to be enslaved by your appetites *and* have the power to fulfill those appetites because you can then keep digging yourself into a progressively deeper hole. This is how he gets to his rather surprising conclusion that the worst possible life is the life of a tyrant. The tyrant appears to control everything, but in fact, he controls nothing, not even himself.

Kant's approach to freedom is different than Plato's in many respects, but there are some key similarities. Like Plato, Kant thinks that the life in which we allow our desires and inclinations to direct our actions is a less good life than one in which reason is in charge. In Kantian terms, the value of living rationally is often expressed in terms of the value of autonomy, which we can think of as a form of self-rule. To be autonomous is to be a lawgiver for yourself. It is to make your own rules and live by those rules. But not just any rules will do.

Sometimes people think of freedom as akin to a kind of license. It's the freedom to do whatever you want with no outside interference. (This is the way in which people often talk about freedom in the United States.) It's just about making your own rules. If freedom is nothing more than license, then it is compatible with making it your rule to spend your entire life sitting on the couch eating Doritos and firing off disparaging tweets about people you don't like. But this isn't the kind of freedom that Kant has in mind. For Kant, we are free when the rules we choose for ourselves are rational ones. If I act on my desire to eat Doritos and send off angry tweets all day, I am making a choice. I am not being forced into it by something outside myself, like a repressive government or manipulative family members. Nevertheless, what I am choosing is something that Kant would undoubtedly say will not withstand the test of rationality. I'm choosing a principle for myself and, in that sense, I am acting freely. But I am choosing a bad principle, one that will not in fact stand up to rational scrutiny. In later chapters, we'll see why Kant would say that a principle like "sit around all day eating Doritos and tweeting angry thoughts" can't survive rational scrutiny. For now, let's just note something important. A life in which I do exactly as I please could still be a life in which I am not really free, one in which I am not fully exercising my capacity for autonomy. True freedom often requires self-constraint.

Remember that project I'm avoiding by watching Netflix? If the project is something that I decided I would do, then there's a sense in which I'm getting in the way of myself. It's my own goal to complete the project, but I'm also the one preventing myself from completing it. There's something irrational about this, and indeed, we're frequently aware of this at the time. How often have you said to yourself that you should really stop doing something and finish off your work, make dinner, get some exercise, or go to bed? When it comes to fulfilling our goals, we are sometimes our own worst enemy. Exercising autonomy, for Kant, means getting a grip on ourselves in a way that enables us to overcome the obstacles we throw in our own paths. It is only when we can manage this kind of self-constraint that we are capable of being free in the sense of being fully autonomous.

In the way that we've been talking about Kantian freedom, it isn't a value that we pursue or a good we try to get more of. It is a capacity that we exercise, and we can do a better or worse job of exercising it. Kantian freedom isn't a means to an end; it's a way of living in which we guide ourselves in accordance with rationally defensible principles. But what does it mean to guide myself by reason? Is it just about getting myself off the couch when I have work to do? For Kant, that's part of the story, but certainly not the whole of it. Reason is far more than a self-help tool. As we'll see in upcoming chapters, Kant has ambitious ideas about our capacity to use reason and exercise freedom in the positive sense. The idea that each of us is an autonomous being, capable of living by rational principles, is the foundation of his entire moral system. But before we turn to that moral system, we should dig more deeply into the various things that stand in the way of our freedom. Although reason *can* guide us down the right path, there's no guarantee that it will. In fact, it's going to turn out that living freely involves a whole lot of work.

3 | HUMAN NATURE

Have you ever looked an advertisement or scrolled through Pinterest and seen pictures of a beautifully organized closet? Have you then opened the doors to your own closet and felt a wave of despair wash over you, as you realize that you will never ever achieve that level of organizational perfection? If so, you have a pretty good idea of how Kant thought about humanity. We have such potential and yet, we're also such a mess. In this chapter, we'll take a look at the many ways in which human beings are basically a disaster. Kant will have plenty of advice about cleaning ourselves up, but we'll get to that later.

In an essay with the (not very catchy) title, *Idea for a Universal History with a Cosmopolitan Aim*, Kant remarks that "out of such crooked wood as the human being is made, nothing entirely straight can be fabricated."[1] He may have been feeling especially pessimistic on the day he wrote that, but it reflects his view that we human beings have a lot of hurdles to overcome in our quest to live more rationally. The hurdles are both internal and external. Some of them come from our internal drives and inclinations and others come from our external surroundings, especially our relationships with other people. Let's take a closer look at some of those obstacles so as to better understand the crooked wood we're endeavoring to make straight.

We'll begin with the biggest obstacle, which is ourselves. We are our own worst enemy when it comes to living rationally. Not only are we a confused muddle of emotions, passions, desires, and inclinations, but we're also prone to misusing our reason in ways that make things worse. It's not just that I have the inclination to sit around binge-watching Netflix when I'm supposed to be working. It's also that I'm really good at rationalizing what I'm doing. ("It's been a tough week!" "The project won't take that long!" "I work better in the middle of the night anyway!") This is going to prove to be a pretty difficult combination of forces to overcome. In later chapters, we'll talk about Kant's strategies for helping us circumvent our tendency to rationalize our actions. But first, let's see what's going on with us when we're sitting on that comfy couch contemplating our options.

Kant's remarks on human nature are scattered over many works, and those works were written over many years. This makes it rather hard to pin down anything like a single, unified theory of human nature. In the *Critique of Practical Reason*, Kant draws a distinction that will prove helpful for us in sorting through the internal obstacles in our path to becoming better. That is a distinction between what Kant calls self-love and self-conceit. Kant describes self-love as "benevolence toward oneself" and self-conceit as "satisfaction with oneself."[2] There are scholarly questions about whether self-conceit is simply another form of self-love, but we'll set those aside and treat them as posing separate threats to morality.

Self-love, as Kant understands it, is primarily directed at my self-interest. What's in my self-interest has to do with my basic human needs for things like food and shelter and what I need to accomplish my goals. If my laptop conks out while I'm writing this book, then self-love will direct me to get a new laptop. If I get hungry while grading papers, then self-love will direct me to go to the kitchen and get a snack. Unsurprisingly, Kant thinks that self-love can get out of control sometimes. Most of us, most of the time, have a natural tendency to put our own needs first. This can lead us to overlook other important considerations, like the needs of other people. It can also lead to a kind of practical irrationality about my own goals, such as if I buy a new laptop with the money that I need to pay this month's electric bill. The requirements of morality, Kant says, "infringe" on self-love. Morality doesn't tell me not to get a new laptop or grab a snack, but it does put some constraints on when, whether, and how I pursue those goals. I should not buy a laptop with money I don't have. I should not eat the snack my daughter was planning to take to school. Self-love needs some boundaries, and morality is what sets them.

But self-conceit is a different story. Morality doesn't just set some limits for self-conceit. It has to "strike it down altogether."[3] Why? It's because self-conceit, unlike self-love, arises from an inclination that is at entirely at odds with morality—the desire to raise ourselves above other people, whether in our own eyes or the eyes of society. As we'll see, Kant's moral system is grounded on the idea that all rational beings are equals. When it comes to pursuing our own needs and interests, we have to be mindful of the fact that other people have equally important needs and interests. If I'm hungry, I can go get a snack, but I can't eat *all* the snacks if there are other hungry people around. Still, so long as there are enough snacks, we can all get what we want. This isn't true about my desire to be better than other people. If I succeed, others will have to fail. It's a zero-sum game by its very definition. And that's the problem with self-conceit. It undermines something Kant takes to be at the heart of morality, which is our fundamental equality with other rational beings.

Kant's wariness about self-conceit doesn't mean that he's opposed to competition or ambition. He was pretty ambitious himself when it came to his own career. Self-conceit is not about wanting to excel on an exam or win a marathon. It's a deeper and more sinister desire, one that leads us to want to be perceived as superior to others and to treat others as our inferiors. It encourages us to (falsely) think of ourselves as having authority over other rational beings. Self-conceit is what's driving the person who barges up to the front of a long line and insists that their problem be resolved first, just because of who they are. It's also behind the secret pleasure we often take in seeing bad things happen to people we don't like. Whether it's expressing the idea that we're amazing or that others are pathetic, self-conceit is a major obstacle to the moral life. And that's why it needs to be struck down, not merely contained.

We're going to encounter self-love and self-conceit frequently in this book. They show up in lots of places in Kant's ethical writings. As we'll see, self-conceit is a particular problem in our social relationships. Kant suggests that we're in a bit of a bind when it comes to social life. On the one hand, we have a deep need to be in society and to interact with other people. On the other hand, those other people tend to get on our nerves. Kant rather aptly describes our situation as one of "unsocial sociability."[4] In some sense, we are social creatures with a deep antisocial streak. This is part of our nature and so not entirely our fault, but it's something we need to fix as best we can. We fix it by doing our best to get rid of those antisocial tendencies in ourselves and working to create better forms of social community.

Lots of things contribute to making it difficult for us to live in society with other people, including our feelings and emotions. Kant distinguishes between the kinds of feelings that come upon us, sometimes in an overpowering way, and the feelings and inclinations that are more settled parts of our character. The feelings in the first category are what he calls affects, and they include things like anger, fear, grief, and shame. Kant thinks that for the most part, we'd be better off if our natural affects weren't quite so powerful, or at least if we had better control over them than we often do. We've all had the experience of being overcome with anger and acting badly as a result. At least sometimes, affects get in the way of clear-sighted moral reasoning. Affects can also have moral benefits, such as when we experience sympathetic feelings upon witnessing the sufferings of others or joy at their successes. Indeed, as we'll see, Kant thinks we should be trying to cultivate positive affects as part of our general project of moral self-improvement. We do, however, need to watch out for the negative ones.

The second category, which Kant calls the passions, are more lasting and entrenched desires and inclinations, ones that permit reflection and even what we might call endorsement. Some passions, like sexual passions, are natural ones, but many others arise from the conditions of social life, like greed. Passions generally pose more serious moral problems than affects because they are capable of interfering with our reasoning in a more fundamental way. They often act as stealth intruders into our deliberative processes, and if we're not careful, they can torpedo the whole project of living a morally good life. Passions have a way of becoming vices, and that's when the Dark Side really starts to beckon.

Moral philosophers often focus on how we can cultivate virtue. As we'll see in the next chapter, Kant does have things to say about virtue and its importance. But when you read Kant, he seems to be awfully concerned about vice. Indeed, when it comes to improving ourselves, he appears to see fighting vice as more than half the battle. We can think of Kantian vice as a bit like poison ivy. You need to be able to recognize it and pull it out before it takes over your yard and causes you no end of trouble. At one point, Kant refers to the vices as the "monsters" we have to fight.[5] If you've ever had poison ivy (or stinging nettles or kudzu) in your yard, you know just what he means. The monsters of vice are a constant threat to moral progress, so we need to be prepared to take them on.

We're going to be talking about a number of specific vices in later chapters. Here we'll just focus on the general threat that vice poses to our ability to live rationally and freely. In the *Religion within the Limits of Reason Alone*, Kant argues that human beings are prone to what he calls "radical evil." Despite its dramatic name, radical evil is actually pretty ordinary. It's simply when we make something other than morality the principle on which we act. That is, we engage in radical evil when we subordinate morality to other kinds of concerns, like those stemming from self-love or self-conceit. Suppose you have a friend who often borrows money from you promising to pay it back, but practically never does. That friend is probably in the grip of radical evil. They'll do the right thing if it suits them, but not if it doesn't. Such a person (who maybe isn't the best choice for a friend) is subordinating morality to their own self-interest. Self-love, not morality, is what's ruling the roost. Kant seems to think that radical evil is entwined in our very natures. We're all in danger of succumbing to it. It's also rather hard to recognize, in part because it is quite sneaky. We're so good at rationalizing our actions that we don't always notice when our reasoning has been overtaken by evil.

At one point in his writings, Kant distinguishes between three "grades" of evil: frailty, impurity, and depravity.[6] Frailty is when we know what we should do, but we're too weak to do it. It's what happens when I sit on the couch instead of working. Impurity is when I need an extra incentive to do what's right, or when the fact that something is the right action isn't sufficient to get me to do it. That's like needing to bribe myself to get off the couch and work. And depravity is when I convince myself that the right action isn't really necessary after all. I *don't* actually have to do the work that I promised I'd do because, after all, my boss is a jerk, I'm underpaid, and so forth. (Here again, depravity is pretty ordinary, so don't be thrown off by the term.) What makes depravity so, well, depraved is that my reasoning process itself is corrupted. I twist things around in my head to get the answer that I want. This, for Kant, is a uniquely human way of being evil. It's also especially perverse because it uses reason as a weapon against itself.

When vices infiltrate our characters, evil reasoning becomes both more likely and more difficult to detect. The more vicious you are, the harder it is to recognize how you are warping your own reasoning processes. We'll see what this looks like in later chapters, and we'll also see what tools Kant thinks we should fashion to combat this danger. It should, however, be evident that Kant thinks we have some serious battles ahead of us if we want to make ourselves better. We all have the potential to have monsters lurking inside of us in the form of vices, and we need to be on our guard against them. As with poison ivy, it's easier to get rid of vices before they spread and do a lot of damage.

I said at the beginning of this chapter that Kant views humanity as somewhat of a disaster. By now, you might be feeling pretty hopeless about our prospects. Perhaps the wood of humanity is so crooked that there's not much point in trying to straighten us out. But Kant would be the first one to say that this is wrong, that there's actually a lot we can do to make ourselves better. Straightening ourselves out isn't easy, but it's within our power. We do, however, have to be ready to put in the necessary effort.

4 | MORAL COMMITMENT

As is probably clear by now, Kant does not think it's easy to become a good person. We have to fend off the worst impulses of our natures and act in accordance with rational principles that we choose for ourselves. That, for Kant, is the way to exercise our autonomy and live as the free rational beings that we are. Needless to say, this is easier said than done. What exactly do we have to do to make this happen? How do we straighten the crooked wood out of which, alas, we are made?

Kant's answer to this is both very simple and very complicated. The simple version of his answer is that we should commit ourselves to doing what's right. But if you don't find that terribly helpful, that's understandable. How do we know what the right thing is? And once we've determined that, how do we get ourselves to do it, especially when there are so many obstacles in the way?

When Kant is taught in introductory philosophy courses, he is nearly always presented as someone who based morality on principles (well, one principle in particular, which we'll discuss over the next few chapters). Being a good person is just a matter of knowing this principle and acting on it. This picture is certainly not wrong, but it is nowhere near the whole story. In fact, it's not even where he starts. Instead, he begins the *Groundwork* by asking us to reflect on the concept of a good person. Kant thinks that this is a useful starting place for ethical inquiry in part because he thinks we already know what such a person is like. It's when we reflect on our conception of what it means to be a good person that we can begin to understand what morality is and what it directs us to do. So, we'll start, as Kant does, by thinking about our ordinary concept of a good person.

You undoubtedly know someone who merits the description of being a truly good and decent human being. Take a minute now to think about that person in all their moral glory. What is it about them that makes you describe them as good? Perhaps they are especially compassionate, always thinking about other people and ready to sacrifice for them. Perhaps they are wise in the choices they make in their life, prioritizing things that truly matter over things that don't. Perhaps they've demonstrated exceptional courage or fortitude in overcoming challenges. Perhaps they are the kind of person you can always count on to show up when you need them, or act with integrity in difficult situations.

This last idea, that a good person is someone you can count on, is especially central to Kant's own conception of a good person, or what he calls a person with a good will. For Kant, a person with a good will is *committed* to morality in a way that means that we can always count on them to do the right thing, no matter what temptations they face or what pressures they're under. It's that commitment that distinguishes the truly good person from the rest of us. And this commitment is what Kant means when he talks about having a good will.

In the *Groundwork*, Kant uses some examples to explain what he has in mind by the commitment to morality expressed in a good will. His examples are controversial, mostly because they are misunderstood. Kant thinks that in many situations, doing the right thing is in our self-interest or coincides with what we want to do in any case. To illustrate this, he gives examples of a shopkeeper who charges fair prices because it's good for business and a person who helps other people because he finds it enjoyable. The shopkeeper acts from self-interest. The sympathetic philanthropist (as he's usually called) acts from his inclinations, which are warm and generous. Kant is often interpreted as saying that the shopkeeper and the sympathetic philanthropist don't have good wills, a view that seems especially implausible in the case of the philanthropist. But that's not quite what he's saying. His point, rather, is that we can't tell from their circumstances whether either of them has a good will or not. They are definitely doing the right thing, but we don't know whether they're doing it because it's right or because of their other motivations. When doing what's right aligns with self-interest or inclination, we can't be sure just how committed a person is to morality. If we want to know what someone is really like, Kant suggests, we should consider how they act when those other motivations are absent. What do people do when the chips are down? That, for Kant, is our best opportunity to understand what it means to have a good will.

And so Kant asks us to imagine the philanthropist in a new set of circumstances, one in which his life has been overtaken by tragedy and troubles. With his mind and heart weighed down, he can no longer take pleasure in helping people the way that he did before. But he still does it. He still gets out of bed and goes to work serving meals at the local soup kitchen or helping refugee families find housing. He doesn't enjoy it the way he did before, but he keeps going because it's the right thing to do. Now, Kant says, we see his real character shining through. The person with a good will has the kind of commitment to morality that will stand up to the most difficult tests.

Kant describes this person as being motivated by duty and says that only actions done from duty have something he calls moral worth. This way of describing good actions is not one that has won Kant many admirers. For one thing, acting from duty doesn't sound very inspiring or compelling as a description of what motivates a really good person. It also seems odd to say that helping actions like the ones performed by the sympathetic philanthropist lack moral worth. There's much to be said about how we should interpret Kant's remarks, but I'm going to set most of it aside. Although the concept of moral worth takes up a lot of space in discussions of Kant's ethics, Kant himself doesn't really do much with it after that early passage in the *Groundwork*. It is not a central idea in his theory. Nor does he talk much about duty as a motive in later works. As we'll see, he mostly thinks of duties in terms of specific actions. This is all pretty confusing on Kant's part, so I'm going to simplify matters and talk about the person with a good will as a person with a commitment to doing what's right because it's right. The rightness of the action matters to them, and it matters to them enough that they are willing to do what's right even when it's unpopular, or when they don't feel like it, or when they have to sacrifice something else that they want. This is what it means to be a good person in Kant's way of thinking.

A slightly different way to explain this commitment to morality is in terms of our reasons. The person with a good will acts for morally good reasons. Now all of us, whether we have good wills or not, act for reasons. This doesn't mean that we always act for good reasons; clearly, we don't! But we are always capable of taking some consideration or other *as* a reason for acting. We can choose our reasons. What is characteristic of a person with a good will is that they choose reasons that reflect a commitment to morality.

Some of what we "do" (say, digesting our lunches) is not under our conscious control. We can't just decide to start or stop digesting. Most of the time, we don't even consider such things to be actions at all. They are more like things that happen to us, such as getting a sunburn. We also have inclinations and desires, some of which we fulfill without thinking. If I'm thirsty, I don't usually consider whether I have reason to take a sip of water. I may even do it without thinking at all. But that doesn't mean that it's not an action. I'm still choosing to drink it and I'm choosing it for a reason, like that I am thirsty. While normally being thirsty is a good enough reason for me to drink from a glass of water, that's not always true. Maybe it's *your* water, in which case just grabbing your glass and sipping from it would be rather rude. The key point is that I am capable of pausing and making a choice about whether to drink the water. I can decide whether to follow my desire to drink, whether my thirst alone is a good enough reason to grab the glass or whether other reasons (like the fact that the glass is yours) come into play. This, for Kant, is what it means for us to be free, rational beings. We are capable of choosing our actions and choosing the reasons on which we act. To be a morally good person, I must act for morally good reasons.

So, what are morally good reasons? They can't simply be reasons that seem good to me. Otherwise, you'd have no grounds for complaint when I swipe your water bottle in the middle of our desert hike. My being thirsty is a reason for me to drink, but it is not always a good enough reason from a moral standpoint. We can see Kant's moral theory in part as an attempt to work out what reasons we should use when we're deciding what to do.

The shopkeeper could be charging fair prices for the reason that he will otherwise get awful reviews on Yelp or for the reason that it's the right thing to do. For Kant, only the second reason counts as a moral reason because it's the one that reflects his underlying commitment to morality. It's the reason in virtue of which we'd say he's a good person. He's not a good person in virtue of the fact that he charges fair prices to maintain high Yelp ratings. He's a good person in virtue of the fact he'd charge fair prices regardless of what happens on Yelp.

This probably seems fairly straightforward in the case of the shopkeeper. The sympathetic philanthropist is a more challenging case, because it looks like his reasons for helping people are pretty good ones. He likes to help them! Isn't that what makes him a good person, that he takes pleasure in helping people? Kant treads carefully here. He does think that the sympathetic philanthropist's inclination to help people is one that should be encouraged and praised. It is not, however, quite what he has in mind by a morally good reason. That's because the philanthropist is still really thinking in terms of what pleases him. I don't mean to say that he's selfish. If helping other people pleases him, he's definitely not selfish. But his reasons for helping are independent of morality, even if they happen to coincide. If he helps people just because he wants to help them, then morality isn't on his radar screen. Does he care who he helps? To borrow an example from contemporary Kantian ethicist Barbara Herman, would he just help a person carrying a heavy package out of an art museum late at night? Or would he stop and wonder whether helping a potential art thief is actually a good idea? If he's not concerned with whether his helping actions are morally defensible, then he doesn't have a good will.

It turns out that Kant has a definite idea of what it means to be a good person. To be a good person, or to have a good will, is to have a commitment to doing what's right because it's right or alternatively, a commitment to acting on morally good reasons. Of course, I still haven't told you how a person with a good will figures out which actions are right. That will come in the next chapter. (It takes Kant a while to get there too, so I'm in good company.) But before we move on to that, it will be helpful to talk a bit about Kant's conception of virtue. That's because we can also express the commitment to doing what's right in terms of virtue.

To some people's ears, the word "virtue" has rather old-fashioned connotations. It's often associated with sexual mores, particularly concerning the sexual behavior of women. That is not at all what Kant means by virtue. (In fact, it's pretty much never what any philosopher, past or present, means by virtue.) The most famous historical account of virtue is almost certainly Aristotle's. For Aristotle, virtue is an excellence. To be virtuous is to be excellent at being the kind of thing you are. On this understanding, it is a virtue of a golden retriever when she reliably returns things that you have thrown. (My own golden retriever seems not to have gotten this particular Aristotelian memo. Fortunately, she has other virtues.) Because human beings are not retrievers, our excellences lie in a different area, namely activities that require reasoning. This means that for Aristotle, it's a virtue in a human being when we engage in excellent reasoning of any sort, whether that's excellent reasoning about the stock market or excellent reasoning about how to handle a morally tricky work situation.

Kant is certainly a fan of excellent reasoning, but he thinks of virtue a little differently than Aristotle. As Kant sees it, virtue is mostly a matter of getting ourselves to *do* the right course of action in the face of temptation to do other things, usually easier or more pleasant ones. It is a kind of strength in maintaining your commitment to morality over time. The sorrowing philanthropist, who helps people even when his own life is falling apart, exhibits Kantian virtue. It takes fortitude to do what's right in such circumstances. We cultivate virtue by cultivating that kind of inner strength.

Let's go back to that morally tricky work situation. Suppose that you think that someone in your department may be embezzling money from company accounts. You don't have solid evidence, but you see irregularities that are best explained by some dodgy bookkeeping on the part of your colleague. You're debating whether to tell your boss, who is not the world's nicest person, or whether to keep silent.

Suppose that you decide that you really must tell your boss. It's possible that your boss will react badly, even blaming you. It's also possible that your boss will fire your colleague, depriving everyone in the office of your colleague's amazing salted caramel brownies, which he brings in every Thursday. So, your boss will be mad at you, your other colleagues will be mad at you, and you'll have to spend Thursdays without salted caramel brownies. The temptation to overlook the bookkeeping irregularities may be pretty strong. After all, you don't own the company and you do like brownies.

This experience of knowing what we should do but not wanting to do it is familiar to all of us. If we give in and don't do the right thing, we're in the grip of what the ancient Greeks called *akrasia*, or weakness of will. Virtue is how we fight weakness of will. Some people read Kant as saying that we show virtue only when we succeed in a struggle against temptation. But one mark of success is that we do not find bad courses of action all that tempting. This is a point on which Aristotle and Kant agree. To say, as Kant does, that virtue is strength doesn't mean that a person with a good will is constantly exhibiting that strength in battle. The more virtuous we are, the fewer battles we'll have to fight. But Kant does think that there's no such thing as winning the war against temptation. We're just too human for that. The best we can do is make ourselves as ready as possible to win each skirmish.

Let's summarize where things stand. We've said that a person with a good will has a commitment to doing what's right because it's right, a commitment that takes the form of acting for morally good reasons. Kantian virtue is strength in living up to this commitment. In my examples, I've mostly been taking for granted that we know what the right thing to do is, whether that's charging fair prices or helping people out or stopping embezzlement. Needless to say, it's not always that simple. By this point you may be wondering if I am ever going to explain how the person with a good will knows which actions are right.

Kant's answer is that the person with a good will acts on a particular principle, which he calls the "categorical imperative." That principle will occupy us for the next three chapters. Before we get there, however, it's important to note something about Kant's methodology. Kant thinks that when he presents the categorical imperative as the principle on which a good person operates, he is simply telling us something we already know about a good person. The principle is already built into our own thinking about morality. We just don't realize it.

In holding this view, Kant is rather unlike Aristotle, for whom moral knowledge is a specialized capacity. For Aristotle, moral judgment requires a virtue called practical wisdom. Practical wisdom is a kind of sound judgment about what to do. The person with practical wisdom can see what is at stake in a given situation and also knows how to value the various goods at stake properly. Thus, the practically wise person will know when it is worth running into a burning building (to save a toddler) and when it is not (to save a Justin Bieber poster). Some decisions are harder than others, which is why practical wisdom is a complex virtue, and one that Aristotle thinks can be acquired only over time and through experience.

Kant takes a different approach, one that more closely resembles the Christian framework in which he was raised. Any religion that holds that we are subject to divine judgment for our actions must also hold that we are capable of knowing which actions are sinful and also capable of avoiding them. Otherwise, that divine judgment would be deeply unfair. As we know, Kant rejects the Pietist religion of his youth, but his claims about our capacities for moral knowledge are consistent with it. We all have the ability to determine what's right and what's wrong. We don't need anyone to tell us the moral principle on which we should be acting. All we need is to shake ourselves free of the desires and inclinations that get in the way, so that we can see it clearly and acknowledge its force.

5 | THE CATEGORICAL IMPERATIVE

EQUALITY

We're now ready to dig into the fundamental part of Kant's moral theory, the principle he calls the "categorical imperative." That is a fancy name for a principle that Kant does not intend to be especially fancy or obscure. He sees this principle as simply articulating a central moral idea that we already have, or at least, that we would have if we were thinking rationally. It is the principle that a morally good person (or a person with a good will) employs when deciding what to do. If we know this principle and more importantly, if we commit to this principle, then we are well on our way to becoming good people.

So now I should just tell you the principle, right? Unfortunately, it's more complicated than that. You see, Kant actually provides us with multiple formulations of the categorical imperative, suggesting that they are all equivalent to each other. Scholars disagree about how many formulations there are and also about whether they are all equivalent. It's possible that Kant was just trolling us, but it's more likely that he himself wasn't perfectly clear about what he had in mind. He spells out these different versions of the categorical imperative in the *Groundwork*, which, as you may recall, is his first major ethical work. But the categorical imperative doesn't actually play a very big role in his later writings. So, although there's a lot of hoopla around this one principle, it's not even one principle and it's not clear how fundamental it is to Kant's overall ethical thought. It gets pride of place in the *Groundwork*, but it plays only a supporting role at best in the *Metaphysics of Morals*.

I mention all this because in understanding Kant, it's important not to get too caught up in the idea that a single principle will contain all the answers we need to live a morally good life. It won't. Principles need to be interpreted and applied, and they don't always provide us with clear direction. Consider a rule like "use the left lane only when you're passing." That's a good rule to teach beginning drivers, but experienced drivers know that there are complexities. Can you stay in the left lane long enough to pass multiple cars? What if there's a left hand exit up ahead? What if someone is threatening to smite half the world's population unless you stay in the left lane? (Okay, that one's a bit far-fetched.) Principles can only take us so far; we always still have to use our judgment in individual cases.

Having said that, it is still true that the categorical imperative is at the center of Kant's ethical system. Before I get to the content of the principle, let me say something about its rather technical name. In calling the principle an imperative, Kant is claiming that it takes the form of a command. If I say, "Make your bed!" I am ordering you to do something. Now if I'm not your parent or your commanding officer, you might very well question my authority to tell you to make your bed. The mere fact that something has the form of a command doesn't make it obligatory. But Kant thinks that the categorical imperative is obligatory on the grounds that its authority comes from reason. More specifically, it comes from my own reason. It's a command I give myself.

Kant distinguishes between two types of imperatives—hypothetical and categorical. A hypothetical imperative has a form like this: "If your aim is to have your room to look nice, make your bed." Taking for granted certain aesthetic standards, we could call this a command of reason. But this command has force only if it matters to you that your room looks nice. If you don't care, you have no reason to make your bed. Whether this command is binding on you depends on whether you have a particular aim. Putting it in more general terms, it depends on facts about you and what you want.

Many people (including many moral philosophers) believe that all moral commands take the form of hypothetical imperatives. If your goal is to be a good person, then you should pay your debts, help the homeless, and be kind to animals. If you don't care about being a good person, well, then you don't have reason to do those things. If moral imperatives are all hypothetical, then morality is dependent on our desires, interests, and aims. Kant thinks that this is exactly the wrong way to think about morality. As he sees it, moral commands have to be able to obligate us regardless of what we want. Otherwise, they won't really be moral commands at all. They'll just be telling us to do things that we already want to do. And so Kant puts forward an alternative, which he calls a categorical imperative.

Now here's where things start to get a little bit complicated. A categorical imperative is a command of reason that I give to myself, and that is independent of any desire or interest that I happen to have. It takes the form "Do X," rather than "If you want A, do X." I may very much want to stay in bed instead of grading papers, or take something from a store that I cannot afford, or lie to someone so as to save face. But if imperatives are categorical, then reason will tell me that I need to get out of bed, keep my hands in my pockets, and tell the truth, regardless of what I want. The command is binding on me no matter what. This is what it means for a command to be categorical.

Why does Kant think that any imperatives have this categorical form? Why aren't all imperatives hypothetical? His argument for this is complex and pretty opaque, but the very short version is that it's because we are rational beings with autonomy. To be autonomous is to be a lawmaker for yourself, and Kant argues that the categorical imperative represents the form that such a law must take. Rationality itself commits us to the existence of a categorical imperative. The categorical imperative expresses the way in which a fully rational being thinks about their actions. That is how it binds us, in virtue of the fact that we are capable of being fully rational beings. (If that seems to have gone by a little quickly, do know that there's a lot more to his argument than this. If you are feeling brave and want to dive into the details, you'll find some resources at the end of the book.)

Let's take a closer look at the first formulation of the categorical imperative, which is usually called the universal law formulation. This formulation is probably the best known one, although it's not necessarily the most useful one. It does, however, bear more than a passing resemblance to two other principles that are familiar to most people—the principle of the "golden rule" that tells us to do unto others as we would have them do unto us and a principle you may have heard from a parent (or said as a parent), one that can be summed up as "What if everybody did that?" Like these two principles, Kant's universal law formulation is going to instruct us to think beyond our own case and imagine what it would be like if other people were proposing to act like we are acting.

Kant's official version of the universal law formulation, as it appears in the *Groundwork*, is this:

Act only on that maxim by which you can at the same time will that it should become a universal law.[1]

In order to get clear on just what he's saying, let's discuss what he means by a maxim, how we would will a maxim to be a universal law, and how that's supposed to show us whether an action is right or wrong. We'll begin with maxims.

A maxim is a kind of principle of action. Suppose that I am worried about global warming and decide to stop eating red meat. In that case, my maxim is that I won't eat red meat so as to reduce my carbon footprint. Less virtuously, I might have it as my maxim to use my neighbor's internet so that I don't have to pay for my own. Or to cut to the front of the line at Starbucks so that I can get my pumpkin spice latte faster. You'll notice that in each case, I've included in the maxim not just my proposed course of action, but also my purpose in acting that way, or what I'm trying to achieve. This is important, because as we'll see in a minute, my purpose makes a difference to what happens when I try to universalize my maxim.

The formulation instructs me to determine my maxim and then see if I can universalize it. To do that, I imagine that everyone else has the exact same maxim that I do. Kant thinks that maxims for immoral actions will fail the universalizing test. They will fail because I cannot will a world in which everyone acts on my maxim.

Kant has his own examples to illustrate his point, but before I get to those, let's go back to that Starbucks line.

There are plenty of cultures in which people don't wait in line for things, but in places where lines (or queues, if you prefer) are standard, it seems pretty clear that you should stand in them and wait your turn to be served. Cutting to the front of the line so that you can get your caffeine fix sooner is rude and obnoxious. Maybe you'd even say that it's wrong. If you would, then Kant's universal law formulation can explain why. (Kant himself never talked about cutting in line, but I feel fairly confident that he would disapprove of it.) Suppose your maxim is that you'll cut in line whenever you don't feel like waiting for your coffee. Now imagine that everyone has that as their maxim, including everyone in line with you. Almost certainly they also don't feel like waiting, which means that they'll all be cutting the line too. Voilà! Chaos!

What makes it chaos, of course, is the line will disintegrate. If everyone is cutting to the front of the line, there is no longer such a thing as a line. But notice that your goal in cutting to the front of the line was to get your coffee sooner. If there's no line for you to cut, you can't achieve that goal. The success of your plan depended on everyone else staying in line, or in other words, not doing what you're doing. Your own maxim is frustrated when everyone else adopts it. And this is the key to seeing why such a maxim would fail the universal law test. It will result in a contradiction of sorts. For the plan of action expressed in your maxim to succeed, you must will that there be a line that you can cut. But if you universalize your maxim, you are *also* effectively willing that the line disintegrate because that's what happens when your maxim is universalized. So, you are willing both the existence of the line and its non-existence, which makes no sense at all. The fact that it makes no sense, for Kant, shows that you can't rationally will your maxim in the first place. And this shows that it's wrong.

Let me put Kant's point in slightly different terms. When I cut in line, I am treating myself as an exception to a rule that I want everyone else to follow. But why should I get to be an exception? My getting my cup of coffee is no more important than someone else getting their cup of coffee. For me to act as though my need for caffeine or my time matters more than the needs and time of everyone else is rude and obnoxious. It's also irrational, as Kant sees it. This is because it's just not true that I'm more important than other people, or that my desires matter more than theirs. Like me, they are rational beings who have plans for their morning and would like to get their drinks and be on their way. On Kant's view, I'm actually making an error of reasoning when I act like I'm the most important person in the universe. Maybe I feel like the most important person in the universe in my own head, but a little bit of reflection should be enough to show me that I'm not. There is nothing about me that elevates me above them. I'm not actually a special snowflake. The universal law formulation serves to remind me of this. It forces me to acknowledge the basic equality of everyone else in line with me.

This acknowledgement of everyone's equality is crucial to Kant's moral picture. Your coffee matters to you in the same way that my coffee matters to me. This, for Kant, is why the universal law formulation is a command of reason. Reason tells me that you and I are equals, that what makes me and my projects important also makes you and your projects important. Universalizing my maxim is a way of making sure I remember this by making sure

I don't treat myself as an exception to rules that I think should bind you.

Now this isn't to say that there aren't circumstances that call for making exceptions. If we're talking about a line at the emergency room and I'm bleeding from a major artery, then cutting to the front of the line does seem warranted. But notice how different this situation is than the Starbucks situation. For one thing, it seems like I could universalize the maxim that I'll cut to the front of the line when I'm bleeding from a major artery. Most of the time, other people's injuries aren't quite so serious, meaning that the line will continue to exist, and my maxim won't self-destruct. (If everyone is bleeding from a major artery, then my ER is in trouble.)

We can make the same point by thinking in terms of the reasons that you could offer to others in line with you. "I want my pumpkin spice latte right now!" is not something that they are likely to see as a good reason for you to cut the line. "I'm bleeding to death!" is a much better reason, and one that others are likely to accept. This is probably how you already think about the justifiability of cutting in line. Sometimes it's okay and sometimes it's not. It depends on the reason. There's nothing especially groundbreaking here. But remember that Kant thinks that the categorical imperative is expressing what morally good people already know and believe. So, if what he says coincides with your common sense, then he'd consider that a win.

Now let me say something about Kant's own examples, in part because he draws a distinction with them that will later prove quite important. Kant uses the universal law formulation to show why four different maxims cannot be universalized: a maxim of ending my life when I no longer value it, a maxim of borrowing money with a false promise to pay it back, a maxim of never cultivating my natural talents, and a maxim of never helping anyone in need. Kant thinks that all four of these maxims will fail the universal law test. But they do not all fail in quite the same way. He thinks that the first two fail in the same way that the maxim of cutting in line failed. Universalizing the maxim will produce a contradiction of the kind that makes my maxim implode on itself. If I borrow $50 from you and promise to pay it back, knowing full well that I won't, I'm counting on the fact that you believe my promise. But if my maxim were universalized, no one would ever pay money back, which means that no one in their right mind would lend it. So, my getting money from you depends on other people not doing what I'm doing. I have to will that you believe my lying promise and also (once I universalize the maxim) that no one ever believes such promises. My maxim implodes when it's universalized, and that's where Kant sees the contradiction happening.

But the fourth example—never helping anyone in need—doesn't produce the same kind of contradiction. I can universalize the maxim "never help anyone" without undermining my own maxim of not helping people or making it implode. My success at not helping people doesn't depend on other people continuing to help. I can keep on refusing to help people, even if everyone else acts the same way. I'm not making an exception of myself in the way that I am when I'm cutting in line or making a false promise.

Here Kant has to come up with a different reason why this maxim cannot be universalized. It fails the test not because it implodes on itself, but because a world in which no one ever helps anyone is a world I cannot rationally will. I may think I prefer that situation, but in fact, it's an irrational preference. If my life ever depends on someone else's help, it will be rational for me to will that they help me. After all, that's the only way my rational human existence is going to continue. What I think is a rational plan of independence and self-sufficiency is in fact an irrational plan that ignores my actual human vulnerabilities. It's like planning to wait out a major hurricane in a rowboat. You may think it will work, but once you're out on the ocean with 150 mph winds, it will no longer seem like such a good idea.

These two different types of contradiction correspond to two different categories of Kantian duties—perfect and imperfect duties. It's a pretty important distinction for Kant, so we'll be returning to it multiple times, beginning in the next chapter. You may have also noticed that the first and third of these examples refer to duties that I owe myself, while the second and fourth refer to duties that I owe to other people. This is not an accident. Kant chose these four examples carefully. I'll come back to the entire structure of Kantian duties in Chapter 9, so don't worry if you're a little confused right now.

Now that you know about universalizing maxims, are we finished? Not quite. While the universal law formulation gets a lot of press, it's not clear that Kant ever meant it to be the main method we use for deciding whether actions are okay or not. That's probably just as well, because the formulation doesn't always work quite as well as it does in cases like cutting in line and making lying promises. For instance, it looks like I can't universalize a maxim of leaving home at 6:00 am to beat traffic; if everyone acted on my maxim, it would just create a traffic jam at 6:00 am. But surely it's not wrong to leave home early to beat traffic. It also looks like I *can* universalize immoral maxims if I just make them extremely specific, like saying that "If your name is Karen Stohr and you teach philosophy at Georgetown University, you can borrow money and lie about paying it back." Perhaps Kant saw the potential holes in this formulation because he did not end up relying on it very often in his later ethical works. More often he reaches for a different formulation, the one we're covering in the next chapter.

The universal law formulation does, however, reflect a crucial concept in Kant's ethics, which is the necessity of seeing ourselves as the moral equals of other rational beings. There is nothing about me that makes me more important (or less important) than anyone else. The universal law formulation is a good way to remind myself of this crucial fact.

6 | THE CATEGORICAL IMPERATIVE

DIGNITY

The universal law formulation aims to get us to acknowledge our fundamental moral equality with other people. I don't get to think of myself as a special snowflake, entitled to cut to the front of the line at Starbucks or borrow money under false pretenses just because I am me. But there is also a sense for Kant in which each of us actually *is* a special snowflake—not in the sense that we deserve better treatment than others, but in the sense that we are each exceptionally important and irreplaceable. To understand what Kant thinks makes us so special, we need to turn to a second formulation of the categorical imperative, usually called the "humanity formulation." Here's how Kant states it in the *Groundwork*:

> *Act in such a way that you treat humanity, whether in your own person or in any other person, always at the same time as an end, never merely as a means.*[1]

It is perhaps obvious why this is called the humanity formulation, but what does Kant mean by humanity and what does it mean to treat humanity as an end and never merely as a means? Let's start with the first question.

As we have seen, Kant thinks that what matters most about human beings is that we have the capacity for rationality. Granted, we do not always use this capacity as well as we might, and it seems almost certain that human beings are not the only creatures capable of reasoning. But rational capacity is, for Kant, the source of a very crucial kind of value. That value is explained through two related claims that he makes about rational beings: 1) that we have dignity, rather than price and 2) that we have absolute or unconditional value, rather than conditional value.

To say that we have dignity is to say that we have value that is incommensurable. This means that our value cannot be traded off, compared, or measured against the value of other people. By contrast, Kant says, objects have mere price. This is what enables me to say that two paintings of dogs playing poker are worth more than one such painting but prevents me from saying that two teenagers playing video games are worth more than one such teenager. The claim that teenagers have dignity means that we cannot make such comparative assessments. Each teenager is incomparably valuable, beyond price. I can't just trade out one for another and call it even. Rational beings cannot be assigned a price tag of any form. We are quite literally priceless. (Side note: you would think that Kant would have seen that this obviously rules out buying and selling slaves. Sadly, you would be wrong.)

To say that we have unconditional value is to say that we have value that is not dependent on our particular qualities or talents, or on whether anyone values us. As I type these words, I am using an ergonomic keyboard, which I like very much. If it were to stop working (say, because I spilled coffee all over it), it would lose its value for me. It was never particularly attractive and a malfunctioning keyboard just takes up valuable space on my desk. It seems totally fine for me to throw the keyboard away and get a new one, perhaps reminding myself to be more careful with my coffee. I am not wronging the keyboard when I put it in the trash can or failing to value it in the right way. Keyboards are valuable only when they are of use to people who need keyboards. Human beings, obviously, are valuable in a different way. We do not lose our value just because other people stop valuing us or stop finding us useful. Unlike a keyboard, our value is not conditional on whether other people value us. Nor is it conditional on whether we value ourselves. To say that I have unconditional value in virtue of being a rational being is to say that I have value regardless of whether I or anyone else thinks of myself that way. It is also to say that my value is not dependent on features of me like my appearance, my talents, or my social position.

To keep things simple, I'm just going to use the word "dignity" as shorthand for the rather complicated kind of value that Kant thinks we have. To respect another person's dignity is to treat them as having value that is both incommensurable and unconditional. Likewise, to respect my own dignity is to treat myself as having value that is both incommensurable and unconditional.

Now here is a very important point. Dignity is something that I possess regardless of what anyone thinks or does to me, or how I think of myself. I cannot waive or forfeit my own dignity, and I cannot diminish or take away someone else's dignity by anything I do or say. The challenge is to make sure that we are always treating ourselves and others in ways that reflect the value that we actually have. Even though we all do have dignity, we do not always treat each other as though we do. This is where the humanity formulation comes in.

The humanity formulation has two parts. It tells us never to treat humanity in ourselves or others as a mere means, and it also tells us always to treat humanity as an end in itself. The distinction is subtle, but important. The first part is a duty to *avoid* certain ways of treating people who have dignity, and the second part is a duty to *promote* the dignity of those same people. These are two very different types of duties. The first type is usually called a *negative* duty, not because it is bad, but because it tells us what *not* to do. It is also sometimes called a *perfect* duty. We can think of it as a duty with which we can comply perfectly. Consider my duty not to kill you because you and your cart are blocking my path down a grocery store aisle. (I'm just going to take it for granted that I have such a duty!) It is a negative duty because it is a duty *not* to do something to you. I must not kill you. It is a perfect duty because it is both possible and reasonable to expect me to comply with it at all times, no matter how great the sale on spaghetti sauce. No one ever *needs* to kill anyone to get through their grocery shopping. And if I pat myself on the back because I killed only two of the five people who got in my way in the cereal aisle, something is seriously wrong with my thinking. I can and should fulfill this duty perfectly, meaning that I can and should fulfill it at all times and in all circumstances.

According to the humanity formulation, I have a perfect, negative duty not to treat myself or anyone else as a mere means. To treat myself or anyone else as a mere means is to disregard their humanity (by which Kant means their rationality) when I am acting. If I kill you because you are in my way, as opposed to politely asking you to move your cart, I am obviously disregarding your rationality. I am destroying your rationality by killing you, and that is certainly a way of disregarding it. But there are other ways. For instance, I would be disregarding your rationality if I shoved you out of the way instead of asking you to move, or if I used you as a stepping stool to reach an item on the top shelf. I am also disregarding your rationality when I make it impossible for you to use it.

Take Kant's example of making a lying promise. If I ask to borrow $50 from you promising to pay you back, but with no intention of doing so, I am disregarding your rationality. True, I'm not destroying it, but I'm certainly trying to do an end run around it. After all, if you knew I wasn't planning to pay you back, you'd never lend me the money. To get you to give me the money, I have to get you to believe that I will pay it back. I do that by creating a false picture of my intentions and presenting it to you as the truth. I am controlling your view of the world in order to get you to do what I want. This is how lying to someone thwarts that person's rationality. In such cases, we often describe what I'm doing as "using" you. I am treating you like an object that I can manipulate for my own purposes, without any regard for your thoughts, feelings, or plans for that $50. It's as if you're an ATM, not a human being. This is what Kant has in mind by treating someone as a mere means—treating a person with dignity like an object that we can just use for whatever purposes we want. He thinks that's always wrong, no matter what our reasons are.

This is why Kant is very troubled by lying. Lying to someone usually amounts to treating that person as a mere means. It does so by manipulating her understanding of her own action. You think you are lending me $50 when in fact you are giving me $50. I deliberately create this misunderstanding so that you will do what I want. I am thus interfering with your rationality by preventing you from using it effectively. Kant sees this as a direct and serious threat to your dignity. When I attack your rationality this way, I am attacking *you*.

Kant never provides a list of perfect duties, but it's safe to assume that besides murder and lying, the humanity formulation also forbids actions like slavery, theft, rape, sexual harassment, and extortion. Such actions constitute treating another human being as a mere means to our own ends. In many cases, it is perfectly obvious that a person is being treated as a mere object. In other cases, the dehumanization of the other person (or of ourselves) is far more subtle. As we will see in later chapters, Kant has concerns about behaviors like making contemptuous remarks about people or mocking them. The duty to avoid treating people as a mere means is a duty not to violate anyone's dignity by treating that person as an object or having only conditional value. In real life, it's not always easy to figure out when that's happening.

This duty not to treat anyone as a mere means, remember, includes ourselves. We have a duty not to treat ourselves as a mere means to our own ends. That may sound strange—how is it possible to use myself in the sense that I can use you as a way of getting $50? But Kant does think that there are ways in which we can fail to treat ourselves as having dignity. Recall from the last chapter that one of Kant's four examples of duties includes the perfect duty to oneself not to commit suicide. His reasons for thinking that suicide is wrong are exactly parallel to his reasons for thinking that killing others is wrong. If I kill you because you are in my way in the grocery store, I treat you as though your value is conditional on my own wishes and preferences. I see you as something that I can move out of my way whenever I want and by whatever methods I want. This, for Kant, is to make a mistake about your value.

The same problem arises when I am considering killing myself. If I don't think that my life is worthwhile or if I regard myself as useless, I am making a mistake about my own value. Now Kant lived in a time when there was little to no awareness of mental health issues and suicide was widely criminalized. Thankfully, things are different now and had Kant had the resources of modern psychology at his disposal, he might have written more knowledgably and compassionately about people contemplating suicide. We may also disagree with Kant's strict stand against suicide in the face of extreme suffering or terminal illness. (Indeed, perhaps assisted suicide in the face of a disease like Alzheimer's is consistent with valuing and respecting one's rationality.) But the basic idea that we owe it to ourselves to treat ourselves with dignity, or we might say, to have appropriate self-respect, is a powerful one.

It is hard to overstate the importance of self-respect in Kant's moral framework. In his *Lectures on Ethics*, he says that duties to ourselves "are of primary importance and take pride of place."[2] This is not because I am supposed to see myself as more important than others; we already know that the categorical imperative requires us to regard ourselves as the moral equals of everyone else. Rather, Kant's idea is that if I do not fully recognize my own value, I will be unable to fully recognize the value of other people. He seems to intend this as a conceptual point about how we come to understand what it means to have dignity in virtue of our rational capacities. My appreciation of dignity begins from the inside, so to speak. Once I have a grasp on my own dignity, I will see that I am rationally compelled to acknowledge the dignity of other people as well. After all, what gives me dignity—my rationality—is also present in them. So, if I have dignity, they must have dignity. This means that if I fail to appreciate my own dignity, I will have trouble appreciating the dignity of others.

Consider a person who values himself only for the number of followers he has on Instagram, or a person who views her worth as lying solely in her accomplishments at work. Kant thinks that such people are mistaking a false source of their value for the true one. Because of this, they are inevitably going to make the same mistake about others. The person who sees his own value as hinging on his social media following is going to value others in the same warped way. This is why we have to get self-respect right before we can get respect for others right. Getting self-respect right means that I have to acknowledge and take seriously my own dignity as a human being. Unless I can do this, I won't be valuing others properly, even if I believe that I am. (We'll talk more about how self-respect goes wrong in Chapters 13 and 14.)

At this point you may be wondering what happened to the second part of the humanity formulation. That was the part that says that we have a duty not just to avoid treating human beings as a mere means, but to treat them (us!) as ends in themselves. Now this may not seem like a very important thing to add, but it actually makes a significant difference to our duties. As we have seen, the duty to avoid treating human beings as a mere means is a *negative, perfect* duty to avoid destroying, thwarting, or otherwise disregarding their rationality. But while undoubtedly the world would be a much better place if we could all just refrain from murder, lying, theft, and rape, Kant does not think that leaving each other alone is sufficient to respect our dignity in the fullest sense. He puts it this way: "For the ends of any person who is an end in himself must, if this idea is to have its full effect in me, be also, as far as possible, *my* ends."[3] This means that that if we're really going to take dignity seriously, we have to up our game. It's not enough just to avoid mistreating people. For Kant, respecting someone's dignity involves a lot more.

What does he have in mind? Suppose you have someone in your life who is never mean to you, who always does what they say they will do, who listens to your opinions, and who doesn't interfere with what you're doing. This would be pretty great because most of us usually fail to live up to this standard. But you probably want something more from your partner and close friends. You might want them to care about what *you* care about, or at least be willing to join with your plans and help you with your goals and projects on occasion. Maybe you are a Marvel Universe fan and really want them to go see the next *Avengers* movie with you, even though it's not their thing. Maybe you need them to help you move some heavy furniture or take care of your dog while you're visiting your elderly parents. We want our friends to do more than just not interfere with our lives; we want them to participate in our lives. And occasionally we need strangers to help us out as well, whether with flat tires or medical emergencies.

Kant agrees. Respecting someone's rationality is not just about not interfering with it; it's also about helping her pursue the ends and projects she has chosen for herself. In Kant's language, it is to treat her as a "setter of ends." This explains why treating someone as an end in herself is not just a negative duty; it's also a *positive* duty. To say that it's a positive duty means that it requires positive action from me, at least on occasion. If your cat has slipped out the door and you are racing after him, it's not enough for me just to refrain from tripping you as you run past me. I should probably get off the couch and help you, even if I don't much like your cat. *You* like your cat and care about its welfare, and that should be enough for me. Now of course it depends on what I'm doing. If I'm desperately performing CPR on an unconscious person at the time, I have a good reason not to stop and help you. This is why the duty to help people is an *imperfect* duty. Unlike the duty not to kill you, it is not a duty I am required to fulfill every time the opportunity arises. There will be times when I am unable to help or when I have good reasons not to help. We'll come back to this in Chapter 9. The key point is that there is more to respecting our dignity as human beings than leaving each other alone. Truly treating humanity as an end requires that we take steps to prevent harm from coming to others and to help them achieve their goals, at least on occasion. That's what it means to treat them as setters of ends.

Thus far we have been working under a quiet, but crucial assumption, which is that all our interactions are with fully rational human beings. This is obviously not true, as anyone who has ever tried to convince a toddler to put on a pair of shoes is well aware. Children lack full rational capacities, and many adult human beings either never acquire them or else lose them to disease or injury. What does Kant have to say about human beings who do not have full rational capacities? Do they have dignity? And what about non-human animals? Like many people, I treat my dog like she is kind of a person, though not the same kind of person as my two daughters. We also know that animals like elephants, dolphins, crows, and chimpanzees seem to have significant rational capacities. Certainly they behave in ways that resemble how humans behave. (Quite possibly it is easier to get a chimpanzee to cooperate with shoes than a two-year-old!)

The short answer is that when it comes to non-human animals, children, and adult human beings with intellectual disabilities or diminished rational capacities, Kant is not at his best. He draws a sharp line between rational beings and everything else. In his worldview, elephants, dolphins, crows, and chimpanzees are mere objects, although he did object to unnecessarily cruel medical experiments on animals and he criticized people who treated their old dogs and horses badly after a lifetime of work. But whatever we owe to animals, we owe to them indirectly, meaning that we owe it to them in virtue of what we owe to other human beings. I may owe it to you to help you find your cat after it has run out the door, but I do not owe it to the cat. Kant does seem to think that there is a connection between how people treat animals and how they treat human beings. A person who is callous to the suffering of an animal is also likely to be callous to the suffering of a person. But in the end for Kant, non-human animals lie outside the sphere of morality.

To be fair, Kant knew much less than we do about the cognitive capacities of elephants and crows. We don't know what he would have said about them if he had known, but regardless, it does not seem true that the moral world should be divided so sharply into the two categories of rational beings and objects. Of course, it is not just this division that poses the problem for Kant; it is also the fact that he places such high value on the first category and seemingly no value on the second. Even if we don't think dogs matter as much as people, surely they do matter, and in ways that inanimate objects do not.

Drawing a sharp division between the rational and the non-rational is also a problem when it comes to our relationships with human beings who lack full rational capacities. Children might be a relatively straightforward case because we are trying to help them become rational beings further down the line. Much of what we think we owe children, like access to health care and education, has to do with making sure that they are in a good position to assume the role of rational adults. But our duties toward people with dementia or who have significant intellectual disabilities cannot be understood this way. It does not seem to us that people in advanced stages of Alzheimer's disease become things or objects just because they have lost their rational capacities, and it would be a major problem for Kant's theory if it had this implication.

I am not going to pretend that these are minor concerns, although I do think there are solutions to them that are consistent with Kant's overall ethical picture. For instance, we could extend the conception of capacity for rational agency to include people who once had that capacity, as well as those who will have it in the future. We could also attend to the moral dimensions of our interactions that do not fall within the scope of Kant's rather narrow conception of rationality. After all, people have deeply morally significant relationships with family members and friends who permanently lack certain rational abilities. People also have morally significant relationships with their pets. It may be that Kant was simply too focused on a particular, albeit extremely important, way in which we interact with others.

Like all ethical theories, Kant's theory has gaps and weaknesses. Moreover, Kant did not always see what now seem like obvious conclusions of his own theory. As I've said, Kant held some deeply racist and sexist views, views that denied the dignity and equal moral standing of many other people. Although he excelled at explaining why it is so terribly wrong to dehumanize people, he did not seem to realize that he was doing just that when he disparaged the rational capacities of women and people with darker skin than his. Kant's framework provides powerful arguments against racism and sexism, but Kant himself did not seem to appreciate those arguments.

We can rightly blame him for that failure; after all, he was an extremely smart man and others knew better at the time. But we should not be too quick to congratulate ourselves on our superior moral capacities. It's true that many of the worst forms of dehumanization, like slavery, are now widely seen as wrong. Still, there are all kinds of subtle ways in which we deny people their dignity and treat them like objects we can manipulate for our convenience or pleasure. If there's a lesson to be drawn from history, it is that human beings are all too ready to dehumanize others when it suits their purposes. We are surely not yet so enlightened that we aren't susceptible to our own appalling moral mistakes. Fortunately, Kant's theory has resources to help us avoid some of them. Indeed, if we just took seriously the strict duty to treat every human being with dignity, we'd be making an excellent start.

7 | THE CATEGORICAL IMPERATIVE
COMMUNITY

We've now arrived at the third and last formulation of the categorical imperative that we'll be discussing in this book, one usually known as the "kingdom of ends" formulation. Thus far I've presented the universal law formulation as expressing the central Kantian concept of moral equality and the humanity formulation as expressing the central Kantian concept of dignity. With the kingdom of ends formulation, we will turn our attention to a third central Kantian concept, that of moral community.

Kant is often held up as a paragon of Enlightenment-style individualism. This is certainly not a false portrait, as Kant does place individual rational agents at the center of his theory. But if we focus just on individuals, we'll miss some important elements of Kant's overall ethical framework. There are several key points in Kant's ethics where he emphasizes the significance of the communities in which we live and the ways in which those communities shape our moral decisions and behavior. The kingdom of ends formulation of the categorical imperative is one of these places.

Kant's statement of the kingdom of ends formulation is not especially intuitive, so we'll have to do some work to figure out what he has in mind. Here's one version of it from the *Groundwork*:

Act on the maxims of a universally lawgiving member of a merely possible kingdom of ends.[1]

That's a little obscure, although as you've realized by now, Kant is sometimes quite obscure. But what he has in mind here is actually pretty straightforward. To see yourself as a member of the kingdom of ends is to see yourself as one among many rational beings, each with the capacity for autonomy and each deserving of respect. As we saw with the universal law formulation, Kant argues that we must think about our actions from a perspective that incorporates the perspectives of other rational agents. The kingdom of ends formulation formalizes this. It instructs us to imagine ourselves as making laws for members of a community of rational agents, including ourselves. In less legalistic language, we could say that it instructs us to develop principles that could be endorsed from a particular standpoint, one that is communal in its form. It commands me to move from what *I* will for *myself* to what *we* will for *ourselves*.

Crucially, Kant does not mean that we have to act only on maxims that all actual human beings would endorse. The kingdom of ends is a hypothetical (or "merely possible") construct. It is a perspective we take up on our actions. From that perspective, I am part of a community of rational agents working together to determine the policies and principles by which we will live. Each member of the kingdom of ends has dignity, and each member is the moral equal of the others. This means that it's not really a kingdom in the usual sense because there's no single reigning monarch. Everyone is their own sovereign, legislating for themselves. They are, however, equal sovereigns. This means that what each one legislates has to be compatible with others legislating for themselves in the same way. The kingdom of ends is a community of people, thinking of themselves and others as rational agents with equal standing.

The kingdom of ends formulation has found concrete expression in the work of the well-known political philosopher John Rawls. In his groundbreaking book, *A Theory of Justice*, Rawls argues that a just society is one based on principles arrived at through a process that resembles legislating in a kingdom of ends. Rawls calls the hypothetical legislative situation the "original position" or the position in which we are rational agents developing laws and policies with other rational agents. In the original position, we operate from behind what Rawls calls a veil of ignorance. The veil shields us from knowledge of our particular situation, knowledge that might interfere with our ability to function as members of the kingdom of ends by allowing self-interest and self-conceit to affect our reasoning.

Suppose we are wondering what would constitute a fair allocation of health care resources. If we think about this question from the standpoint of our actual situations, facts about our real-life selves are almost certainly going to affect our conception of what is fair. It will matter to my thinking whether I am healthy or whether I have a serious chronic disease. It will matter to my thinking whether I have good access to health insurance. It will matter to my thinking whether I have a disability that requires considerable medical care. But if I am aiming to be fair, I need to make sure these facts about me don't warp my reasoning about what is good for an entire community of people. For Rawls, the best way to do this is for me to take up a hypothetical standpoint in which I don't have certain kinds of information about myself and my situation. What principles would I endorse if I didn't know whether I would get cancer, or whether I'd lose my job and so my health insurance? What kinds of policies would I want in place if I didn't know whether I'd have the use of my legs or whether I'd be in a wheelchair?

Rawls sees this as a tool to get us to think about laws and policies in a more just way. What I would will in the original position reflects what it would be rational to will for an entire community of rational agents, each with dignity and autonomy. Rawls thinks that this method will produce laws and policies that protect the dignity and freedom of the weakest and most vulnerable members of society. If I am not someone who uses a wheelchair, I may not see the need to spend lots of money to make buildings and other public spaces fully accessible to people in wheelchairs. From behind the veil of ignorance, however, things will look different. I set aside the question of what I personally need or don't need and instead consider the situation from a hypothetical standpoint in which I do not know my specific situation. All I know is that the community includes rational agents with dignity and who have ends, projects, and goals of their own. That community will contain people who need wheelchairs; indeed, I could be one such person. In that case, it will be rational for me to will whatever is necessary to treat people in wheelchairs with dignity and as setters of ends. This is what the kingdom of ends formulation is intended to make apparent to me. By taking on its perspective, I am able to see what a fully respectful moral community would be like.

To say that the kingdom of ends formulation directs us to take up the standpoint of the moral community is not to deny the importance of individual rational agents. In the kingdom of ends, we still function as autonomous individuals, giving laws to ourselves. That is crucial to Kant's overall picture. But of course, it's also true that we are autonomous individuals living with other autonomous individuals, to whom we owe duties and on whom we can make claims. The kingdom of ends formulation is what helps us navigate our shared world together.

It is possible to see the kingdom of ends as nothing more than an aggregation of individuals working out principles that function like traffic rules. When we're driving in traffic, we are sharing the road with other vehicles, each heading on their own path. Perhaps you're going to work while I'm heading to the hardware store. Traffic rules govern our use of shared space by setting out procedures for how we can jointly use the space without causing injury to others or being injured by them. When the light is green for me, it's my turn to occupy the intersection while you wait at your red light. When your light is green, you're the one with the right to occupy the intersection. It makes sense for us to obey these rules, because doing so is what enables each of us to get where we want to go efficiently and safely. But nothing in the system requires us to approve of each other's ends, much less share in them. Most of the time when we're driving, we give no thought to where other people are going or why. So long as they follow the rules and stay in their lanes, it makes no difference.

There's something appealing about this as a vision for living with other people, particularly in a diverse society in which people have different ideas about what constitutes a good life. You do you, I'll do me, and everything will work out fine. Insofar as Kant values the ability of each of us to set and pursue our own ends, he would certainly endorse principles and rules that allow each of us the largest space for expressing our freedom and directing the course of our lives. We don't all have to be driving to the same place. We just need to figure out how each of us can get where we want to go.

Lots of people interpret Kant's kingdom of ends formulation as requiring nothing more than this. But this doesn't really do justice to Kant's vision of moral community. In fact, Kant seems to think that there's a sense in which we're all going somewhere together. More specifically, we're on a shared mission to build what he calls an ethical commonwealth. Kant's fullest discussion of the ethical commonwealth appears in the *Religion*, which is part of the reason why people who read only his ethical works sometimes miss it. It is, however, quite central to his way of thinking about our relationship to other human beings. Moral community is not simply a matter of staying out of each other's way. Kant thinks we should be working to create something that extends beyond the boundaries of our individual lives and pursuits.

What exactly should we be working to create? It might be helpful to start with what Kant thinks we need to escape, which he describes as the ethical state of nature. The concept of a state of nature is probably best known through the work of seventeenth-century British philosopher Thomas Hobbes. In his famous book, *Leviathan*, Hobbes argues that in the absence of any form of civil organization or society, we'd be existing in a natural state that is, to put it mildly, unpleasant. The Hobbesian state of nature is a place in which each of us is out only for ourselves, with our primary goal being to stay alive. The effect of this is that we are constantly in danger of being killed, or at least having all our possessions taken by someone who wants them more. Hobbes memorably describes the state of nature as "solitary, poor, nasty, brutish, and short," going on to argue that it is rational to accept even a powerful and potentially oppressive form of government as an alternative.

Kant has his own, less grim account of the state of nature and the formation of political community. Like Hobbes and many other Enlightenment philosophers (and their heirs, like Rawls), Kant argues for a version of what is broadly known as social contract theory. According to this theory, individuals join together in a hypothetical agreement (a social contract!) to set up a central government, which then has the authority to create and enforce laws. We can see this theory reflected in Kant's conception of a kingdom of ends, as well as the Rawlsian version of it that relies on an original position from which we make decisions.

Kant's conception of an ethical community, however, is not quite the same as his conception of a political community. Political communities exist to regulate our external behavior. They generate the authority for a government to exercise coercion over us so as to keep our external behavior in check. The law forces me to acknowledge your claims on me by providing me with a compelling self-interested reason for me to do what the law says.

But an ethical community is different. Crucially, it lacks the coercive authority of a political community. It also involves our internal attitudes, as well as our external behavior. An ethical community is a place where we see the claims of others as having authority for us in virtue of the fact that those others are rational beings, just like ourselves. I'll borrow an example from contemporary Kantian ethicist Kyla Ebels-Duggan to explain. Suppose that you're trying to take a picture of the Grand Canyon and I decide to photobomb your shot. There's no property claim here. Neither of us owns the Grand Canyon and you don't have a legal right to take an unobstructed picture of it. And yet, it's clear that I'm being annoying. More to the point, you'd be justified in asking me to step aside and also justified in resenting me if I refuse. The mere fact that you want to take a picture, Ebels-Duggan points out, is sufficient to generate a reason for me to stay out of your way. To be member of the ethical community is to see others as having the authority to make claims on us and give us reasons, even in the absence of any kind of government power backing them up.

Kant thinks that political community is what makes possible political freedom in its fullest sense. Laws constrain me through their coercion, but those constraints, exercised justly, actually enable me to live more freely, more able to pursue my own ends and projects. (Think about traffic rules here.) Likewise, the ethical community makes possible a kind of ethical freedom. It is through a system in which we each recognize the authority of others to make claims on us and give us reasons that we are best able to exercise our own freedom as rational agents. My ability to make claims on you and give you reasons to act is essential to my being able to function well in the world, something I have reason to want to do. The only way I can acquire that authority over you is to acknowledge your equal authority over me. It is the reciprocity that makes the difference.

Of course, the actual world contains people who are free riders and moochers. On Kant's view, such people are behaving immorally and, by extension, irrationally. In acting as though they can make claims and issue demands without also being subject to the claims and demands of others, they treat themselves as having a different status than everyone else. They are failing to do what the categorical imperative requires of them. We can see this with any of the three formulations. The maxim of being a free rider cannot be universalized, as not everyone can be a free rider. Free riders also treat others as a mere means to achieving their own ends. And free riders fail to see themselves as members of a community of equals. For Kant, these amount to three somewhat different ways of saying the same thing. What the kingdom of ends formulation offers us is a new way of thinking about ourselves in relationship to others, one in which we are joining up with other people, working out the terms of our shared life, and striving toward the shared goal of creating a better form of community. In the real world, people act like they can opt out of this endeavor. Kant thinks that we can't rationally opt out. Like it or not, we're all in this together.

The refusal to accept that I'm part of a moral community is, for Kant, a manifestation of those natural propensities toward self-interest and self-conceit. A world in which I am concerned only with myself is a world in danger of being overtaken by vice. In Chapter 3, I described Kantian vice in terms of poison ivy. But we can also think of Kantian vice as a battle against mosquitoes. If you live somewhere where mosquitoes are a problem, you are likely well aware that in order to keep them at bay, you have to get rid of standing water because that's where they breed. And unless your nearest neighbors are some distance away, you probably also know that it's not enough for you to get rid of all the standing water on your property. Your neighbors have to do the same, or else their mosquitoes will simply come over and visit you. Given what mosquitoes are like, getting rid of them has to be a joint effort. The same thing is true of Kantian vice.

Vice, alas, is somewhat contagious. It's crucial to make efforts to extricate myself from its grip, but unless my neighbors do the same, I'm going to be at significant risk of backsliding. We'll see just how Kant thinks this works in later chapters, when we talk about vices like contempt and ridicule. Kant worries that in the absence of collective vice-fighting efforts, we're much more likely to succumb to our worst impulses. Like mosquitoes in August, vice is all around us:

> Envy, addiction to power, avarice, and the malignant inclinations associated with these assail his nature . . . as soon as he is among human beings. Nor is it necessary to assume that these are sunk into evil and are examples that lead him astray: it suffices that they are there, that they surround him, and that they are human beings, and they will mutually corrupt each other's dispositions, and make one another evil.[2]

This doesn't sound very promising. But Kant, ever the optimist, thinks there's a solution. The solution is to form a community of people committed to cultivating their own good wills and supporting each other in doing the same.

Kant suggests that the ideal version of such a community would be a religious community, something like a small parish or church. In principle, there's no reason why a secular community couldn't serve the same purpose, so long as people band together to fight vice and develop virtue together. Basically, we need to form a vice-fighting squad in which we join forces and squash evil wherever it rears its ugly head. As Kant rather memorably puts it:

> In addition to prescribing laws to each individual human being, morally legislative reason also unfurls a banner of

virtue as rallying point for all those who love the good, that they may congregate under it and thus at the very start gain the upper hand over evil and its untiring attacks.[3]

For those who think of Kant as locating the entirety of morality in our individual wills, this picture of us rallying around a banner of virtue may come as a bit of a surprise. But as we'll see, the idea that we need to work together to fight vice in ourselves is one that shows up in lots of places in Kant's ethical works. Although each of us is responsible for our own moral improvement, we are more likely to succeed in our efforts when we work together to create an ethical community, that, as much as possible, resembles the kingdom of ends.

8 | LOVE AND RESPECT

We've just been on a whirlwind tour of Kant's primary moral principle, the categorical imperative. It might seem as though we have the basics of his theory down. I'm sorry to report that we're not quite there yet. You can blame that on Kant. As I've mentioned, the way he thought about our duties in the *Groundwork* does not neatly correspond to the way he thought about them in the later *Metaphysics of Morals*. In fact, it's actually rather difficult to map these two works on to each other, despite the fact that the names suggest that we can.

In the next chapter, I'll set out a more systematic picture of Kantian duties as they appear in both works. Before we get to that, it will be useful to focus on one particular distinction that Kant draws in the *Metaphysics of Morals*, a distinction between love and respect. As we'll see shortly, this distinction will form the basis of a division between types of duties we owe to other people. The distinction, however, is more than a categorization system. Kant describes love and respect as two "great moral forces" that at least sometimes pull us in opposite directions.[1] This idea that there is a tension between love and respect, and their corresponding moral demands, is both insightful and puzzling. What makes it insightful is that it nicely illustrates some of the complexities we face in trying to make good moral decisions. But because it is also puzzling to say that love and respect are in tension with each other, we'll start with an example to help us see what Kant might have in mind.

Imagine that you're strolling through a park when you come across a stranger sitting alone on a bench weeping. You might very well have two conflicting thoughts about what you should do. The first thought is that you should approach them, ask what's wrong, and see if there's anything you can do to help. The second thought is that it's really none of your business and that the person might be angry or embarrassed by your interference, even if it's well-meant. If you do have these two thoughts, you will likely find yourself stuck, not at all sure what to do.

Congratulations. You've just experienced the tension between love and respect that Kant is talking about. Kant describes it by saying that love directs us to come close to people while respect tells us to keep our distance. And that's exactly what is happening here. Our justified concern for the weeping stranger's well-being draws us toward the park bench, but our equally justified concern for their privacy keeps us rooted in our spot, worried that approaching them will be an unwelcome intrusion.

These two great moral forces play an important role in Kant's thinking about what it means to be a good person. For Kant, both love and respect generate moral obligations for us. We owe people respect. Often that means leaving them alone or giving them space. We also owe people care and concern. Often that means coming close enough, literally or figuratively, to take on some of their burdens and ease their pain. But on occasion, someone's attempt to help us can feel intrusive or overbearing, even when it's well-meant.

Likewise, someone's efforts to give us space can sometimes seem cold or unfeeling. It's not easy to find the right balance between expressing our love for people and treating them respectfully, even when we're talking about our family members or closest friends.

Actually, it can be especially difficult when we're talking about the people we love most. We all know how hard it is to stand by and watch a loved one suffer. It's natural to want to step in and help them, maybe by fixing their problem or getting them to take a different course of action. We also know that this very natural feeling can generate problems. We can become *too* invested in someone else's life, treating their choices as if they were ours to make instead of theirs. Feelings of love can also interfere with our ability to exercise good judgment. If my friend's partner breaks up with her and she's miserable, I'm understandably going to be angry at the jerk who broke her heart. That can make it hard for me to perceive the situation accurately and be fair to everyone involved. Sometimes love needs to be reined in, and for Kant, respect is what does the reining.

Of course, sometimes the problem is that we don't feel *enough* care and concern for people, particularly if we dislike them. Love does not always pull us as close to people as it should. We even sometimes hide our indifference to people by claiming that we're simply respecting their independence or giving them space. As Kant reminds us it's not enough just to leave people alone. Truly treating other people as ends, as beings with dignity, often demands that we step up to the plate and help when we're needed. It's not all about respect. Love matters too.

Kant sometimes talks about love and respect as attitudes, and sometimes as duties that require specific actions from us. We'll be covering some of those specific actions in later chapters, so here I'll focus mostly on love and respect as attitudes. Now when I say that they are attitudes, I don't mean that they are simply feelings. Feelings come and go, but attitudes reflect our underlying moral beliefs, commitments, and priorities. This isn't to say that love and respect don't ever produce feelings. But it would be a mistake to reduce Kantian love and respect to mere feelings.

As we all know, it's possible to love someone dearly (say, your cranky toddler or prickly teenager) without constantly "feeling it" in the sense of having positive emotions toward them. The over-powering love that wells up in your chest as you watch your adorable two-year-old sleeping with her stuffed dog clutched in her arms may disappear the next morning as she flings her oatmeal across the room when you're already late for work. Of course you still love your two-year-old, but you'd have to be a saint to feel complete adoration for her every second of the day. Kant doesn't expect you to be a saint, but he does expect you to be able to get past your irritation and deal with your toddler. And your unreasonable boss. And the unhelpful parking attendant. And the person taking forty-two items through the express checkout lane in the grocery store. People are annoying. We need to find a way not just to deal with them, but to treat them as the valuable creatures that they really are. That is why we need to cultivate the attitudes of love and respect.

Let's start with respect. In some ways, all Kantian duties are duties of respect, but Kant has something specific in mind when he is talking about respect as a moral force that bids us to keep our distance. As we've seen, respecting people means treating them with dignity. Much of the respect that we owe to others takes the form of non-interference. I respect you by not harming you, lying to you, manipulating you, and so forth. But respect is also present in my desire not to get into the business of someone weeping on a park bench. It's true that we're not always expressing respect when we leave people alone. Sometimes we're just being self-centered or indifferent. Sometimes, though, when we're refraining from interfering with someone's life, it reflects a morally important attitude toward that person. This is what Kant has in mind when he says that respect is a moral force.

Kant does occasionally talk about respect as a feeling. It's not always easy to know what he means by that. Insofar as Kantian respect is a feeling, its nearest neighbors might be feelings of awe or reverence. Although Kant doesn't really use terms like "sacred," he does think that our response to rational agency should be something like an acknowledgment of its sacredness. Now this doesn't mean that we have to walk around constantly feeling awestruck by every rational being in our midst. That would be quite a challenge! In some ways, cultivating the attitude of respect is a matter of getting over other kinds of feelings, the ones that get in the way of our ability to see people as we should. In the *Metaphysics of Morals*, Kant names several vices that he says are contrary to the duties of respect that we owe to others. These include vices like contempt, arrogance, and the enjoyment of ridiculing people. We'll be coming back to these vices in later chapters, so I won't say much about them here. The broader point is that respect can only operate properly in us if we are able to squelch these vices and the self-conceit that so often gives rise to them.

Respect as a moral attitude means seeing people in the right way, which is as beings who *warrant* our awe and reverence. This is especially difficult when the beings in question do not seem to be worthy of it. Contemporary philosopher Stephen Darwall draws a useful distinction between what he calls recognition respect and appraisal respect. Appraisal respect is something that we earn through impressive actions and good behavior. It is also something we can lose through bad behavior. Recognition respect, however, is something that we warrant simply in virtue of being rational agents with dignity. Kant is not saying that we always have to treat others with appraisal respect. Some people don't deserve it. But we do owe recognition respect to everyone, regardless of what they've done. Recognition respect consists in the acknowledgment of each person's fundamental value as a rational being. This is not a kind of value that we can waive or forfeit through our actions. Nor is it a value that we can decide that others don't have. (Remember, it's unconditional value.) When Kant talks about the importance of maintaining respect for people, it's recognition respect that he means.

For Kant, respecting people is about more than how we act around them. This isn't to say that acting respectfully isn't important; obviously it is. But respecting people is not just about pulling off the correct outward behavior. It's also about our inner attitudes. We have to do what it takes to make sure that we are always seeing other rational beings as having the value that they have, and regarding them with the recognition respect that they deserve in virtue of that value. This isn't always easy. Lots of things are working against us, including their bad behavior and our own self-conceit. We have to work at maintaining the requisite moral attitude of respect toward all rational beings. Some of this work involves ensuring that we think about others in the right way. Some of it involves presenting ourselves in the right way so that others can maintain their respect for us. We'll dive into those details in later chapters. For now, though, let's set aside respect and turn to love.

In one of his sermons, Martin Luther King Jr. remarks that it's easier to love people than to like them. Kant would agree. There are always going to be people we don't like. But even though loving people isn't as hard as liking them, it doesn't mean that loving them is easy. As Kant points out in the *Lectures on Ethics*, "it is a good thing to love one's neighbor: it makes us good natured; but how can we love him if he is not lovable?"[2] The challenge of loving one's unlovable neighbors is one that Kant takes very seriously. Perhaps it was a challenge he himself faced. Luckily, he has some ideas for us.

In both the *Groundwork* and the *Metaphysics of Morals*, Kant distinguishes between two different kinds of love—practical and pathological. (The word "pathological" is kind of a technical term for Kant. It just means that the love in question is based in *pathos*, or emotion.) Insofar as love is pathological, it isn't something we can summon up on command. It's more like something we experience. Nor are the feelings and inclinations characteristic of pathological love always a good thing. In his discussion of sympathy, Kant shows some impatience with people who are overcome by their feelings and end up not being very useful to the people in distress. The love that we owe to people as a matter of duty is practical love, which is a kind of responsiveness to their actual needs. Sometimes our feelings can get in the way of this responsiveness, as when we "help" them by easing our own pain, not theirs. The aim of practical love is to benefit people, not to assuage or express our own feelings.

But Kant isn't dissing emotions entirely. We don't need to have warm and fuzzy feelings toward people in order to carry out our duties of love to them. It's possible to be extremely helpful to people you don't like. It is, however, much harder than helping people you do like. Kant's solution is to direct us to work on ourselves so that we're more likely to find people lovable and sympathize with them in their troubles. In other words, we should try to cultivate those warm fuzzies as best we can. It's true that some people are really hard to love. We owe duties of love to such people anyway, but it will certainly be easier to recognize and fulfill those duties of love if we can find *something* lovable about them, even if it's just that they're kind to their dog. The more we're able to nurture attitudes associated with love, especially toward people we find annoying, the more responsive we'll be to the needs of others, and the readier we'll be to meet those needs.

How do we cultivate those loving attitudes? As usual, Kant focuses on warning us about the vices that tend to interfere with feelings of sympathy. These vices, which he calls the vices of hatred for human beings, include envy, ingratitude, and malice. It's worth noting that Kant thinks such vices are very serious problems when it comes to our capacity to feel love and meet our obligations. At one point, he even calls them devilish vices. So, the first step in loving people is to ensure that we are not harboring vices that will get in the way of love. And then we have to work on acquiring more substantive feelings of care, compassion, and sympathy, so that we're not simply indifferent to the sufferings of others.

Kant believes that one way to cultivate love for people is to go ahead and help them. He suggests that in helping them, we will eventually come to love them. He says this in several places, so he is clearly pretty confident about it as a practical strategy for cultivating the right kinds of feelings. Unfortunately, he doesn't say much about how he thinks it works, but we can try to fill in the gaps. One possibility is that when we help people, we become invested in their fates ourselves. We want things to go well for the people we've helped. Perhaps we just want proof that our help has worked so that we can pat ourselves on the back, but it's often more than this. To help someone effectively, you have to learn something about their situation. Kant seems confident that this process will encourage natural sympathy in us. For instance, he recommends that we visit sickrooms and debtors' prisons so that we can fully appreciate the difficult situations that people are in. And on this point, he seems to have common sense on his side. We're not going to be able to help people if we shut our eyes to what is happening to them. Part of the duty of love involves taking steps to understand the problems that other people are facing and develop sympathy for them.

The upshot is that if we are really going to fulfill the duties spelled out in the categorical imperative, we have to work on our attitudes toward other people. Although Kant would not deny that it can be pretty hard to see certain people as worthy of respect and love, the problem is very often with us, not them. Things like self-interest and self-conceit get in the way of seeing other people properly. Respecting people means regarding them as my equals, with dignity and absolute value. In respecting people, I grant them the space to make their own decisions and treat those decisions as an expression of their rational agency. Loving people means learning to view them with sympathy and cultivating concern for their needs, so that I will be more responsive to those needs. Kant does think that love needs to be constrained by respect, lest we draw too close and end up interfering more than we should. But he is very clear that both attitudes are important. He warns us that "should one of these great moral forces fail, 'then nothingness (immorality), with gaping throat, would drink up the whole kingdom of (moral) beings like a drop of water.' "[3] That might be a little melodramatic, but it points to the centrality of love and respect to Kant's entire ethical framework. In later chapters, we'll see how these two great moral forces shape our specific duties.

9 | KANTIAN DUTIES

Take a deep breath because this chapter is going to be a little intense. I'm about to sketch a picture of the various types of duties that Kant thinks we have. It's a pretty complicated picture, in part because Kant himself did not provide anything like a consistent, systematic account of our duties. The good news is that you've already encountered some of these duties in previous chapters. The bad news is that you'll need to remember them for later chapters. I'll include some summaries along the way to help you keep track of where we are.

Kant's ethics is often described as an ethics of duty. This isn't entirely wrong, although it's also not entirely right. Still, there's no doubt that duties play a huge role in Kant's theory. In Kantian terms, a duty is simply something that we're morally required to do. To modern ears, using the word "duty" to describe our moral obligations may sound a bit old-fashioned. Alternatively, it may call up images of military duties. We do tend to think of people who serve in the military as having made a commitment to their country that implies explicit duties. We routinely refer to a soldier's duty to deploy or to her duty to follow her commanding officer's orders. Kant's conception of duty is actually not all that far off from this military sense, but for current purposes, it's fine simply to think of "duty" as synonymous with "moral obligation" or "moral require-ment." As we saw in Chapter 4, Kant talks about duty as a motive for action, where he means being committed to doing what's right in a general sense. But he also uses it to describe specific actions and attitudes that are required of us. That's the sense in which we'll be talking about duties in this chapter.

Kant draws a lot of distinctions among types of duties. This can get confusing pretty quickly, but it is also one of the features of his ethical theory that makes it so useful. Kant thinks that our duties are not all the same. Some are more pressing than others. Some can be enforced by the law if we don't live up to them, while others can't. Some can be overridden by other obligations, while others are more like unbreakable vows. If we want an ethical theory that is sensitive to these intuitive variations in our moral obligations, we're going to have to accept some complexity. And that's going to mean working through the various distinctions that Kant draws among different categories of duties. Hopefully the usefulness of these distinctions will become clear as you read this chapter. We'll also be employing the distinctions in later chapters, which will help you see how they work and why they matter.

Let's start with a fundamental distinction between what Kant called juridical duties (or duties of right) and ethical duties (or duties of virtue). This distinction corresponds to the divide be-tween the two halves of his work, the *Metaphysics of Morals*. The first half of that book is called the *Doctrine of Right* and the second part is called the *Doctrine of Virtue*. Kant's political philosophy is outlined in the *Doctrine of Right*, while the *Doctrine of Virtue* ex-pands (kind of) on the ethical framework spelled out in the ear-lier *Groundwork for the Metaphysics of Morals*. The easiest way to explain the difference between juridical duties and ethical duties is in terms of whether they are subject to external enforcement by the state.

Here's what I mean. I have a duty not to kill you. This is a juridical duty, one that I owe to you as a matter of right. In Kant's terms, that means that the state may coerce me in ways that prevent me from killing you. It may also punish me for having killed you if those deterrence methods don't work. For Kant, the main task of the state is to create and maintain conditions in which we can all exercise our rationality together. If we were all perfectly rational beings, we would never do the things that the state prevents us from doing. But (and I know this will shock you) we're not perfectly rational beings. I may very well harbor a desire to do you harm. For you to live your life as freely as possible, you need some kind of state with the authority to restrict my actions. The state protects you by enforcing certain claims that you have on me, like the claim that I refrain from gratuitous violence against you. Should I come after you with my sword, the state may permissibly step in and stop me. This is what it means to say that I have a juridical duty not to kill you.

But you might be thinking, wait, don't I have a duty not to kill you regardless of whether it's against the law? Indeed, I do. It is certainly true that killing you would be illegal, but let's hope that I do not need the threat of jail to get me to put down my sword. I should refrain from killing you because killing you would be wrong. And this is why Kant holds that all juridical duties have parallel ethical duties. I do have a juridical duty not to kill you, but I also have an ethical duty not to kill you. That ethical duty rests in your status as an end, or a being with dignity. If I kill you, I would be treating you as a mere means to my end of having a world free of your presence. This is true regardless of what the law says.

This means that there's a sense in which for a person with a good will, some (maybe most) laws are superfluous. But the concept of a juridical duty is still important because it marks out a specific terrain of action that the state has the authority to regulate and coerce. Crucially, that terrain extends only to my external behavior. The state can prevent me from performing certain actions and require me to perform others. What it cannot do, however, is demand that I act for particular reasons, have particular motives, or adopt particular attitudes. It can order me not to kill you, but it cannot regulate my motives in refraining from killing you. This is why Kant thinks that ethical duties overlay all our juridical duties. If I refrain from killing you because I don't want to go to jail, I may be fulfilling my juridical duty toward you, but I'd still be failing in my ethical duty.

In this book, we are primarily concerned with ethical duties, not juridical ones. So, we'll leave juridical duties behind for now. Instead, we'll turn to another distinction, one that separates some ethical duties from others. This is the distinction between perfect and imperfect duties. We've discussed this distinction a few times already, but let's review it because it's quite important to Kant's overall picture. Perfect duties are duties to do or refrain from doing specific actions, like killing and lying. Imperfect duties are duties to adopt ends or take on commitments. They do not point us toward specific actions, at least not in most cases. Instead, they take the form of commitments like, "help people who are in need" or "make something of your life instead of sitting around binge-watching Netflix." You aren't violating an imperfect duty if you don't help everyone or if you occasionally sit in front of your TV all day. After all, you might have run out of spare cash, or you might have symptoms of COVID-19 and need to self-isolate. Or perhaps you are just tired and grumpy and not in the mood to volunteer at the animal shelter or practice the flute.

Perfect and imperfect duties are names for two categories of duties. Within these categories, Kant identifies specific duties that he thinks we have. We'll be talking about many of these specific duties in later chapters. Here, though, I will focus on the two duties that Kant puts into the category of imperfect duties. The first is a duty to improve ourselves. (Technically, this is actually a duty to perfect ourselves. This will become important in Chapter 29, but not until then, so I'm going to stick with calling it a duty of self-improvement for the time being.) The second is a duty to promote the happiness of others. To say that these are imperfect duties is to say that they are ends or commitments that we take up as a central part of our lives. If I adopt my own improvement and the happiness of others as ends, those commitments will frame my thinking and my decisions. Crucially, Kant argues that these two ends are morally obligatory. They are not optional extras. We don't have a choice about whether to adopt them. (Confusingly, the fact that we are morally obligated to adopt these two ends means that we have a perfect duty to adopt the ends that generate our specific imperfect duties.) Morality itself requires me to take up my own improvement and the happiness of others as life-shaping commitments.

Let's start with the duty of self-improvement. In saying that I have a duty to improve myself, Kant means that I have to take seriously my own development. This includes both my moral development and what we might call my personal development, or the cultivation of my talents and capacities. We'll return to personal development in Chapter 20, so I will focus on moral development here. Basically, Kant says that we are morally obligated to work on our moral characters. It's something we owe to ourselves as a matter of self-respect. Moral improvement is a way of perfecting ourselves as rational beings. When I make myself morally better, I make myself more capable of acting in accordance with my own rational principles and so more capable of acting autonomously. In some sense, making ourselves better is a way of making ourselves free.

Kant explicitly says that we have no parallel duty to improve other people. This is largely because it is not something we can actually do. Becoming better is a matter of committing more fully and thoroughly to morality, and I cannot do this on behalf of someone else. Each of us is responsible for the state of our own wills. Now Kant does make exceptions for parents and teachers engaged in the moral education of children. And as we'll see in later chapters, my ability to make myself better is affected by my social environment. There will be some sense in which moral improvement is a collective project. Kant also claims at one point that we have a duty not to corrupt people. I should not go around making other people worse. Not only would it be disrespectful to them but engaging in corrupting activities also poses a rather large threat to my own moral character. The upshot is that this duty of moral improvement, while technically a duty I owe only to myself, has social dimensions that we will explore in later chapters.

The second big imperfect duty is the duty to promote the happiness of others. We will be talking about this duty extensively in Chapter 23, but it's so important to Kant's account that it's worth spending a few minutes on it here. This duty is a crucial way in which we express both love and respect for other people. Remember that in order to treat someone as an end in themselves, we have to take seriously the fact they have goals, projects, and ends of their own. That's why I have a reason to help you with your runaway cat, even if I don't like the cat. The fact that the cat matters to you is the part that matters to Kant. (Kant never discusses his feelings about cats, but one gets the sense that he's more of a dog person.) My imperfect duty to promote your ends is something I owe to you as my fellow rational being. It's how I show positive respect for you as a setter of ends.

If you're hoping that Kant will say that we also have a moral duty to promote our own happiness, I'm sorry to have to disappoint you. He claims this isn't a moral duty, in part because it's something we are inclined to do anyway. It's not that Kant thinks that I should ignore my own needs and focus entirely on other people. As we'll see in Chapter 13, that would be a failure to treat myself with respect. It's just that when I take myself out for ice cream, I'm not doing something *morally* good in the way that I am if I take my next-door neighbor out for ice cream.

To review, the main difference between perfect duties and imperfect duties is that perfect duties are duties to perform or refrain from performing particular actions. (Most perfect duties are duties to refrain from doing things.) Imperfect duties are duties to take on commitments. Taking on those commitments means regarding them as priorities in our lives and acting accordingly.

A very important element in Kant's ethics is that perfect duties always take precedence over imperfect duties. This has the implication that you can never justify violating a perfect duty to fulfill an imperfect duty. So, you can't kill one person to use their organs for life-saving transplants into five other people. Neither can you push a person onto a trolley track to stop an oncoming train and prevent it from hitting five people further down the track. Kant sees both these actions as using the one person as a mere means to saving the other five. In general, saving someone's life is a way of fulfilling the imperfect duty to promote their happiness. But there are moral constraints on the ways in which we promote the happiness of others, such as the duty to avoid treating people as a mere means. It's never all right to use anyone as a mere means in your efforts to promote someone's happiness. If I were to kill you to save five others, I'd be using you as a mere means toward saving them. While it's good to save them, I can't do it by violating your right to be treated as a being with dignity. The imperfect duty to help them has to give way to the perfect duty not to harm you as a way of helping them.

Perfect duties have no wiggle room. Imperfect duties do come with some wiggle room. Importantly, there is no wiggle room at all when it comes to committing ourselves to our own improvement and the happiness of others. We are required to have those commitments—no squirming our way out of them! The wiggle room comes into play when we start thinking about how to act on those commitments. I get to make some choices about the kinds of helping actions I perform and the ways in which I develop my talents and capacities. This doesn't mean that helping people is always optional. In concrete situations, imperfect duties can produce more or less stringent obligations. If someone is having a heart attack in front of me, I need to do CPR or at least call 911 (or both). But for the most part, I'm not acting wrongly if I decide not to give money to a particular charity or if I decline to help you move house for the fourth time this year. When it comes to imperfect duties, we're generally looking at the bigger picture. Do I *ever* donate money to charity? Am I *always* busy when you or anyone else needs a hand? If the answer is no, then I'm almost certainly failing in my imperfect duty to commit myself to the happiness of others. The same is true if I never take any steps to improve my moral character or develop my personal talents and capacities.

What I'm calling wiggle room is more technically known as latitude. We have no latitude when it comes to performing perfect duties. We also have no latitude when it comes to adopting the two ends of my own improvement and the happiness of others. We do have latitude when it comes to the specifics of how we fulfill those duties. There are all kinds of ways to improve myself or contribute to the happiness of others. I can go to medical school or become an accomplished violinist. I can volunteer at the homeless shelter, or I can work with refugee families. Any of these would be good paths by Kantian standards. He recognizes that we have to use our judgment when it comes to determining how best to make something of ourselves and to help others. Each of us is different, and we all have different circumstances. The person who is truly committed to those two obligatory ends, however, will make sure that her commitment shines through in her life choices.

Now from the fact that imperfect duties have latitude, it does not follow that any given imperfect duty is optional. Some imperfect duties are more stringent than others. The duty to improve ourselves morally is a stringent one. I can't decide that I'm going to work on my moral character only on Wednesdays. The duty to promote the happiness of others usually has lots of latitude, but not when we're talking about emergencies. If someone's life is in danger and all I have to do is call 911 from the phone I'm currently holding in my hand, it's not optional. It's my obligation, even if I've already spent all day helping people. Kant also thinks that there can be better or worse reasons for not helping people. If I choose to help only people I like, or only people who belong to my political party, something is going wrong. We'll talk more about all of this when we get to the duty of beneficence in Chapter 23. The take-home message is that although imperfect duties have latitude built into them, there is no "get out duty free" card that we can use to shirk our responsibilities for the welfare of others or our own improvement.

Let's do a quick summary of what we've said about Kantian duties. Some duties are juridical (enforceable by the state) and some are ethical. We're focusing just on ethical duties. Ethical duties can be either perfect or imperfect. Perfect duties are duties to do or refrain from doing specific actions. They require perfect compliance from us. There's never a justification for violating a perfect duty. Imperfect duties are duties to take on particular commitments or ends. Kant thinks there are two ends we are required to adopt— our own improvement and the happiness of others. Perfect duties allow no latitude. Imperfect duties usually allow for latitude, although things get complicated in emergencies. Perfect duties also always take priority over imperfect duties. Indeed, this is part of why imperfect duties need to have some wiggle room. If the only way I can help you win the science fair is to knock your main competitor senseless, I'm going to have to take a pass on giving you a hand. While both perfect and imperfect duties are essential to treating ourselves and others with respect, there's a sense in which perfect duties are more fundamental to respecting ourselves and others as rational beings.

One consequence of Kant's system of duties is that there are never any moral dilemmas. By a moral dilemma, I mean a situation in which you are both morally required to do something and morally required not to do that thing (or morally required to do something incompatible with it). I'd be in a moral dilemma if I were morally required to be in the town of Hadleyville at noon to face down three villains in a gunfight and *also* morally required to be at my Quaker meeting in the next town over at noon, reaffirming my commitment to pacifism.[1] Kant thinks there aren't any moral dilemmas. This is in part because he took seriously a principle usually expressed as "ought implies can." If it's true of you that you ought to do something, it must also be true of you that you can do that thing. This is why I can't have a duty to get myself to the moon or develop an effective malaria vaccine by Tuesday morning. I can be obligated to do only those things that are possible for me. A moral dilemma is a situation in which I have two conflicting obligations. I must do both, but I cannot do both. I'll inevitably be violating one obligation or the other. Although a whole lot of Greek tragedy revolves around moral dilemmas, Kant does not seem to believe that fate puts us into such lousy positions.

Kant's theory rules out moral dilemmas because perfect duties, being primarily negative duties, never present us with conflicting obligations.[2] I can fulfill all my perfect duties at the same time. For instance, right now I am not killing a single person, thereby fulfilling a perfect duty to everyone on the planet. (Aren't you impressed?) Imperfect duties can conflict with each other, but no particular instance of an imperfect duty is ever strictly required of me. That's what it is for something to be an imperfect duty. This means that I always have a way to resolve any conflict, whether between an imperfect duty and a perfect duty (the perfect duty wins) or between two imperfect duties (I use my judgment to decide). Some people see this as an advantage of Kant's theory. Others are skeptical that the moral life works out so neatly.

We're getting close to the end, but we still have a few more distinctions to power through. As you may remember from earlier chapters, Kant thinks that we have duties both to ourselves and to other people. There is a sense in which these duties are parallel, at least in terms of their importance. They all derive from the same source, which is the value of rational agents. The duties I have to myself are just as important as the duties I have toward you, particularly when we're talking about perfect duties. But as you've already seen, there is another sense in which my duties to myself and my duties to others are not parallel. The actual duties are not the same, and Kant, rather confusingly, uses quite different terminology in developing subcategories within each type of duty.

Let's take up duties to ourselves first. Kant divides my duties to myself into two subcategories: duties I owe to myself as an animal being and duties I owe to myself as a moral being. The duties I owe to myself as an animal being are all in some way related to my body. These duties include a duty not to commit suicide, a duty not to commit certain sexual acts that Kant regards as unchaste, and a duty not to drink or eat myself into a stupor. (Yes, I know this is a strange collection of duties.) These are all perfect duties, although the third is a bit tricky. The line between eating and overeating, or drinking and getting drunk, is not exactly straightforward. We'll be coming back to drunkenness in Chapter 19.

The duties I owe to myself as a moral being are all about how I relate to myself as a rational agent. Here again Kant mentions three: a duty to avoid lying, a duty to avoid avarice or greed, and a duty not to be subservient or servile to other people. These are also perfect duties. I owe it to myself not to misuse my reason, as I do when I'm lying, or allow it to be controlled by outside forces like money or other people. I also have that large looming imperfect duty to improve myself, both in terms of my natural capacities and my good will. We'll come back to most of these duties in later chapters.

You might expect Kant to divide our duties to others into the subcategories of animal and moral as well. Alas, he does not. But you'll be glad to know that you've already encountered the subcategories he uses for our duties to others—love and respect. We have duties of respect to others that include things like a duty not to hold them in contempt, not to be arrogant, not to spread nasty gossip about them, and not to mock them. These are perfect duties, although as we'll see, there are also associated vices. Kant lists three duties of love that we owe to others—a duty of beneficence, a duty to cultivate sympathy, and a duty of gratitude. The duty of beneficence is an imperfect duty. (It's sort of the same as the general imperfect duty to promote the happiness of others.) The duty to cultivate sympathy is also an imperfect duty because it's not a specific action. The duty of gratitude has elements of both perfect and imperfect duty. It tells us to do specific things, like express thanks when people do us favors. But it's also an attitude we have to cultivate, like sympathy. For the most part, though, our duties of respect are perfect duties, and our duties of love are imperfect duties.

I promise, we're really almost finished! There's one more kind of duty that is not an official category, but that shows up rather sneakily in a number of places in Kant's ethics. This is what he calls a "duty to humanity as such." What makes this an odd duty is that it is not a duty to a particular person. We might think of "humanity" in this context as functioning like it does when we talk about crimes against humanity. A crime against humanity is often a crime against specific individuals. When we call something a crime against humanity, however, we generally mean something that is over and above the specific violations of duty toward those individuals. It's a crime against the human race—past, present, and future. Kant's duty to humanity as such seems to rely on a similar sense of humanity. It's a duty that we owe to humanity over and above the duties that we owe to specific human beings. To keep things simple, I'm going to talk about the duty to humanity as such as a duty to the moral community, in the sense of the ethical commonwealth. This is not perfectly accurate, but it's close enough for our purposes. And anyway, by this point you're probably running out of mental space for additional distinctions.

We now have quite an array of duties before us. You do not need to memorize them. There is no quiz at the end of the book. When we talk about specific duties in later chapters, I'll remind you about where each of them fits into this overall schema. Still, you might find it helpful to refer back to this chapter once in a while to keep some of these duties straight in your head. And congratulations! You just survived Kantian duty boot camp!

Part II

Moral Assessment

10 | KNOWING OURSELVES

Know thyself. These words were said to have been inscribed at the Temple of Apollo in Delphi, Greece. This temple was the site of a famous oracle, an oracle that once declared that no one running around ancient Athens was wiser than Socrates. Now Socrates claims that he found this puzzling, as he took himself to be ignorant of most things (nearly everything, in fact). He spent his days seeking wisdom in those who claimed they had it, only to be disappointed at their consistent inability to hold up under his questioning. When the Athenians finally got tired of Socrates humiliating them, they put him on trial for his life. His defense, recorded by his student Plato in a work called the *Apology*, was unsuccessful, in that he was sentenced to death by drinking hemlock. But it was successful in enshrining a fundamental principle in western philosophy, which is that knowledge is both very important and very difficult to acquire. This is especially true of self-knowledge.

Socrates famously says that his wisdom, such as it is, consists in awareness of his own ignorance. On his view, the best we can do is rid ourselves of our false beliefs. Kant is not quite as skeptical about the possibility of knowledge as Socrates, but he does share his predecessor's concern about the dangers of overestimating what we can and do know. This is especially true when it comes to self-knowledge. It might be natural to suppose that self-knowledge is the easiest, most reliable kind of knowledge around. After all, we are constantly with ourselves, so we have plenty of time and opportunity to observe ourselves. And surely no one knows us better than we know ourselves.

Alas, we are no more immune to self-deception than the ancient Athenians. For instance, sometimes when we are not in fact very good at something, we mistakenly take ourselves to be much better at it than we are, a phenomenon known in psychology as the Dunning-Kruger effect. Bad drivers tend to think they are good drivers, bad teachers tend to think they are good teachers, and so forth. It takes skill to recognize a lack of skill in yourself, which means that those who are unskilled are often especially short on self-awareness. More generally, there's plenty of evidence to indicate that many of the operations of our minds are opaque to us. Much of the time, we're unaware of what's really motivating us and causing us to act as we do. We are, as psychologist Timothy Wilson puts it, strangers to ourselves.

These challenges about self-knowledge put us in a difficult position when it comes to cultivating a good will. After all, how can we make ourselves better if we aren't even in a position to see ourselves clearly? Kant is fully aware of this problem. As we've seen, his list of duties includes a duty to ourselves to improve our moral characters. But Kant also acknowledges that human nature makes it challenging to fulfill this duty. Although he didn't have the resources of modern psychology at his disposal, he does recognize the difficulties we face when it comes to accurate self-assessment. For Kant, much of the problem lies in our strong interest in getting what we want (self-love) while maintaining a high opinion of ourselves relative to others (self-conceit). When we combine these propensities toward self-love and self-conceit with our capacity to engage in rationalization and self-deception, the result is a major hurdle to self-knowledge.

Consider for a minute how easy it is to talk yourself into believing that some incident or argument is entirely the other person's fault. When I'm not involved in an argument or invested in the outcome, I can usually see how both sides are fanning the flames and making things worse. But when I'm one of the parties to the conflict, it becomes much more difficult to take up that perspective. After all, most of us prefer being right to being wrong. We definitely prefer blaming others over accepting blame ourselves. This means that I'm likely to construct a scenario that supports the worldview I favor, the one in which I am the hero and my opponent is the villain. It's unlikely that this scenario is always (or even ever!) fully accurate. Self-deception, however, is a powerful force, particularly when it serves our interests.

As we've seen, Kant thinks we are all capable of recognizing the categorical imperative and its authority. It is not a mystery what the categorical imperative says, or what it requires of us. But that doesn't mean it's easy for us to know how well we're living up to its demands. This puts us in a bit of a bind when it comes to assessing how we're doing from a moral standpoint. Even though I'm supposed to be striving for a good will, I cannot ever know if I actually have one. I'm strongly invested in believing that I'm a good person, but in truth, I don't have a lot of evidence one way or the other. There is no giant accounting system, à la *The Good Place*, that we can consult to see how we're stacking up. All we have is what we observe. Unfortunately, that's not always so helpful.

As Kant notes in the *Anthropology*, self-observation is fraught with challenges. As most of us are aware, when we're being observed by others, our behavior tends to change. The same thing happens when we try to observe ourselves. We just can't get a good look at what we're doing. Much of what we need to know remains a mystery. Self-examination is also not a lot of fun. We have strong motivations not to seek out unpleasant truths about ourselves and our behavior. Even when those unpleasant truths are basically staring us in the face, we prefer not to acknowledge them. In fact, we're quite skilled at reasoning our way around them. And yet, if we really want to be better, there's no way around the difficult and unpleasant task of looking at ourselves in the moral mirror. Kant puts it this way: "Only the descent into the hell of self-cognition can pave the way to godliness."[1] Acquiring self-knowledge is a potentially hellish, but necessary task. If we're going to commit ourselves to our moral improvement, as Kant says we must, we have to be willing to be as honest with ourselves as possible.

Honest self-assessment is a real challenge. Of course, it's not like we can't know *anything* about how we're doing. I am surely capable of knowing whether I've killed anyone today, or stolen a widower's life savings, or made my employees work overtime illegally. I can know these things about myself in the sense of knowing what external behaviors I have performed or failed to perform, although we should not underestimate how powerful self-deception can be here too. But there's a lot more to being a good person than what's observable from the outside. Maybe I'm releasing my employees from work on time because I don't want to be fined or be targeted in a lawsuit. Maybe I'm refraining from killing you because I know you have black belts in several martial arts and I doubt I'll succeed. From the outside, it can be hard to tell the difference between a person who refrains from murder or theft because it's the right thing to do and a person who refrains from murder or theft because they're afraid of getting caught. But the difference certainly seems to matter to what kind of person they are on the inside.

We also frequently have mixed motives, as Kant's example of the sympathetic philanthropist in the *Groundwork* illustrates. Suppose I'm the kind of person who just enjoys helping people. Suppose that in a particular case, helping people is also my moral duty. If I go out and help them, am I doing it because it's right or because it's enjoyable? If it's the latter, does that make me selfish? Kant thinks that most of the time, we really can't know what our motives are. As he says:

> The depths of the human heart are unfathomable. Who knows himself well enough to say, when he feels the incentive to fulfill his duty, whether it proceeds entirely from the representation of the law or whether there are not many other sensible impulses contributing to it that look to one's advantage (or to avoiding what is detrimental) and that, in other circumstances, could just as well serve vice?[2]

Usually, we can't tell much about our motives unless our circumstances happen to force a kind of reckoning on us. Even that, however, has its limitations.

Suppose it's my week to help make lunch at the local homeless shelter, but I wake up tired and hungover after a night of partying.

Suppose further that it's raining and that my car has a flat tire, meaning that I'd have to take a long and inconvenient bus ride to get to the shelter. As we know, Kant thinks that these are the kinds of situation that provide us with some insight into our real characters. Am I a person who, despite having absolutely no desire to go help at the shelter today, nevertheless gets out of bed and goes? If so, then I have some evidence that my will is good.

Still, it's only *some* evidence. Even if I can tell that my will is good here, I may well deceive myself about it in other cases. Remember, we're really good at rationalizing our choices, especially when those choices serve our self-interested desires. And so, as I'm lying there in bed, I might start to think that my throat feels a bit scratchy, or that my stomach isn't quite right. What if I'm actually sick, not hungover? It would be a terrible thing to go make food at a homeless shelter if I'm in the grip of some contagious illness. A responsible, morally sensitive person would avoid spreading germs to others. Clearly then the right thing is for me to stay in bed and protect all those people from what is surely an unpleasant and potentially serious illness lurking in my throat.

See how easy it was for me to get myself to the conclusion that I wanted? The one that allows me to continue to think of myself as a selfless person even as I'm lying comfortably in bed? Kant knows that we do this sort of thing all the time. Probably he did as well. In fact, he must have been engaged in some pretty hefty rationalization and self-deception, given the sexist and racist views that he held. He is hardly alone among his eighteenth-century compatriots in being sexist and racist, and yet we might still wonder why, with all his emphasis on self-examination, he often seems so very unaware of his own prejudices and biases.

Let's return to the issue of slavery. Kant was never a vocal advocate of slavery, but neither did he oppose it until the very end of his life. Even then, he did so rather weakly. Given that slavery clearly violates the categorical imperative, treating people as a mere means in about the most obvious and awful way possible, how could such a smart man not arrive at the conclusion that it is deeply morally wrong? There were certainly opponents of slavery in his academic circles; it's not as though he had never heard arguments for abolitionism. And yet, those arguments seem to have carried little weight with him. At the very least, it's disappointing, and at the most, it's a damning indictment of Kant's moral character and capacity for moral insight. What good is an ethical system that can't even illuminate the wrongness of slavery for its creator?

In some ways, Kant predicted his own failures, insofar as he recognizes the deep challenges of self-knowledge. Kant's racism was motivated by features of his thinking that are familiar to us and hardly absent today—an overly quick willingness to accept false portrayals of people of other races, a desire to have the superiority of his comfortable Northern European culture reinforced, and more generally, a failure to acknowledge the humanity of other people. If nothing else, Kant's own racism and sexism should remind us of the dangers of self-assurance and rationalization. Kant's brilliance was no remedy for his moral failings. It may even have exacerbated it insofar as it led him to place too much confidence in his own judgment. Probably like most of us, Kant found it hard to be wrong.

What, then, does Kant suggest for us when it comes to overcoming the problems of self-knowledge? He does have a remedy of sorts, although perhaps not a perfect one. Obviously, it did not always work for him. But it's something. The remedy is a tool that he calls the "court of conscience." It's not quite like having Judge Judy in your head to cut through all the nonsense, but as we're about to see, it's also not that far off.

11 | JUDGING OURSELVES

Have you ever done something kind of shady and then felt guilty about it afterwards? Would you consider this the work of your conscience? Kant would. He believes that each of us has a conscience and that if we use it properly, it's an extremely important tool for making moral progress. In Chapter 8, we saw that Kant thinks of moral improvement as a duty. It's one of the two required ends, or one of the two ends that we are morally obligated to take up. I have a duty to cultivate my good will. And self-reflection, guided by my conscience, is a key part of that cultivation.

Kant talks about this self-reflection in terms of a rather elaborate legal metaphor—the court of conscience. In Kant's court of conscience, we call ourselves to account in a way similar to how we call suspected offenders to account in a courtroom. But in my personal court of conscience, I'm playing all the roles. I'm the defendant, the defense attorney, the prosecutor, *and* the judge. In the court of conscience, my job is to determine the truth about myself, so far as I can. Now Kant isn't proposing that we put on robes and set up mock courtrooms. What he means is that we need to step back and take a hard look at ourselves from the standpoint of a less partial observer.

Suppose that, having bailed on my commitment to serve lunch at the homeless shelter, I am now reflecting on my action, perhaps in response to a feeling of mild guilt. In the court of conscience, I might ask myself: was my scratchy throat really a sign of illness, or was it an after-effect of last night's drinking? Would I have made the same call if it had been a beautiful day, if my car was functioning, and if my latest crush was also scheduled to work at the shelter that day? These are the kind of questions we are supposed to pose to ourselves in the court of conscience.

Kant believes that everyone has a conscience, in that everyone has it within their power to know what's right. He also seems to have confidence that if we really subject ourselves to the court of conscience, in good faith and with the right attitude, we'll be able to see through the ruses that we use to rationalize our actions, at least many of them. But we do have to be willing to allow reflection to take us where we don't want to go. We have to let go of our desire to see ourselves as the victim, the hero, or whatever narrative about ourselves suits us best, and instead take ownership of our own moral mistakes and failures. This means that if we're going to use the court of conscience effectively, we need to develop a sense of humility.

For Kant, humility is very important to effective self-reflection. We must be willing to look in the mirror, even if we don't like what we see there. Crucially, being humble doesn't mean that we try to shoulder all the blame for everything or see ourselves as worthless. If the court of conscience ends up making us feel inept or hopeless, something has gone amiss. Kant himself focuses mostly on our unwillingness to accept that we've been in the wrong, probably because he worries a lot about our propensity toward self-conceit.

We are too prone to thinking unreasonably well of ourselves. But it's also a problem if self-examination in the court of conscience produces a feeling of failure or despondency. As he warns us, "self-conceit and dejection are the two rocks on which man is wrecked if he deviates, in the one direction or the other, from the moral law."[1]

When the court of conscience is working properly, we will be able to avoid both these two rocks. We'll avoid self-conceit because we'll have to come to grips with the hard truths about ourselves that we don't want to hear. And we'll avoid dejection because, Kant thinks, we'll be reminded of our own dignity and moral capacities. Indeed, if we do the court of conscience right, we'll end up even more committed to morality than when we started. To understand this, we'll need to consider in more detail how the court of conscience is supposed to work.

Actually, it helps to start with how Kant thinks it's *not* supposed to work. When we're in the court of conscience, we're assessing our behavior in light of some standard. One thing Kant argues that we should not be doing is using other people as that standard. He regards comparisons as a dangerous business. On Kant's view, using other people as the measure by which we judge ourselves is counterproductive. Not only does it not help us improve, but most of the time it actually makes us worse. (Do you ever feel annoyed and miserable after an afternoon of scrolling through Instagram? Kant would not be surprised.)

Kant's skepticism about comparisons is a bit unusual, both within moral philosophy and outside of it. The idea that we should look to others as examples for behavior, whether positive or negative, has ancient roots. Exemplarism, as it is often called, is a central tenet of Confucianism and it appears in many strands of

Western philosophical thought as well. In ordinary human life, it's common to seek out role models that we admire, doing our best to imitate them. We also frequently look at what others do as a way of identifying behaviors and character traits that we want to avoid. Given all this, Kant's distrust of comparisons as a way of altering our behavior needs some explaining.

What exactly is his problem with comparing ourselves to others? Sometimes the issue is that we are using the wrong criteria to make comparisons of worth. I may compare myself to someone who is more (or less) financially successful than me and draw conclusions about my relative social worth. Kant, like most people, would reject this kind of comparison as a mistake, at least if we're assessing our moral value. My dignity does not depend on my income.

But Kant is also opposed to using comparisons that rely on moral characteristics. As we've been discussing, he worries about the ways in which our propensities toward self-conceit and self-love warp our perspective on our own behavior. We give ourselves too much credit and are often unwilling to face up to our own flaws. Kant thinks that these propensities infiltrate our perspective on other people too. It's not just that we are inclined to go easy on ourselves. We are also inclined to be hard on others. And when these two inclinations come together, as they do when we are comparing ourselves to others, trouble ensues.

Proponents of using moral exemplars as a way of inspiring us to become better often assume that the comparison will have a positive effect on our motivations. Jonathan Haidt describes an emotion called elevation, which is essentially a warm and fuzzy response to the noble deeds of other people. If reflecting on the virtues of other people inspires elevation, we'll be motivated to emulate them and reach new moral heights ourselves. Kant, however, has his doubts about whether things really work this smoothly in practice.

In the *Lectures on Ethics*, Kant claims that there are two methods we can employ to measure ourselves. We can compare ourselves to the ideal of rational behavior represented by the categorical imperative, or we can compare ourselves to actual people. He strongly favors the first method over the second. But why? To understand Kant's reasons, we have to reach back into his theory of human nature and what he thinks actually happens when we measure ourselves against other living, breathing human beings.

In a rather entertaining passage, Kant describes the aftermath when a parent attempts to encourage better behavior in her child by pointing to "young Fritz next door" as an exemplar. (So well-behaved and industrious!) As Kant sees it, her efforts are not likely to have the desired effect of inspiring her own child to become more like Fritz, or to see him as a role model. No, the most likely consequence is that her child will just end up disliking his neighbor: "By setting up [Fritz] as a pattern for imitation, I anger my son, and make him feel a grudge against this so-called paragon, and I instill jealousy in him."[2] Not exactly "Parent of the Year" material there. Kant goes on to warn that the child may resort to disparaging and belittling poor young Fritz in an effort to fend off an assessment that makes him look and feel bad by comparison.

Kant's point is that when we find ourselves being compared against someone else and coming up short, we can take one of two paths. Either we can put in the hard work of making ourselves better or else we can bring the other person down to our level. The second path is certainly the easier one and usually also the most pleasant. (For Kant, that alone is probably enough to warrant a red flag.) But it is the more dangerous path because it allows me to wallow in the false illusion that I am just fine as I am. It's also deeply unfair to the Fritzes of the world, who probably don't deserve to be the target of my jealousy. This means that the second path interferes with our ability to improve ourselves and to relate well to others.

Being compared negatively to someone else threatens my self-image. The natural way for me to protect myself from the threat is to turn the comparison on its head. In doing so, however, I distort my perception of myself and of the person to whom I am being compared. This distorted perception makes it impossible for me to see myself accurately. I'm likely to shut down in response to the criticism and refuse to consider whether there's something in it. This is not exactly a good tactic for self-improvement. To make matters worse, I'm also likely to feel resentful of the person to whom I'm being compared. Belittling that person may be how I deal with my resentment because it enables me to bring them down to my level, or even below it. But throwing shade at other people is hardly the solution to fixing my own moral shortcomings. If anything, it exacerbates them. This is why Kant thinks that comparisons are downright harmful when used as a tool for self-assessment and self-improvement.

Perhaps, though, this problem is confined to comparisons that come from outside of us. It's worth noting that comparisons imposed by others sometimes stem from their attempts to control or manipulate us. Advertising, for instance, often operates by first making us feel bad about ourselves in comparison with others and then trying to sell us something that will fix whatever is supposedly wrong with us and get us up to par with others. There is plenty of Kantian justification for resisting attempts by other people to "improve" us, although Kant would undoubtedly make exceptions when it comes to parents and teachers improving children. (Kant wasn't a parent himself, but he did spend years working as a tutor and had plenty of experience with adolescents.) His concern about the parent comparing her child to Fritz is primarily about her method, not about her right to influence her child's moral development. It's true, though, that we often have compelling Kantian reasons to dismiss comparisons imposed on us by others.

But what about comparisons that we draw for ourselves? Can those be useful in helping us improve? Suppose that I'm the one who looks at Fritz and sees the kind of person I'd like to become. Many of us really do feel inspired by people like Rosa Parks, and regard them as moral exemplars. In such cases, we are often identifying particular character traits (like courage, persistence, or wisdom) that we see the other person as having and that we would like to develop ourselves. If I'm the one choosing the exemplar and working to become more like her, it seems unlikely that I would end up belittling or disparaging her. Am I really going to read about Rosa Parks and decide she is overrated or that she has flaws that lessen her achievements? That might happen if I'm being really cynical, but we're not usually cynical about our role models. (If we were, we wouldn't be using them as role models!)

Kant himself doesn't seem to see much of a positive role for exemplars when it comes to improving ourselves. He suggests that when we do choose our own comparisons, we tend to select competitors over whom we can achieve an easy victory. (Real estate estimates offer a useful analogy here. If I am trying to justify a high estimate for the house I'm selling, I'm going to deliberately seek out comparisons that make my house shine.) No doubt he is right that this is sometimes what happens. Sometimes we really are just trying to make ourselves look good. But that isn't always what we're doing when we compare ourselves to people. Haidt and his colleagues have compelling research showing that reflecting on moral exemplars can at least sometimes motivate us in the right direction.

Let us grant that Kant may be unduly pessimistic about our ability to use comparisons constructively. But before we jump fully on the exemplar bandwagon, it is worth considering Kant's proposed alternative. Instead of comparing ourselves to other people, he suggests, we should compare ourselves to the "ideal of perfection" represented in the moral law. What does this mean and how could it help us become better?

Kant, recall, believes that the requirements of morality are no mystery to us. If I am being honest, it will be clear to me whether or not I have lived up to moral standards, at least in terms of my external behavior. (My motives, alas, are likely to remain opaque to me.) I am fully capable of assessing my own behavior against what it should have been. I don't need to compare myself with Rosa Parks to see where I fall short. Examining my own conscience, with proper humility, will make my moral failings clear to me. Of course, this implies that the court of conscience is a pretty unpleasant place to hang out. We sometimes have to force ourselves to spend time there.

But Kant adds an interesting twist. It's true that comparing ourselves to a perfect moral ideal is a deeply humbling experience. We will inevitably fall short of what morality demands of us. Crucially, though, humbling need not mean humiliating. When we feel humiliated, we feel that we have been lowered, that we have lost our value and are not worth very much. Kant's twist is that comparing ourselves to the moral ideal actually counteracts that tendency toward feeling humiliated by our failings. In reflecting on the moral law within me (Kant's fancy way of saying my capacity to govern myself by reason), I will not only see my shortcomings. I will also be filled with respect for my own dignity and by extension, the dignity of others as well. In the court of conscience, I am reminded that I am more than my worst moments, that I am not hopeless or evil. I am a rational being, with all the moral possibility that entails. My failings do not and need not define me. This is why Kant thinks that spending time in self-reflection can actually leave us feeling inspired. The inspiration comes not from delusions about our own behavior. It comes from our realization that we are capable of so very much more.

As Kant sees it, subjecting ourselves to the court of conscience is a challenging but important tool for the necessary task of understanding ourselves and becoming better. We will never have perfect clarity about ourselves and our motives. But if we're willing to reflect on our actions in the spirit of humility, we can gain some important insight into what went wrong. And although it will be an unpleasant experience, it will also motivate us to do better in the future.

In its ideal form, the court of conscience is a place where rationalization and self-deception fall away, where we see ourselves as we really are. This is painful, but it is also a path to freedom. The false reality to which we are clinging is actually holding us back. It is as though we are mired at the bottom of Plato's famous cave, chained to rocks and convinced that the shadows we see on the walls represent the truth. Only when we free ourselves from our chains and ascend upward towards the light can we see things properly. For Kant, honest reflection in the court of conscience is how we free ourselves from our self-imposed chains of delusion and self-conceit and clear the way for something better.

12 | JUDGING OTHERS

Let's just admit it. It can be fun to judge other people, especially when they are people we don't like very much in the first place. It's much less fun to be on the receiving end of someone else's judgment. Whether we're being judged for our fashion sense, our mannerisms, or our parenting style, we often feel like the people who are judging us are being rude, unfair, close-minded, and perhaps even hypocritical. This is why calling someone judgmental is a way of criticizing them. A judgmental person jumps into someone else's business, often without knowing all the facts, and delivers a negative verdict on the other person and their choices. It seems to come with a built-in presumption of superiority. No wonder we don't like being judged, and no wonder we also enjoy being a bit "judgy" ourselves.

Kant worries about this tendency to be judgmental about other people, although as we'll see, he could be pretty judgmental himself. There are two different kinds of problems with being judgy. The first is what philosophers call an epistemic problem, or a problem about knowledge. We often lack enough information to justify our negative judgments about other people. The second is a problem about self-conceit. The person who is being judgy is putting themselves on a higher plane than the other person. When

I judge you for your weird Facebook post, I am implying that there is something wrong with you and maybe also something right about me because (naturally!) I would never post something so weird. In judging you, I am asserting my superiority over you, as a Facebook user and as a person. We'll talk about these two problems in turn, starting with the epistemic problem.

But first, a caveat. Kant is *not* saying that we can't ever judge anyone at all. In particular, he's not saying that we can't make judgments about people who do terrible things. If Lucius deliberately runs over Lily with his motorcycle because Lily is holding up a protest sign that Lucius doesn't like, then it's perfectly fair to judge Lucius for what he has done. He doesn't exactly seem like someone committed to the categorical imperative, so we can be pretty sure he lacks a good will. Of course, we have to make sure it was really Lucius driving the motorcycle and also that he ran over Lily deliberately. The first part is pretty easy to determine. The second part is a bit more complicated, but hardly impossible. Lucius might claim that he accelerated by mistake, or that he didn't see Lily, but much will depend on the plausibility of that explanation, especially if we have other evidence about his political views or his tendencies toward violence. The mere fact that Lucius said it was an accident doesn't make it true. We're in a pretty good position to make judgments about what Lucius did. To the extent that his outward behavior shows a total lack of respect for Lily, we can also make moral judgments about him.

But of course much of the time when we're judging others, we don't really have lots of evidence for our judgments. Even when we're in a good position to see what the other person did, we rarely know *why* they did it. Remember that Kant thinks we have trouble knowing our own motives. Usually we can't be sure if we're doing actions because they're right or because they happen to suit our purposes (or because not doing them will make us feel guilty.) This is exacerbated when we're talking about other people. We have even less insight into their behavior than we have into our own. What this means is that when I make a judgment about someone, I'm often basing it on lots of assumptions about their motives, assumptions that may not be grounded in reality or that may reflect unconscious biases on my part. This is the epistemic problem about judging people.

We tend to form beliefs very quickly, and we often form them based on what we see coming through our social media feeds or what our friends tell us. This is not necessarily a bad thing; perhaps these are reliable sources of information. It's also pretty hard to avoid forming beliefs, even if we try. In his *Meditations*, the seventeenth-century French philosopher René Descartes introduced a method for assessing whether we know what we think we know. (Socrates would have been pleased!) This method involved Descartes rejecting all beliefs about which he could be mistaken. For Descartes, that means rejecting every belief except for one— the belief that I exist. His famous saying, "*cogito, ergo sum*" ("I think, therefore I am") means that I cannot be deceived or deluded about my own existence.

Descartes went on to argue that from that one foundational belief, we can reliably get ourselves to lots of other beliefs. He is not advocating total skepticism, and neither is Kant. But like Descartes (and like Socrates before them), Kant thinks that our inclinations to believe things can get ahead of our evidence for them. This is a real problem when we're judging other people. Evidence from psychology that suggests that we use different standards in assessing others than we use when we're assessing ourselves. For instance, when we fail to act as we should, we tend to blame our circumstances. But when others fail to act as they should, we tend to blame their characters. I might chalk up my own crankiness with a Starbucks barista who messed up my order to my high stress job or my lack of sleep. But if I see someone else being rude to a barista, I'm more likely just to think they're a jerk. And maybe they are. Then again, maybe *I'm* a jerk and I'm just making excuses for myself by pointing to my sleep-deprived state.

Let's suppose that Kant (and the contemporary psychologists who agree with him) are correct that we use different standards for judging ourselves and other people, and that we judge others more harshly than we judge ourselves. At best this is inconsistent. If sleep deprivation is an excuse for my rudeness, it ought to be an excuse for the other guy's rudeness. And if it's not an excuse for his rudeness, it shouldn't be an excuse for mine. But it's worse than just inconsistency. The problem is that in judging you more harshly than I judge myself, I'm getting my responsibilities mixed up. Plus, I'm doing so in a way that actually hinders my own efforts at self-improvement.

Remember that Kant thinks we have a duty to improve ourselves. Remember too that he thinks we do not have a duty to improve other people. For Kant, moral improvement is the kind of thing you have to do for yourself. It's not something I can do for you. In the end, your moral character is your own responsibility. Now I shouldn't be trying to corrupt you, say by encouraging you to go to the casino with me when I know you're trying to break your gambling habit. That would be interfering with your rational capacities and choices in a way that I should not. But in the end, your decision to gamble or not is your own. It's not really my business. Perhaps more importantly, if I'm focused on your moral flaws, it's likely that I'm ignoring my own. As the Christian Bible says, get the log out of your own eye before you start looking for specks in the eyes of others.

This takes us to the second problem with judginess, which is about its relationship to self-conceit. The reason why being judgy is enjoyable is that it makes us feel good about ourselves in relation to other people. When I judge you, I look down on you from my superior plane of existence. I express the attitude that I am better than you, that you don't meet my standards, whatever those happen to be. Likely you'll resent me for taking this attitude, and probably you won't want to be my friend. That might be one reason to hold my judgmental tongue. But my judginess is also a problem for me, even if I manage to keep it to myself. It's bad for me because it feeds that natural propensity toward self-conceit that Kant seems to think we all harbor. It's not just that I'm being inconsistent when I judge you more harshly than I judge myself, or that I'm basing my judgments of you on false beliefs. Even when I'm right about you, being judgmental enhances my own smug sense of my superiority over you. That's why it's bad for me as well as for you.

Kant had his own judgmental moments. He could be pretty brutal in his criticisms of other scholars, especially when he felt aggrieved by what he regarded as misinterpretations of his work. And he certainly judged Maria von Herbert, his young correspondent with the complicated love life, whom we met in Chapter 1. Having decided that she did not meet his standards for appropriate sexual behavior in a young woman, he stopped engaging with her in intellectual terms and instead relegated her to the metaphorical eighteenth-century dustbin of used goods. That's pretty darned judgmental on Kant's part.

Kant's theory, however, gives us plenty of reason to be less judgy of other people overall. We rarely know enough to be able to make those judgments accurately. Even when we do, the point of judging people is generally to enable us to feel superior to them, which is something we should be avoiding for their sakes and for our own. A less judgy world is going to be better for all of us. But Kant goes beyond the idea that we should simply zip our lips. Instead, he suggests that we should throw what he calls the "veil of charity" over the failings of other people.[1] He doesn't exactly explain what he means by this phrase, but here's one interpretation.

When we make judgments about other people, we generally need to make up some stuff. This isn't always as bad as it sounds. After all, we can't see into people's heads and sometimes it's really important to understand what they were intending, as in the case of Lucius. It matters a lot whether he ran over Lily deliberately, and we can't necessarily trust him to tell us the truth. Instead, we have to make inferences based on other features of the situation and of Lucius himself. We construct a narrative that explains what Lucius was doing. The narrative is based on things that we know for certain. (Lucius was driving the motorcycle, Lily was holding a sign protesting racism, Lucius has a long history of making racist posts on social media, Lucius has run over someone with his car before, Lucius told his roommate that morning that he was really angry and felt like hurting someone, etc.) The more of these things we know, the more confident we feel in the truth of our narrative. There will still be some gaps, of course, and Lucius's defense attorneys will do their best to find those gaps and widen them. That's their job—to cast doubt on the narrative that the prosecutors are telling.

But most of the time when we're judging people, we're not in a courtroom. We're just making judgments about them based on what we observe, and rarely are we observing the whole story. Our tendency is very often to fill in the rest of the story in the way that suits us. This can go both directions. We may be inclined to come up with narratives that let our friends and family members off the hook, or we may be inclined to come up with narratives that make them look bad. Crucially, we have some control over what narratives we use. We can choose how we decide to see people, what stories we tell about them.

One way to understand Kant's veil of charity is to see it as a way of choosing charitable stories, particularly when we really don't have evidence for the less charitable ones. This doesn't mean that we should ignore or dismiss evidence we don't want to accept, like I might be inclined to do if Lucius is my friend. But it does mean that I should be careful not to tell negative stories about other people simply to make myself or others feel better about ourselves.

Indeed, there's a lot to be said on behalf of letting go of our tendencies to compare ourselves to other people and to be judgmental about them. Although it's undeniably satisfying to feel superior to others, it's a hollow kind of satisfaction. It's also unstable because any feeling of superiority is likely to come undone the next time I scroll through Instagram and witness the photographic perfection of other people's lives. The moral ideal represented in Kant's conception of the good will, by contrast, is a fixed point. By focusing on that, we can let go of the superficial values that so often drive our judgments of ourselves and other people. Instead, we can keep our attention on what really matters. It's possible that we might even find this liberating.

Being judgmental is common enough, but that doesn't mean that it's harmless. If Kant is right, a tendency to be judgy is a pretty serious character flaw. We can do a lot of damage when we're quick to criticize and blame other people. Even more importantly, focusing on what other people are doing wrong distracts us from the really important questions we need to be asking ourselves about our own behavior. We'd be better off giving other people the benefit of the doubt and concentrating instead on the logs in our own eyes.

Part III

Vices

13 | SERVILITY
ACTING LIKE A DOORMAT

Maybe it was the effect of those long, cold Prussian winters, but Kant seems to have spent a whole lot of time thinking about vice. You may remember from Chapter 3 that he refers to vices as the monsters we have to fight. Making matters worse, these monsters aren't external enemies; they live inside us. And they're not always easy to recognize, much less fend off. Vices are sneaky beasts. They steal their way into our very capacity to reason, which is why Kant thinks we really need to be on our guard against them. Vices enslave us from the inside, preventing us from exercising our freedom and making rational choices. If we're going to avoid them, we need to know what they look like.

Most casual readers of Kant focus on what he says about duties, not vices. But in fact, Kant often frames his discussion of duties in terms of the vices that give rise to violations of those duties. This is important because for Kant, becoming a good person is not simply a matter of learning a long list of dos and don'ts. It isn't that duties don't matter; they definitely do. The point is that if we're in the grip of vice, we're not going to be very good at recognizing our duties, much less fulfilling them. That's why it's so important to free ourselves from vice.

Some Kantian vices are familiar. Others may be less so, like the vice that Kant calls servility. Servility is essentially a failure to have adequate self-respect. We've seen in previous chapters that Kant takes self-respect very seriously—so seriously that he describes it as a necessary condition for being able to respect others. If we can't get self-respect right, we're going to have trouble getting respect for other people right. A person's failure to have adequate self-respect affects all their moral relationships, making servility a much more serious vice than it might seem. It is also an especially devious vice. We don't always recognize when it shows up on our doorstep. Indeed, it often disguises itself as humility or agreeableness or selflessness. Identifying servility is thus the first step to getting rid of it.

Perhaps you know someone who is constantly prioritizing the needs and wants of others, rather than their own. We usually think of such people as being virtuously unselfish, and we tend to think of that as a good thing. Often such people truly are praiseworthy. But sometimes there is something a bit more troubling underlying a person's tendency to engage in constant self-sacrifice. Sometimes it reflects their assessment that they themselves aren't important enough ever to come first, either in their own minds or the minds of other people. A person who really believes that she is worth less than others, or who treats her needs, projects, and interests as subordinate to the needs, projects, and interests of others, has a self-respect problem.

As we're going to see in the next few chapters, there are all kinds of self-respect problems. In fact, arrogance is also a self-respect problem. But for now, let's focus on one particular form that a lack of self-respect can take, the form that Kant calls servility. To be servile is to put yourself at the service of others in a way that implies that you are beneath them, that you aren't their equal. Now there are plenty of contexts in which other people outrank us and recognizing that fact doesn't mean we're acting in a servile way. If my boss asks me to do something that is part of my job and I do it because she is my boss, I am not necessarily being servile. I'm just doing what I'm being paid to do.

But of course, not all jobs are alike. Some are downright exploitative. Others raise more subtle problems about respect. Consider, for instance, the traditional job of a secretary. Secretaries have always done important and often challenging administrative tasks.[1] As most of us know, either from our own experience or from watching *Mad Men*, the job of a secretary also used to carry unwritten requirements that we now regard as demeaning, such as the expectation that secretaries be physically attractive and carry out personal errands for their bosses. No doubt there could be a long debate about exactly what kinds of tasks it is demeaning to ask someone to take on. At this point, all we need is the idea that there are *some* things that it would be wrong for a boss to ask an employee to do, and probably also wrong for an employee to agree to do, on the grounds that it would be degrading. We don't think people should ask others to do things that are beneath them and we think people asked to do such things should refuse.

For Kant, self-respect means understanding your own worth and acting accordingly. As we know, Kant would say that my worth depends on my status as a rational being with dignity, a status that is shared equally by all rational beings. To understand my own worth, then, is to regard myself as the moral equal of others. Acting in accordance with my moral worth means expecting others to treat me as their moral equal and refusing to stand for it when they do not. Of course, this is easier said than done. For one thing, a person's ability to understand their true self-worth will depend on the social and cultural environment in which they live. What we regard as demeaning or degrading treatment will depend on how we were brought up and how we learned to think about ourselves in relation to various other people in our society.

Contemporary Kantian ethicist Thomas Hill distinguishes between two forms of servility. The first is when a person genuinely doesn't understand their own moral status. Imagine a woman who grew up steeped in sexist views about the intellectual capacities of women and their supposedly proper place in the world. Imagine that she was raised to think that women are meant only to be wives and mothers and so don't need access to higher education. Or that women are too emotional to make important decisions, or that they lack the authority to contradict their fathers or husbands. It would not be surprising that a woman in this situation would be unable to recognize her own status as the moral equal of the men in her lives. Nor would we necessarily want to blame her for failing to recognize it. Her ignorance of her own value is a direct result of her oppression, after all. Still, it seems right to say that she suffers from a lack of self-respect.

Hill's second form of servility shows up when a person recognizes their status but chooses to participate in activities or relationships that are degrading, perhaps because it's a good way to make money or become famous. This is a somewhat different way to be servile because now it's a matter of a person refusing to claim her status, rather than failing to recognize that she has it. It's probably also a form of servility that we're more likely to find blameworthy. Imagine that you have a friend who is in an unhealthy relationship with a very rich person. Although his rich partner treats him badly in any number of ways, your friend stays in the relationship because he likes the lifestyle that he gets to enjoy while traveling and socializing with his uber-wealthy partner. In this case, it makes some sense to say that he is degrading himself by staying in the relationship. You might be inclined to think he's not showing enough self-respect because he's willing to put up with poor treatment just to enjoy the benefits of his partner's money.

That is exactly what Kant would say. The Kantian way of framing the problem with your friend is that he is treating himself as having price, not dignity. He is prepared to trade himself for something that he sees as having higher value. But what it means to have dignity is to regard yourself as having value that can't be sacrificed for things like money or a month on a yacht in Greece. (Yes, I know that sounds really tempting. Get it out of your head!) We sometimes say of people behaving like your friend that they are selling out. To be a sell-out is to betray yourself and your own ideals for the sake of something that isn't worth the sacrifice. For Kant, nothing could be worth sacrificing our dignity. This means that when we sacrifice our dignity, even to get something that we want, we're making a lousy trade.

In his discussion of servility, Kant instructs us to "be no man's lackey" and not to "let others tread with impunity on your rights."[2] When we let other people walk all over us, we're undermining our own self-respect and allowing others to treat us disrespectfully. This is bad for us, bad for them, and bad for the moral community more generally. It's bad for us because of course we are not being accorded the standing that we should have. It's bad for others because they end up in a position where they are encouraged to act badly themselves. (Think back to that unhealthy romantic relationship. It's not really good for either partner.) And it's bad for the moral community more generally because it disrupts the very important principle that each of us is the equal of everyone else.

It's crucial to remember that on Kant's account, no matter how poorly someone treats us, it's not possible for them to *actually* take away our dignity. Dignity is something we have regardless of whether it is acknowledged by the people around us. We are worth just as much, whether or not that worth is recognized. Someone who is a victim of racial oppression may never be treated with the respect that they deserve, but no amount of racism can actually make a person less valuable than they are. In the same vein, it's not possible for us to waive our own right to respectful treatment. Even if I say it's just fine for you to treat me badly, that doesn't mean that it really is just fine. In Kantian terms, we might say that there's no such thing as genuine consent to being degraded. Technically, I can sign a contract in which I agree to subordinate my will to yours, but the contract will not be valid in the eyes of Kant's moral law.

This may seem counterintuitive to those of us accustomed to thinking that autonomy means something equivalent to total freedom. Saying that I can't really consent to degrading treatment seems like a way of impinging on my freedom to act according to my own judgment. If I want to humiliate myself on YouTube for large sums of advertising revenue, why can't I make a rational choice to go for the money? If I don't mind other people laughing at me, it's not clear why it's anyone else's business, including Kant's.

The intuition that there's something wrong with servility also depends on the assumption that we can distinguish demeaning behavior from non-demeaning behavior, when in fact, that can be fairly tricky. What is the difference between humiliating yourself on YouTube and just doing something funny? Why are some uses of our bodies degrading (Kant's example is allowing your body to be tossed around for the sport of others) whereas others presumably are not, like working for a moving company?

At one point, Kant considers whether we are treating ourselves disrespectfully if we sell parts of our bodies, like our teeth or our hair. He opposes selling teeth, but reluctantly agrees that selling one's hair might be all right, presumably on the grounds that hair grows back. Selling teeth and hair is no longer common in our world of dentures and hair extensions, but the same issue arises when we consider the sale of body parts like blood or kidneys for transplant. It is illegal in most places to buy a kidney and often illegal to sell one as well. (It happens anyway, especially in impoverished countries.) Most people agree that there is a real danger of exploitation because selling your kidney puts you at risk and desperate people are more likely to take such risks. But there are other jobs that are very dangerous, like guiding tourists up Mount Everest. So long as people are being paid well, what difference does it make how they are earning the money?

It's not easy to put one's finger on exactly what is troubling about the sale of one's own body parts, and perhaps that intuition is simply irrational and outdated. (Kant would almost certainly oppose all forms of sex work. We'll see why in Chapter 26.) Yet Kant does seem to be on to something when he suggests that there are limits to how we ought to allow ourselves to be treated, even for large sums of cash. It's not that Kant isn't sympathetic to people in dire straits. He would certainly come down much harder on those who exploit desperate people than on the desperate people themselves. Anyway, most of his discussion is focused on people we might call sycophants (if we're being polite), who "bow and scrape" to higher ups for the sake of gaining some kind of advantage. As Kant sees it, such people are making an enormous mistake. They are sacrificing something precious for something that will always be worth much less in the end. There's no reason to envy the servile person, no matter how many worldly advantages they gain. Whatever they acquire will never be worth the price they pay.

Remember that Kant thinks that if we don't understand our own value, we aren't going to be able to understand the value of other people. If I don't appreciate that my worth rests on my dignity, I will not be able to appreciate that about the people I encounter. The person who willingly surrenders her dignity is unlikely to value or respect it in others. But self-respect is not simply a way to fulfilling duties to other people. Kant sees it as extraordinarily important in its own right. I owe myself respect, and I owe it to myself to insist that others treat me with the respect that I deserve. Anything less is a failure for everyone.

14 | ARROGANCE
BEING FULL OF OURSELVES

Do you know someone who thinks they're better than you? Maybe this person even thinks they're better than everyone. We have a lot of expressions to describe such people. They think of themselves as God's gift to humanity, they're too big for their britches, they should get off their high horse, they're a tall poppy that needs to be cut down to size.[1] Whatever we call them, they're certainly annoying. Kant, however, thinks that arrogance is far more than an annoyance. It's a full-fledged vice, one that will prove to have interesting parallels to servility.

It may seem as though the problem with an arrogant person is that they have too much self-respect. They respect themselves so much that they think everyone else should see them in the same light in which they see themselves. In fact, they tend to complain if people don't treat them as having the status they think they deserve. Arrogant people are the ones who storm up to the maître-de at a restaurant, demanding their table right away. They're the ones who turn every conversation to themselves or make a point of emphasizing how many famous people they know. Arrogant people expect other people to acknowledge and respond to their perceived greatness. They think they are amazing, and they insist that other people treat them as the outstanding specimens of humanity that they take themselves to be.

It does seem right to say that arrogant people have excessive self-regard. Kant would agree, in the sense that they think too highly of themselves in relation to other people. But self-regard is not the same as self-respect. In fact, as Kant sees things, the arrogant person actually has too little self-respect. More specifically, the arrogant person is wrong about what it means to have self-respect. The arrogant person ties their self-respect to facts about their job, their intelligence, their wealth, their strength, their family background—you name it. As we know, Kant doesn't think that any of these things is the true basis of self-respect. That basis is our status as beings with dignity, a status we share equally with others. And that is the part that the arrogant person, like the servile person, does not understand.

We can derive some insights into arrogance by considering narcissism. Not all arrogant people are narcissists, but there does seem to be a close connection. Psychological research tells us that narcissists tend to have high self-esteem. (No surprise there!) But there are some complexities to this picture. The self-esteem of a narcissist is often fragile, making it unstable and vulnerable to challenges or threats. Because of this, some narcissists may need to seek out validation of their status as a way of bolstering that fragile self-esteem. This would explain why a narcissist is constantly demanding that others defer to them, honor them, or otherwise respond to them in a positive way. They are often on the defensive, and what they're defending is a sense of self that feels under threat. But of course, if they really understood their dignity, they'd realize that it can't be threatened. Their narcissism is evidence that they don't actually understand the true basis of their self-worth.

In Chapter 8, we distinguished between recognition respect and appraisal respect. Appraisal respect is tied to our accomplishments and deeds. Recognition respect is what we warrant simply in virtue of being rational beings. What the arrogant person seeks is appraisal respect. Perhaps that's the only kind of respect they think exists. Or perhaps they confuse appraisal respect and recognition respect, believing that succeeding on one dimension (like running a successful business or being an outstanding athlete) warrants extra recognition respect. This distinction is important, because sometimes arrogant people really do deserve appraisal respect. Highly talented athletes, for instance, could be arrogant and also properly deserving of appraisal respect for their skills and achievements. When Muhammed Ali said, "It's hard to be humble when you're as great as I am," he wasn't entirely wrong. He was certainly a great boxer. Still, even the world's greatest boxer is one among equals when it comes to moral value.

Now it's not necessarily arrogant to believe that you are the world's greatest boxer if, in fact, you are. Kantian arrogance comes in when a person demands more recognition respect than other people on whatever basis. In Kantian terms, that's a demand that doesn't even make sense, at least not if you understand what recognition respect is. We deserve recognition respect in virtue of our dignity, which is something we have purely on the basis of having rational capacities. In this sense, no one could have "more" dignity than someone else, so no one *could* deserve more recognition respect than others. Failing to see this is failing to appreciate what it means to have dignity in Kant's sense.

On Kant's view, if an arrogant person really understood the source of their own value, they would not insist on special treatment. The special treatment would be unnecessary to mark their status as a valuable individual. It is only because they are confused about the basis on which people deserve respect that they fail to realize this. In this regard, the arrogant person has a lot in common with the servile person. Both make mistakes about their own status in relationship to other people. Both locate their value in features of them that aren't actually essential to their true moral status. The servile person takes themselves to have less value than others. The arrogant person takes themselves to have more value than others. But it's the same mistake underlying both responses.

This helps explain why it seems that arrogance and servility can sometimes coexist in the same person. A marvelous literary illustration of this can be found in Jane Austen's *Pride and Prejudice*, in the form of Mr. Collins. Mr. Collins clearly thinks himself superior to other people in virtue of his role as a clergyman and, more specifically, the clergyman installed in the parish controlled by Lady Catherine de Bourgh, who is herself exceptionally arrogant. Mr. Collins is so awed by Lady Catherine's greatness that he debases himself whenever he is in her presence. He falls over backwards conforming his every move to her wishes, whatever they might be.

Unfortunately, his brush with greatness isn't actually humbling for him. Instead, it makes him feel superior to other, lesser creatures who lack his connections with the aristocracy. Mr. Collins puts on the appearance of humility because he thinks that it enhances his charm, but the more perceptive characters in the novels are not deceived by it. They can see how absurdly pompous and self-important he is, even as he behaves in what seems like an exceptionally deferential manner. His deference toward them doesn't express genuine respect. He just thinks (mistakenly) that it's a good look for a clergyman like him. He's actually thoroughly self-satisfied, even though he has many flaws, as does his patroness. But he lacks the self-awareness to recognize them. He prefers to bask in the glow of false greatness.

For Kant, someone like Mr. Collins is relatively easy to explain. Collins mistakes social status for moral status. (He also makes mistakes about his own social status, but that's not important for our purposes.) He gives and demands respect according to what he perceives is due to others in virtue of their social rank. The result is that he demands too much respect from people he sees as beneath him (making him arrogant) and too little respect from Lady Catherine (making him servile). In making these demands, he is showing his own failure to appreciate the actual source of his moral status, namely his dignity as a rational being.

The ways in which arrogant people demand respect from others can be subtle, even manipulative at times. Arrogance doesn't always manifest itself in huffing and puffing about who one is. Consider the phenomenon that has come to be known as humblebragging. The humblebragger says or posts something that, on the surface, appears to be self-deprecating or self-critical. In fact, though, the person is actually bragging. We know this because the humblebrag is an attempt to get people to respond in a way that reaffirms the person's importance. Suppose I post a humblebrag on Facebook about how I am so undeserving of some award I just won. It's likely that at least some of my Facebook friends will respond by telling me that I do deserve the award, perhaps more than anyone they know. My humblebrag alerts people to the fact that I won an award *and* elicits congratulations for it, perhaps with an extra dose of applause for my humility. It's a way of bragging that doesn't actually seem like bragging. That, of course, is kind of the point.

Of course, we often see through humblebrags, but that doesn't really eliminate the pressure to respond to them reassuringly. There's pretty strong social norming that works against leaving self-criticism or self-deprecation unchallenged. If your friend puts out a humblebrag on social media, it's hard not to feel like you have to say something positive in response. No doubt this helps explain why it's so prevalent. Ordinary brags can be ignored or even mocked. Humblebrags are harder to ignore and even harder to mock, at least directly. It's an especially manipulative way of drawing out compliments and affirmation.

If arrogant people, including humblebraggers, annoy you, you'll be glad to know that you have Kantian reasons to resist their arrogance. Arrogant people are claiming something from us that they have no right to claim. Our own self-respect probably demands that we not hand it over. Most of us are glad when the arrogant would-be diner at a restaurant is denied their table (and disappointed when they are seated anyway to avoid the scene they are intent on making). We like to see people put in their place. Crucially, though, we have to be careful that we're not taking *too* much joy in seeing them put in their place. It's possible that my own self-conceit is being pricked by the arrogance of other people. Is my pleasure in seeing arrogant people taken down a notch righteous satisfaction, or is it spite? It's not always easy to tell the difference. We'll be coming back to this problem over the next few chapters.

It might even make sense to feel sorry for arrogant people. After all, there's something pathetic about having to resort to humblebragging to shore up your self-confidence. If you really had a sense of your own dignity, you wouldn't need to humblebrag because you wouldn't be so dependent on outside affirmation. This isn't to say that praising others for their accomplishments, or being satisfied with your own, is a bad thing. Appraisal respect is important. Kant's point is simply that we need to separate those accomplishments from our value as human beings. Nobel prize winners and Olympic athletes have achieved impressive, laudable things. But they have exactly the same moral status as the person who swept the fancy ballroom in which they are honored, or who handed them a towel as they returned from their workout. In that sense, we are all on the same level.

Arrogance, like servility, is a vice because of the way in which it becomes rooted in our way of thinking about ourselves in relationship to other people, as well as our expectations for how they should treat us. It can be so inculcated into our perceptions of interactions that it's hard to recognize in ourselves. The arrogant person demanding his table *right now* probably thinks that he's just standing up for himself. He may regard it as a matter of self-respect that he be granted the privileges that he thinks are his due. He's wrong, of course, but that doesn't mean that it will be easy for him to see that. The same is true of the servile person, who really believes that they deserve a lesser place at the table (literally and figuratively). They may even think it would be arrogant for them to claim what is their actual due.

The categorical imperative is useful when it comes to remedying both vices, although it might be slightly more useful for arrogance. Arrogant maxims are likely to be captured by the universal law formulation, but it may be harder for someone trying to apply the humanity formulation to see what's going wrong. Both the arrogant and servile person need to undergo a fairly radical revision in their understanding of what it actually means to have dignity, as well as what that dignity requires of us and of other people. Until they can let go of the idea that their respect-worthiness rests in their accomplishments, skills, bank balance, or social position, they will have trouble treating themselves and other people in the way that they should.

15 | CONTEMPT
LOOKING DOWN ON PEOPLE

Stop reading and take a minute to think about a person that you really, really dislike. It can be someone you know personally, or it can be someone famous. As you think about this person, consider all the different things you find so unappealing about them. Reflect on their many faults and how they exemplify everything terrible that human beings are capable of doing and being. If you want to take it a step further, imagine that this person has just done something truly morally appalling, something that you think should land them in jail or at least ruin their life.

Unless you're an unusually charitable person, you're probably experiencing feelings of contempt toward the person I asked you to imagine. Let's just assume for the moment that your feelings are justified. The person really is as bad as you think they are. In that case, contempt seems like exactly the right response. If someone is a poor excuse for a human being, surely we should recognize that and act accordingly. Otherwise, it's as though we're ignoring, or even condoning, their bad behavior Those people who kept inviting Jeffrey Epstein to their parties long after it was abundantly clear that he was a cold-hearted sexual predator were making a major moral mistake. In fact, they probably deserve contempt too.

Kant is sympathetic to these feelings and accepts that there are some lowlifes toward whom we can't help feeling contempt. But then he throws a surprising and perhaps counterintuitive curve ball at us. Even though the Jeffrey Epsteins of the world deserve contempt, it's wrong for us to express it. This doesn't mean that we can't lock such people up in jail for the rest of their lives. We can and should protect ourselves and others from dangerous predators. We do, however, have to restrain ourselves from giving voice to those very natural human feelings of contempt, and we definitely have to refrain from acting on them. Why would Kant take such a stand?

To see what Kant thinks is wrong with contempt, let's step back from people like Jeffrey Epstein and think about contempt in a more general way. (We'll return to Epstein later.) Although Kant doesn't specifically label contempt a vice, his main discussion of it occurs alongside a section on what he calls the vices that violate the respect we owe to others. Kant clearly thinks that contempt is at odds with specific duties that we owe to others. But its impact is much broader. Contempt can become a more general way of thinking about people, in which case it starts behaving like a Kantian vice. Moreover, it's a particularly destructive vice because contempt has features that make it damaging to society as a whole.

In psychology, it's standard to treat contempt as an emotion, which is how I was treating it at the beginning of the chapter when I asked you to call it up. Some psychologists categorize contempt as a basic emotion, one with distinctive and easily recognizable manifestations in facial expressions. The person feeling contempt characteristically has a sneer on their face, with a tightened mouth and one corner of a lip raised. (Try thinking about the person you

despise in front of a mirror!) It's certainly possible to feel contempt and not express it. It's also possible to express it through
tone of voice or through the words typed in the comment section
of a blog or news article. In fact, once we start looking for it, we
can see contempt in a lot of different places, expressed in a lot of
different ways.

In the context of relationships, contempt appears to be the har-
binger of doom. Psychologist John Gottman has done extensive
research showing that contempt in a marriage is an outstanding
predicter of divorce. We can deal with a lot of negative emotions
in relationships, but contempt seems to be in a category of its own.
There's a reason for this. In most philosophical accounts of contempt, contempt is not like other emotions or attitudes. One of
the things that makes it different is that it encompasses the person
as a whole, not just one aspect of them. This is often expressed by
saying that contempt is a globalist emotion. It's global because it's
directed at the entire person.

To make this clear, consider the difference between anger
and contempt. When we're angry at someone, we're generally
angry at them for something in particular that they've done (say,
leaving food-encrusted dishes lying around for days). Our anger is
directed at the person, but if they apologize and change their behavior, the reason for the anger dissipates. It's about the dishes, not
about the person. Contempt, however, works differently. When
we hold someone in contempt, our negative reaction is toward the
person themselves, not just something they've done. If my anger
about your dirty dishes turns into contempt, I will start regarding
you as a kind of lesser being, one who isn't really worth my time
and effort. Anger is a reaction to people in virtue of something

they've done. Contempt is a way of dismissing people altogether. No wonder Gottman thinks that contempt is a death knell for a marriage.

Think of the contempt that underlies racism. A white supremacist takes the view that people of color are beneath him, occupying a lower rung on a ladder of worthiness. Even a white supremacist who keeps his views mostly to himself can be said to be harboring contempt if his underlying attitude is that he is superior to people of other races. In the case of racist contempt, it's not hard to accept Kant's point that contempt is a really bad thing. The white supremacist is violating a fundamental duty of respect toward the targets of his contempt. He does not treat them as his moral equals, meaning that he denies that they have the same moral status that he has. He refuses to acknowledge their dignity.

Racist contempt is obviously a violation of a duty of respect toward its target. But this is not the only problem that it poses. Racist contempt is also bad for the racists who harbor it, insofar as it enables them to hold on to a false belief about their own superiority. The racist, like the arrogant person in the last chapter, is making a mistake about the basis of his own self-worth. Racists try to draw rationally unsustainable lines between themselves and other people. In doing so, they diminish their own moral standing, although they may not see it that way. Contempt of any kind is a form of denial of recognition respect to its target or a denial of another's dignity. This implies that the person who expresses contempt toward another is doing damage to the moral status that all of us share. We might put it this way: a world in which anyone can be held in contempt is a world in which everyone can be held in contempt.

This is why contempt is an especially dangerous vice, and not just for racists. It is a vice that potentially affects our relationship with all human beings, including ourselves. If we think that even one rational being doesn't deserve recognition respect, we are no longer treating dignity as the basis of our decisions about treating people respectfully. Instead, we're making that distinction on the basis of their race, or their political party, or just whether we like them. Of course, Kant does not think that these features of us are what make us the valuable beings that we are. Recognition respect reflects a worth that we have in virtue of being rational beings. In a way, denying recognition respect to one rational being is effectively denying recognition respect to all rational beings.

For Kant, this means that even the Jeffrey Epsteins of the world must be treated with recognition respect. They are rational beings with dignity, even if they fail to live up to that standard and fail to treat others according to that standard. The fact that they have failed does not, on Kant's view, entitle us to fail alongside them. However difficult it may be, we need to treat awful people better than we might think they deserve. We owe it not just to them, but to humanity itself. Vile people are, after all, still people. Ignoring that crucial fact poses a major threat to the foundations of morality in our dignity as rational agents.

Kant criticizes certain forms of judicial punishment as incompatible with respect for the dignity of humanity. (Drawing and quartering is his example. If you don't know what that is and you have a strong stomach, go look it up. Otherwise, I'll spare you the details.) As Kant sees it, there are some things that human beings just shouldn't do to other human beings. He doesn't try to convince us that Jeffrey Epstein and his ilk aren't really all that bad.

Instead, he points to our duty to uphold humanity itself as having absolute value. The source of my dignity, the thing that makes me worthy of respect, is something that I share with the worst criminals. I cannot deny respect to the criminal without undermining respect for all of us. This is why contempt threatens the moral community as a whole.

Again, this doesn't mean that we can't hold people responsible for their morally despicable acts. Indeed, Kant thinks that punishing people within a judicial system is actually a way of respecting them, strange as that might sound. As we've seen, Kant believes that everyone is capable of recognizing and following the categorical imperative. This is part of his justification for holding lawbreakers accountable for what they've done. In holding someone accountable, we treat them as a rational being who could and should have known better. But it's possible to hold someone accountable without holding them in contempt. And that, according to Kant, is what morality directs us to do.

The fact that we're all capable of knowing and doing what's right also means that we have reason to believe that everyone is also capable of moral reform, even the most hardened criminal. (Granted, this is a bit hard to square with Kant's rather fervent support of the death penalty. Executing someone is obviously a pretty solid way to ensure that they won't have the opportunity to reform their ways.) This doesn't mean that we should just throw open the prison doors and hope for the best. But this background belief that we're all capable of doing better plays a very important role in Kant's overall ethical approach. Contempt implies that its target is a lost cause. On Kant's view, however, no one is truly a lost cause. We are all better than our worst actions. And even if we have reason to think the terrible person in front of us is extremely unlikely to reform, we should still be hoping for a miracle of sorts. As we'll see in Chapter 29, Kant thinks we have to be able to maintain hope in the possibility of moral progress. That hope is going to be very hard to sustain unless we take the attitude that our fellow rational beings are capable of contributing to that moral progress. Maintaining hope in humanity requires maintaining hope in individual human beings.

Avoiding contempt is, for Kant, extremely important. Avoiding it is also pretty difficult at times. Contemptuous attitudes can show up anywhere and everywhere, even in our ordinary encounters with people. People behave contemptuously on Twitter, at high school reunions, at restaurants, and at the dog park. Sometimes contempt is very subtle, disguising itself as supposedly constructive criticism. Kant's own remarks on contempt include a specific warning to be careful to avoid it when we're correcting mistakes, both moral mistakes and mistakes in reasoning. It's not that he's opposed to engaging in criticism, particularly when people are making false statements. Kant places an exceptionally high value on the pursuit of truth, a topic we'll discuss in Chapter 18. Correcting false statements and errors in reasoning is important, whether we're talking about our own errors or the errors of others. But when we do engage in such corrections, we have to do it without letting ourselves slide into contempt. Kant's remarks on this are worth quoting directly:

On this is based a duty to respect a human being even in the logical use of his reason, a duty not to censure his errors by calling them absurdities, poor judgment, and so forth, but rather to suppose that his judgment must yet contain some truth and to seek this out, uncovering, at the same time, the deceptive illusion, and so, by explaining to him the possibility of his having erred, to preserve his respect for his own understanding.[1]

There are two points to note in this passage. The first is that when we call out people for their mistakes, we have to do it without ridiculing them or otherwise treating them as if they weren't really capable of reasoning. If you've ever been on the receiving end of such treatment, you'll know why Kant sees it as such a problem.

The second point is that we're supposed to assume that the person's judgment is based on something that they genuinely believe to be true, even if it's not. It's not that we have to believe that what they are saying is true. But we should accept that *they* believe themselves to be speaking the truth. Our task is to try to figure out the source of the "deceptive illusion" that is causing their mistake. Kant explains why he thinks this is so important. It's because in treating people like they are intelligent people who have made understandable mistakes, rather than treating them like idiots, we enable them to preserve their self-respect. Although Kant doesn't say this outright, it also enables us to preserve our respect for them.

The mutually respectful exchange of ideas, which includes the mutually respectful correction of errors, is, for Kant, at the very center of human society. If we cannot pull off a highly charged conversation without devolving into contempt, we are in trouble as a community. It's not just that it's unpleasant for us as individuals when others respond to us and our ideas with contempt, although of course it is. No one wants to be disrespected or treated like a fool. The ramifications of a generally contemptuous culture, however, extend far beyond these individual relationships.

When we expect contempt from others, we're not going to engage with them. This means that expressing contempt is a surefire way to stop people from working with each other toward our common goals. Kant sees this as a major impediment to our progress as human beings. We can't move forward in our collective pursuit of truth unless we share ideas. We can't share ideas successfully unless we regard ourselves as all being on the same team, so to speak. This is what makes contempt so dangerous, not just to individual relationships, but to the broader human community.

We're going to be coming back to these broader dangers of contempt in later chapters because Kant brings them up in the context of other vices as well. Before I close out this chapter, though, I want to take up something that may or may not be bothering you. It's the idea that despite what Kant says, contempt may sometimes be justified. Consider someone who is treating *you* with contempt. If that person thinks of themselves as superior you, it might seem that treating them with contempt in response is a way of cutting them down to their proper size.

Contemporary philosopher Macalester Bell has made a case for meeting racist contempt with what she calls counter-contempt. Counter-contempt rejects the racist's attempt to diminish the target's dignity by using contempt to deflect it. We might even see this kind of contempt as an expression of self-respect. Indeed, maybe contempt is at least sometimes a way of *preserving* our self-respect in the face of threats to it. In that case, shouldn't Kant be okay with it?

If it were true that contempt could preserve our self-respect, then perhaps Kant would endorse it or at least not criticize it. But at the risk of putting words in his mouth, I think he would say that it's not true. This is because insofar as contempt requires regarding the person as beneath you, there's no way to take up that attitude while still maintaining recognition respect for the target of your contempt and for that matter, for yourself. Kant thinks we must see people as our equals. By definition, contempt requires that you see yourself as superior to the target of your contempt. Of course, an anti-racist really is superior to a racist in the sense of deserving greater appraisal respect. What Kant denies is that any of us can ever deserve more recognition respect than someone else. So racist contempt must be met with something that preserves recognition respect all around, which contempt does not. This is not just for the sake of the racist; it's for the sake of all of us. Kant's concern is that we can't build a moral community on a foundation of disrespect.

This doesn't mean that we should let racist comments slide. Anger, outrage, righteous indignation—these are all responses that have the effect of holding racists responsible for their behavior while still acknowledging their status as members of the moral community. Remember, our ability to hold them responsible depends on the assumption that they are capable of doing better, that it's within their power *not* to be racists. But contempt, as Kant understands it, operates beyond this. It exiles people from the moral community entirely. And this, Kant thinks, is something we're simply not entitled to do.

This can be a difficult pill to swallow, particularly when it comes to people who really do seem to deserve contempt, like white supremacists and Jeffrey Epstein. But for Kant, recognition respect is not really a response to what people deserve. It's a response to what they are. Contempt is at odds with our deep-down nature as beings with dignity. People can never lose or forfeit their dignity, no matter what terrible things they've done. Kant knows it can be extremely difficult to remember this. He's asking a lot when he asks us to give up all our contemptuous feelings. It's just that he thinks the alternative is worse. If you spend a lot of time on Twitter or in the comments section of newspapers, you might see his point. For all its virtues, the internet makes it very tempting for us to dehumanize each other. It's easy for me to forget that the person on the other side of the keyboard is also a person, with the same dignity that I have. If, however, we lose sight of this fact, we're going to have a very hard time maintaining a community at all.

I'll close with one final reason to worry about contempt, one that has to do with our propensity toward self-conceit. Contempt, even toward terrible people, runs the risk of exacerbating our already existing tendencies to want to feel superior to people. Righteous indignation can easily slide into contempt if we're not careful. Sometimes we don't even notice it, particularly if we're surrounded by like-minded people. Remember that we aren't very good at distinguishing our own motives. Think back to the person I asked you to call to mind at the beginning of the chapter. Consider the basis on which you made your judgments about them. Possibly those judgments were well-founded. But if the person you called to mind is someone you didn't like in the first place, it's possible that you were letting your dislike of the person affect your assessment of them. It's also possible that you enjoyed the exercise because it made you feel just a little bit superior to the person you were contemplating. This is the kind of space in which Kant thinks contempt can grow and spread into a deeply entrenched vice.

In the next couple of chapters, we'll be talking about two more vices that are closely related to contempt—enjoyment of negative gossip and pleasure in mocking people. Before we leave contempt behind, though, let me ask you do to one more mental exercise. Consider the worst meeting, email exchange, or Facebook argument that you've witnessed. Likely it involved contempt on someone's part, or maybe everyone's part. Probably it was not a terribly productive exchange or meeting. Kant worries about the future of a world in which contempt becomes a settled way of interacting with others, whether we're talking about a school board meeting, a Twitter exchange, or the floor of the Senate. We can't cooperate with people we hold in contempt. And if we can't cooperate, we can't make progress in the ways that Kant thinks we must. To put it plainly, contempt is toxic to our most fundamental moral relationships. That's why Kant thinks we need to yank it out like poison ivy, before it can take root in ourselves and our culture.

16 | DEFAMATION
SPREADING GOSSIP

Everybody loves a gossip. Alice Roosevelt Longworth supposedly had a pillow with the embroidered inscription, "If you
can't say anything nice, come sit by me." Of course, if you're the
subject of gossip by other people, it's not quite so enjoyable. If
you've made it this far in the book, you might be able to guess
what Kant thinks about gossip, at least the negative kind. Kant
worries about the effects of gossip on us, on others, and on the
moral community. When the love of gossip becomes a deep-seated
enjoyment of spreading nasty rumors about other people, he sees
it as a full-fledged vice, one he calls the vice of defamation. But
before we get to his concerns about gossip, let's pause to get a grip
on what it is.

In her book *Secrets*, contemporary philosopher Sissela Bok
gives a definition of gossip that will be a useful starting point.
According to Bok, gossip has four key features: it's informal,
it's personal communication, it's about other people, and those
people are either absent or treated as absent. The first two features
are about the mechanism by which gossip is transmitted and the
second two are about the target of the gossip. We'll start by talking
about the mechanism.

If gossip needs to be informal and personally communicated as a matter of definition, then a press release or a newspaper article could not count as gossip. That's both because they're formal and because they aren't forms of personal communication, at least not as that is usually understood. Now it's true that we do usually consider things like gossip columns in newspapers as methods for transmitting gossip, which means that Bok's definition might be a little narrow. It gets even more complicated when we start thinking about the ways in which gossip is transmitted over social media. Bok's definition predates the internet, but it seems clear that at least some instances of messaging, texting, and emailing could count as informal personal communication. And then of course there are Facebook posts, tweets, TikTok videos, and other ways in which people communicate the information that we ordinarily put into the category of gossip. To keep things simple, let's just grant these methods of communicating with people do sometimes count as vehicles for engaging in gossip. Although the traditional image of gossip as two people whispering in a corner still resonates with us, it's clearly not the only way in which we engage in it. So, let's turn to the second two features, which involve the target of gossip.

According to Bok, gossip has to be about other people, and those other people have to be absent or treated as absent. This would mean that I can't gossip about myself, only about other people. If I tell you that I am getting a new puppy, I am not gossiping. If I tell you that I really dislike my husband's brother, I'm confiding in you, not gossiping.[1] In fact, it's pretty hard to imagine a situation in which it would make sense to say that I am gossiping about myself. I'm also not gossiping if I tell you something about you, such that I've noticed that you really don't seem to like your husband's brother. Gossip always seems to involve third parties. If I tell you that our mutual friend Jane dislikes her husband's brother, *then* we're gossiping about Jane and probably also about her husband's brother. The fact that you and I can't gossip about ourselves might explain why the target of the gossip needs to be absent. If the target is part of our conversation, it's not gossip! Presumably we could talk about a person who is standing right there as if they weren't standing right there, but that would be a pretty strange situation.

Let me add a feature to Bok's list. Gossip also seems to be primarily about people we know or feel like we know. If you know Jane, you're likely to be interested in her feelings about her brother-in-law, particularly if you also know him. But if you don't know Jane or her brother-in-law, you may wonder why I'm telling you because you likely don't really care what she thinks about her brother-in-law. It may not even feel like gossip from your end of things. Now it's true that lots of us enjoy gossip about celebrities, none of whom we actually know. Probably all of us who have clicked on a link or picked up a magazine in the grocery store line have wondered to ourselves why we care about where Kim Kardashian goes on vacation or how Prince Harry is getting along with the rest of his family. Such magazines sell copies by making us *feel* as though we know them. This is why it still seems like gossip when we're talking about them. But gossip can't get started if we're just talking about someone whose name we've randomly pulled off the internet. (It would also be extremely boring.)

It's not always easy to tell the difference between sharing gossip and simply sharing news. Perhaps there is no difference, except that gossip usually seems to have something salacious about it. Telling you that Jane got a new puppy doesn't really feel like gossiping about Jane. Telling you that Jane hates her brother-in-law does feel like gossiping about her. Maybe this is because it uncovers something about Jane herself, something that she may very well not want other people to know.

This takes us to a crucial point about gossip, which is that it is usually about more than simply sharing information. This isn't to say that the information isn't important. Very often it is, say, if I'm interested in blackmailing Jane down the line. But when we share gossip with each other, we're also engaging in a bonding experience. It's an experience that, according to psychologists, triggers reward responses in our brains. Indeed, this is almost certainly why it's such a popular activity. When you and I exchange information about a third party, we feel more connected to each other, particularly if we take the same view of the third party.

Consider how much more satisfying it is to pass along the information that Jane hates her brother-in-law if I expect you to mirror my own reaction to it. Maybe we both think the brother-in-law is a jerk and deserves the cold shoulder from Jane. In that case, we could be sharing useful information with each other. (Some research indicates that we pay closer visual attention to faces when negative information is attached to those faces.) Or maybe we both dislike Jane. Indeed, if I dislike Jane and I know you do too, I may well have sought you out to share this information. If our exchange of gossip reinforces our mutual dislike of Jane, it brings us closer together by way of setting us apart from our common enemy.

And here we start to get to the thing about gossip that worries Kant. Kant is actually a big fan of sharing information, as we'll discuss in later chapters. Gossip, however, he treats differently on the grounds that it isn't *just* information. As Kant describes the information-sharing that characterizes what he calls the "vice of defamation," it is information that casts another person in a negative light. As the philosopher Bertrand Russell once pointed out, no one gossips about secret virtues—only about secret vices. This is the part that Kant finds concerning, even when the information is true.

Of course, we do sometimes have to pass along negative information about other people. Sometimes informal channels of personal communication are the best way to do this. It's not always possible or safe to, say, report a sexual harasser, but spreading the word can certainly be a good way to warn potential victims and limit the damage. If this counts as gossip, then gossiping as a way of spreading negative information can't always be wrong. And anyway, Kant's concern about negative gossip is more specific. What he describes as the vice of defamation is more like a settled tendency to *enjoy* telling and hearing negative information about other people.

Kant describes defamation as "the immediate inclination, with no particular aim in view, to bring into the open something prejudicial to respect for others."[2] This definition suggests that spreading information about sexual harassers wouldn't count as expressing the vice because it has the aim of warning potential victims and enabling them to protect themselves. His focus is on the inclination to spread negative gossip for the entertainment value. It's the pleasure that we get from negative gossip that concerns him. The duty to avoid the vice of defamation is the duty "not to take malicious pleasure in exposing the faults of others so that one will be thought as good as, or at least not worse than, others."[3] The malicious pleasure is the real problem.

It's not really surprising that we enjoy hearing negative information about people that we already dislike. But we sometimes also enjoy hearing negative information about people we do like, or people we don't even know. Why would that be true? There's a Kantian explanation for this in the form of that natural propensity toward self-conceit we've been encountering so frequently. We like to feel superior to other people. Hearing negative information about people helps us feel superior to them. When I expose your faults, I make you seem worse than me (as naturally I wouldn't be gossiping about faults that I believe myself to share). Plus, sharing negative information with others allows us all to form our own, smug little group of insiders, throwing shade at those on the outside.

You can probably see why this raise red flags for Kant. He knows we enjoy gossip. He likely enjoyed it himself. But he doesn't like where it leads us, which is to a place where we get to reinforce our own inflated sense of our own importance with our like-minded friends, at the expense of others. This is bad for us because self-conceit is a major impediment to having a good will. Anything that exacerbates it is going to make us worse as individuals. It also makes us worse as a community.

One of the interesting things about Kant's discussion of defamation is that he spends only a little bit of time on how it affects the person about whom gossip is being spread. Instead, he emphasizes the effects that negative gossip has on the person who practices it and what happens to the social world when that practice becomes widespread:

The intentional spreading of something that detracts from another's honor—even if it is not a matter of public justice and even if what is said is true—diminishes respect for humanity as such, so as finally to cast a shadow of worthlessness over our race itself, making misanthropy . . . or contempt the prevalent cast of mind, or to dull one's moral feeling by repeatedly exposing one to the sight of such things and accustoming one to it.[4]

Kant's concern is that the habit of spreading negative gossip for fun is a habit that drags us all into the mud. The mud is actually a bit more like quicksand. As Kant sees it, the danger of defamation is that it encourages a widespread attitude of contempt and even hatred for other human beings. We know that Kant thinks this is a real problem for us. This is why we need to work so hard to cultivate the attitudes of love and respect, which counter our tendencies to think the worst about others. Negative gossip makes those attitudes even more of a challenge than they would otherwise be.

Consider the effects of a constant stream of negative gossip across your social media feeds. If your entertainment consists mostly in scrolling through snarky comments about other people, their habits, their clothes, etc., you're likely going to be feeling pretty snarky yourself. That snarkiness is probably going to find its way into your own social media posts and perhaps to other areas of your life as well. Kant treats certain vices almost as if they were contagious diseases. If you breathe in the air of contempt and defamation, you'll be infected by it as well. And if you're breathing it on others, they're going to fall victim. This is why Kant thinks we need to mask up and keep the ugliness out of our collective oxygen supply.

As is often the case, Kant discusses defamation as a vice together with the particular actions we need to avoid in order to avoid the vice. The actions are straightforward enough—don't spread negative gossip or listen to it just for fun. But like contempt, defamation has deeper roots. There's a mindset behind it that is bad for our characters and our communities. That pleasure we take in hearing some juicy gossip is worrisome, even if we manage to keep our own mouths more or less shut. Not only does it feed our self-conceit, but it hinders us from the morally necessary task of seeing other people as deserving of our respect and assistance.

In Chapter 12, we saw that Kant believes we should avoid being judgmental about other people. This is in part because we really don't know their motivations. But it's also because when we're judgmental, we lose out on an opportunity to help them become better. In that chapter, I discussed Kant's concept of a veil of charity, which he directs us to throw over the flaws of other people. It is in his discussion of the vice of defamation that he introduces that idea. He claims we have a positive duty to "throw the veil of [charity] over their faults, not merely by softening our judgments but also by keeping these judgments to ourselves; for examples of respect that we give others can arouse their striving to deserve it."[5]

There are two aspects of this duty that we should notice. The first part of the duty is to soften whatever judgments we do make about other people. Negative gossip often involves the opposite—playing up the flaws and failings of people—because that's the part that makes us feel better by comparison. The second part of the duty is to keep our judgments to ourselves. The veil of charity should affect our external behavior—what we are willing to say and hear. But it should also affect our internal attitudes toward others—what we think about others in our heads.

In Chapter 12, I interpreted this as a duty to choose certain stories rather than others. We are usually missing pieces of the narratives needed to fill in our accounts of what other people are doing and why. We can decide how we fill in those missing pieces. I suggested that we can think of Kant's veil of charity as a duty to fill in those missing pieces as sympathetically as we can, at least when doing so doesn't risk harm to anyone else. At the very least, we should avoid jumping to the worst possible interpretation of other people's actions. Contemporary philosopher Ryan Preston-Roedder calls this an expression of the virtue of faith in humanity. As Preston-Roedder describes the virtue, it includes both a belief in the basic decency of people and a desire that they will act well. It's kind of like rooting for a beloved, but bad sports team. You keep showing up for games and hoping that they'll win. Faith in humanity is what the vice of defamation threatens to destroy, and what the veil of charity helps preserve.

Kant's reasons for thinking the veil of charity is a good idea are twofold. First, it helps us develop those all-important attitudes of love and respect. Charitable narratives help me to view others through a more optimistic lens. Second, Kant suggests that treating people in accordance with those charitable narratives can help make those narratives come true. This is nicely exemplified in Victor Hugo's *Les Miserables,* when the desperate Jean Valjean steals silver from the bishop who offered him hospitality for the night. After Valjean is caught, the bishop not only refuses to say to the police that the silver was stolen. He also hands Valjean even more silver, telling him that he has now been redeemed. And indeed, Valjean commits himself to living a different life thereafter. What the bishop does for Valjean is very much what Kant thinks we should do for each other. (Okay, Kant might not have approved of the bishop lying to the police, but we'll come back to that in Chapter 18.) The broader point here is that Kant believed that the veil of charity can help us make each other better. The malicious pleasure we take in defamation undermines our love and respect for humanity. The veil of charity helps us maintain it.

So negative gossip is a no-no. That may seem kind of depressing because it's also usually quite a lot of fun. But steel yourself because we're about to see some Kantian worries about another rather pleasant activity—making fun of people. You might want to go catch up on your favorite comedy sketches now, before you move on to Chapter 17.

17 | MOCKERY
MAKING FUN OF OTHERS

On to the next stage of our Kantian quest to take all the fun out of life! I'm only sort of kidding. Kant is not opposed to fun, but he's a bit suspicious of some of the things we consider to be fun, like spreading salacious rumors about people we don't much like. Here we're going to focus on another fun activity—ridiculing or mocking people. Like defamation, this sounds more like an action than a vice. And like defamation, the associated vice of mockery will be a tendency to engage in the activity and, moreover, to enjoy it. But mockery might even be worse than defamation. To understand why, we're going to have to do some digging into Kant's writings about it, as well as some additional exploration of what's going on when we mock people.

Mockery has a very long history, especially in the arts. The ancient Greek playwright Aristophanes famously mocked Socrates in his work, *The Clouds*, where he portrayed Socrates as something of a con artist, taking people's money and teaching them nothing of value. This portrayal almost certainly shaped the way in which Athenians saw him, including the members of the jury who sentenced him to death. In the case of Socrates, this was undoubtedly unfortunate, but mockery is often a valuable way of taking down corrupt political leaders, monarchs, or other important personages. Indeed, mockery's track record as an effective method of moral and political criticism creates a pretty compelling case for it.

Given Kant's commitment to equality and his dislike of arrogance, it's reasonable to think that he might appreciate a good smack down of a politician abusing his power or otherwise failing at his job. And maybe he would. But he'd still be worried about what the practice does to us and to our communities. His concern is that mockery, like defamation, tends to bring out the worst in us. It also makes our shared social world worse. Like defamation, the vice of mockery contaminates the air we all breathe.

Kant describes mockery as the propensity to laugh at people for their flaws, real or perceived. The flaws don't necessarily have to be moral ones. It's possible to mock people for their appearance, their accent, their background—really, just about anything. The key thing is that the feature of the person in virtue of which they are being mocked is being singled out for negative assessment. In mocking someone, I take something about them (say, their accent) and hold it out for others to see and ridicule. Although it's possible to mock people in private, it's common for mockery to be public in the sense that it's done for an audience. When we mock people, we generally want not just to laugh at them ourselves. We want others to laugh at them as well.

Probably everyone agrees that mockery is *sometimes* wrong. Mocking someone for stuttering, or for having an unusual facial feature, or for being clumsy in gym class is both disrespectful and cruel. What makes it disrespectful (at least in Kant's sense) is that the target of the mockery is being portrayed as inferior for some characteristic that has no bearing on their value as a person. The mocker seeks to get the audience to think less of someone because of their stutter or their unusual appearance. This is how mockery diminishes its target. By implying that the target is worth less than others in virtue of having that feature, the mocker attacks their dignity. So do the people who laugh at the mockery. It's a way of denying respect to the target.

Kant points out that the pleasure of mockery tends to involve malice, or the enjoyment of watching someone suffer. It's malice that makes it plausible to see mockery as cruel as well as disrespectful. Mockery standardly causes pain to its target because, of course, being treated in a dehumanizing way is painful. It also tells us something about the character of the one doing the mocking, as well as those responding to it with laughter. The able-bodied person who mocks someone for their disability aims to denigrate someone and moreover, enjoys doing it. This is why Kant is inclined to call such people vicious.

Obviously, disabilities are not flaws. No one is less deserving of respect in virtue of having a disability. But in a society that consistently discriminates against people with disabilities, whether overly or covertly, it's all too easy to get people to see a person's disability as a flaw and so to perceive the person who has the disability as lesser than others. In this way, mockery of a person's disability becomes an effective way of diminishing them. It denies the person with the disability the recognition respect they deserve. The fact that this is how mockery works is important to understanding why Kant worries about it. Mockery is an invitation to an audience to see its target in a negative light. The negative portrayal is standardly generated by taking a perceived flaw and exaggerating or caricaturing it in a way that the audience is likely to find entertaining. When the so-called flaw is something like a disability, it's not hard to see why the mockery is so disrespectful. It seeks to turn something into a flaw for the purpose of denigrating them and denying them recognition respect.

But what if we're talking about actual flaws? If we're mocking someone for having done a morally terrible thing, isn't that denying them appraisal respect, not recognition respect? And isn't that sometimes okay? We don't all deserve appraisal respect just in virtue of being rational. It seems just fine to criticize evil people for what they've done. If so, then we might see this kind of mockery just as an especially entertaining form of moral criticism.

Unfortunately, mockery can still go badly wrong, even when it's an actual flaw that we're talking about. It's not the moral criticism part that's the problem. It's the entertainment value of mockery-as-moral-criticism that bothers Kant. He puts it this way:

> Holding up to ridicule a person's real faults, or supposed faults as if they were real, in order to deprive him of the re-spect he deserves, and the propensity to do this, a mania for caustic mockery, has something of a fiendish joy in it; and this makes it an even more serious violation of one's duty of re-spect for other human beings.[1]

Fiendish joy might seem a little strong, but it reflects the depth of Kant's concern about how quick we are to take pleasure in the fail-ings of other people. Self-conceit is rearing its ugly head again here. As Kant sees it, other people's flaws aren't really an appropriate ob-ject of entertainment, even when the flaws are genuine. Laughing at people for having them may be fun, but it poses hidden risks.

Kant makes a point of distinguishing mockery from what he calls banter, which is when friends make fun of each other in a light-hearted way. The way that Kant draws this distinction is pretty insightful. He describes a situation in which friends "make fun of their peculiarities that only seem to be faults but are really marks of their pluck in sometimes departing from the rule of fashion."[2] That's a somewhat roundabout way of saying that we sometimes banter or tease our friends about characteristics that we don't really believe to be flaws at all. In such cases, we're not trying to deprive our friends of respect. If anything, we're expressing our respect and affection for them by joking around with them in this way.

As we know, though, this line gets a bit tricky to draw in practice. There's often a lot going on under the surface when it comes to banter. Suppose that I tease my friend about her unusual decorating style. A great deal depends on whether I actually admire her decorating style or whether I think it's tacky. I may very well be admiring her "pluck" in going against current trends, but it's also quite possible that my so-called teasing is not merely harmless banter. It may be a standing joke between us that she has no eye for color. But standing jokes are not always entirely jokes. If that's the situation, then she would be right to feel as though I'm disrespecting her. After all, in mocking her decorating style, I'm actually mocking her. And in mocking her, I'm claiming a position of superiority over her. Even if it's just about whether those pillows look good on that couch, my setting myself up as having better taste than her has the effect of diminishing her.

Maybe you're beginning to see why Kant worries so much about self-conceit and why he thinks it's at the heart of so many vices. Self-conceit is very often what underlies our desire to diminish people. It enables us to feel superior to them and we find that pleasant. As we saw with defamation, this can be exacerbated when it's a group behavior. Mocking someone together can help us bond with our fellow mockers, but it does so by setting us above the person being mocked. We get to feel superior together. This is why people who are engaging in mockery are usually focusing on flaws that they don't think that they share, and that their audience won't think that *they* share. Otherwise, the mockery won't have the desired effect.

There do seem to be forms of self-mockery, mockery that makes us laugh at ourselves. Possibly Kant would say that such mockery is a good thing insofar as it pricks our bubbles of self-conceit. It's also not impossible that mockery could be a good way of dealing with someone else's arrogance. (Probably it is not such a good way of responding to servility, as it runs the risk of making it worse.) Mockery that is aimed at restoring everyone's sense of moral equality would not have the features that make Kant want to call it a vice. But even in those cases, it's not easy to keep mockery in its proper boundaries. Just as teasing can sometimes cross the line into bullying, so mockery intended to burst someone else's arrogant bubble can easily turn into self-congratulatory smugness.

Mockery sometimes explicitly aims at depriving people of respect. Even when that's not the explicit aim, it's very often the effect. Suppose that I really was joking about my friend's decorating style, but that I did so in front of a large group of her friends, family members, and co-workers. Then it matters how they interpret what I'm saying. As Kant points out, sometimes teasing comes off as a compliment to its target. Sometimes it comes off as a derogatory remark about them. And sometimes what makes the difference is how everyone is already disposed to feel about the person being teased. The less we like someone, the more likely it is that our pleasure in seeing their flaws put on display is going to devolve into fiendish joy.

Take, for instance, a comedy sketch like *Saturday Night Live*'s cold open. (If you've never seen one, you may want to put down this book and go watch one on YouTube so you'll know what I'm talking about.) *SNL* cold opens usually mock political figures. In many cases, they serve as a form of moral criticism of those figures, using satire as a way of making a deeper moral point about the target's behavior or policies. It is of course possible to make moral criticisms without using mockery. People do it all the time on Twitter and in newspaper op-eds. But mockery is especially effective, perhaps because it's more fun to watch an *SNL* cold open than to read an op-ed piece in the *New York Times* or *Wall Street Journal*. (No offense to the editorial teams at either paper!) The criticisms are more searing, the images more memorable. Mockery takes a flawed figure and cuts that person down to size more thoroughly than almost any other method can manage.

In the case of powerful politicians doing terrible things, it's hard to think of mockery as a bad thing, especially if it has a positive effect. Consider, though, that how you react to a given *SNL* sketch will probably depend on what you think about the person being mocked in it. Mockery works by getting you to see the target as ridiculous or absurd. It may get you to see the target as ridiculous or absurd by mocking the specific moral flaw for which they are being mocked. Or it may get you to see the target as ridiculous or absurd in virtue of some other flaw, one that is perhaps not as worthy of mockery or perhaps not even a flaw at all.

Here's what I mean. Suppose that *SNL* or a newspaper cartoonist mocks a politician who has done some truly awful things and hence deserves moral criticism. But suppose that the humor in the mocking portrayal lies in something else, like the politician's weight or receding hairline. Then the humor stems from something that is not actually a flaw. So even though the person is rightly mocked for their actual flaws, the mockery is not trading on those actual flaws, but on something else. It's getting you to laugh at something irrelevant, something that perhaps ought not be mocked at all.

Many comedy writers and comedians recognize this, and regard some forms of mockery, like mocking people for their race or disability status, as off limits for just that reason. Notice, however, that the pleasure we take in mockery often makes it difficult for us to recognize when mockery is going awry. If we're already inclined not to like the target, we may be less likely to notice when the mockery has wandered over the line separating righteous moral criticism from gratuitous denigration. Even if a person actually deserves to be mocked, it doesn't follow that any form of mockery of them is okay. Whether it's okay depends on whether it violates our duty to treat others respectfully. Kant is not opposed to criticizing people, but he insists that it be consistent with everyone's dignity.

It's not impossible for mockery to meet that standard. We may be able to engage in mocking behavior without descending into the associated vice, if we can keep it focused on the actual moral flaw. But it takes a great deal of caution because we're not always the best judges of what exactly we're doing. We may take ourselves to be mocking a politician's words when we're actually mocking their accent or speech patterns in a way that reflects class-based prejudice. Making mockery compatible with respect is harder than it seems, even when it's in the service of moral criticism. And if we find ourselves using mockery as our primary form of moral engagement with others, especially those with whom we disagree, then we need to be honest with ourselves about our reasons and about its effects on our moral characters. The fact that mockery entertains us isn't sufficient to make it okay.

18 | DECEITFULNESS
BENDING THE TRUTH

Suppose that one evening, you answer a knock at the door only to be confronted by a suspicious character wielding a knife and asking for the whereabouts of your friend Percy. You happen to know that Percy is in your backyard toasting marshmallows over your firepit. But being a perceptive person, you have a hunch that the man at your door is not there to help Percy slice chocolate bars for s'mores. Do you tell him the truth and let Percy take his chances on defending himself with a toasting fork? Or do you lie and tell him that Percy has gone to the 7-11 down the street?

Very few people would say that it's wrong to lie to a would-be murderer at the door. And yet Kant seems to say exactly that in an infamous essay with the clunky title, *On a Supposed Right to Lie Because of Philanthropic Concerns*. Kant's stance in that essay has caused many people to throw up their hands and decide that Kant is clueless, deluded, neurotic, or all of the above. Some people even use this essay as the basis for dismissing Kant's ethical thought entirely. This would be a mistake, both because his views about lying comprise just a small part of his broader ethical outlook and because those views, including the ones expressed in this essay, are often misunderstood. Kant's actual views about lying are subtler and more nuanced that most readers (including philosophers!)

realize. Even if you yourself have no qualms about lying to would-be murderers at your door, it's worth considering what Kant has to say on the subject.

To appreciate why Kant is so horrified by lying, it helps to begin with what, in Kant's mind, is so important about truth. By now you won't be surprised to learn that it comes back to the importance of reason. As we'll see, Kant thinks that when we tell lies, we are fundamentally misusing reason in a way that he sees as a devaluing of our dignity, resting as it does on our rational capacities. This is why he considers a propensity to lie to be a vice, one that is contrary to what we owe ourselves as rational beings. Lying is also contrary to the duties we owe to other rational beings. But there's still more to Kant's concern about truthfulness, which is that it is foundational to the possibility of human community, as well as its progress. Essentially, a bunch of liars cannot form a functional society. We'll get to all these issues in turn, but let's start with looking at what Kant says about the wrongness of specific instances of lying.

As we saw way back in the first few chapters of this book, in the *Groundwork*, Kant sets out four examples of wrong actions. One of those examples involves borrowing money from someone while making a lying promise to repay it. Like most people, Kant thinks this is a wrong action. What makes it wrong is not that you are breaking a promise, but that you are making a promise that you have no intention of keeping. And what makes *that* wrong is that it violates the categorical imperative.

Using the universal law formulation, we might say that your proposed course of action (making a false promise) relies on the existence of a practice (keeping promises) for its success, a practice that would be undermined if everyone constantly made false promises. A world in which promises were never kept would be a world in which your false promise would fail to yield money in your pocket because no one would trust you enough to lend you money. The success of your false promise depends on others *not* making false promises themselves. This, as we saw in Chapter 5, constitutes making an unjustified exception for yourself. Using the humanity formulation, we might say that in lying to the person from whom you are borrowing money, you are treating them as a mere means to your end. You get them to do what you want by manipulating their understanding of reality, getting them to believe falsely that they will get their money back. When you do this, you interfere with their capacity to use their rationality effectively. You interact with them not as a person, but as an object you can use for your own purposes.

So far, so good. But when we apply this to the murderer at the door, things start to fall apart. It seems like we might be able to universalize a maxim of averting murder through lying. After all, averting murder is pretty important, and if everyone has it as their maxim to lie to murderers, there will presumably be fewer murders and no lasting harm to society. The humanity formulation might seem to suggest that in lying to the murderer, we're bypassing his rationality, which amounts to treating him as a mere means. On the other hand, he's not exactly acting as a rational agent at the moment. True, you may be implanting false beliefs in his head if you convince him that Percy is at the corner store, where you happen to know that several police officers are conveniently congregating over coffee. Given his dastardly plans for Percy, however, it seems like he has forfeited his claim to a truthful answer from you.

This sometimes comes as a surprise to people who think they know Kant, but he doesn't actually disagree. In that controversial essay, Kant makes clear that your duty not to lie to the murderer at the door is not a duty that you owe to *him*. He acknowledges that the murderer is acting unjustly in trying to force you to tell him Percy's current location. Because of that, he has no personal claim on you that you give him a truthful answer to his question. (He does, however, still have a claim to basic respect as a rational being, even if he is not acting very rationally at the moment.) So why should you tell him the truth? Kant's answer is that truth-telling is something that we owe not just to other people, but to ourselves and to the moral community more generally.

Before we delve into those duties, let's pause to introduce another important clarification to Kant's view. A strange thing about this example, one that often goes unnoticed, is that Kant seems to be working with the background assumption that you have no choice but to answer the would-be murderer's question. It's not simply that you have good reason to fear for your safety if you don't answer. Rather, it's that this guy at the door somehow has the authority to compel you to make what Kant calls a statement or a declaration. This is going to require some explanation.

When it comes to asking and answering questions, Kant seems to accept two very sensible ideas. The first is that we are not morally obligated to answer a question just because someone has asked it. I may ask you for your social security number, but you are usually under no obligation to provide it (unless, of course, I work for the IRS). You may want to know where I live, whether I have children, or whether I go to church on Sundays. That doesn't mean I have to tell you. We don't owe people all the information in our possession, even if they would very much like to have it. (In fact, Kant thinks that it's a really good idea to keep certain stuff back. More about that in Chapter 22.) That's the first sensible idea.

The second sensible idea is that in asking questions, we aren't always seeking a truthful answer. If, upon seeing you, I greet you with, "Hey, how are you?" I am not really hoping that you will give me a full account of how worried you are about your pet gerbil's digestive habits. In most contexts, that question is what we'd describe as a rhetorical one. You are supposed to say, "Fine. You?" (or maybe, "Getting by" or "Can't complain," depending on local customs and the general state of the world). Likewise, the minefield-like question "How do I look?" is usually asked by someone seeking reassurance, not a critical assessment of whether their last haircut was a major mistake.

In general, however, reasonable questions deserve answers. If you ask me the time or whether this is the right stop for the Natural History Museum and I happen to know the answer, it would be churlish of me not to tell you. It would be even worse if I lied to you instead. When people ask us questions that we can reasonably be expected to answer, and to answer truthfully, then Kant thinks our answers must be true. This is what Kant has in mind by a statement or declaration. If I say something that I am purporting to be true and that my listeners reasonably expect to be true, then I am making a declaration. If you ask me the time, and I answer by saying that it's 3:15, I am making a declaration in Kant's sense. And as he sees it, that declaration had better reflect the truth as I know it. In fact, Kant seems to think that the very existence of human community depends on the practice of making only declarations that we believe to be true.

That may seem a little dramatic but consider for a moment what the world would be like if people routinely made statements either knowing them to be false or without any regard for whether they are true or false. (This may not be very difficult if you think we already live in such a world.) It's not just that we'd constantly be in danger of getting off at the wrong subway stop, although we would. A world in which we couldn't trust the stated qualifications of the engineers who design bridges, or the published findings of scientists doing medical research, or the stories written by reporters telling us what is happening three thousand miles away would be a world in which we could not function, either as individuals or as a community.

Each of us needs to know things, and many of the things we need to know extend beyond our own capacities and expertise. As Kant points out, we have only two ways of acquiring knowledge—our own experience and the testimony of other people. We are all limited in our experience. The time I spend acquiring knowledge about Kant is time I cannot spend learning about bridge construction. This means that we depend on each other's information in crucial ways. When I drive my car over the (rather scary!) Chesapeake Bay Bridge, I have to trust the engineers, contractors, regulators, and everyone else who had a hand in building it. In particular, I have to trust that they know what they say they do and that they did what they said they would do. My life literally depends on their trustworthiness.

This is why Kant thinks that truth is so very important and so very worth defending, even at a great cost. As he puts it: "We can only know what a man thinks if he tells us his thoughts, and when he undertakes to express them he must really do so, or else there can be no society of men."[1] Without truth-telling, we can't have trust, and without trust, we can't have society as we know it. If we want bridges and medications and edification about Kant, we must commit ourselves fully to the practice of truth-telling. Our interdependence leaves us with no other choice.

Now you might be wondering whether we could maintain this general commitment to truth-telling while still telling the occasional lie. It's hard to see how lying to a would-be murderer to save a life would undermine society, even if everyone did it. (If anything, that sounds like a maxim we *want* people to adopt.) Kant's description of the murderer case is missing key details, such as exactly why the murderer has the authority to compel an answer from me. If the murderer is, say, an official of the state, that might change things. Lying to the authorities is not quite like lying to random people on the street.

Still, even if you think Kant was wrong about this particular situation, he is surely right to value the widespread practice of truth-telling as a social good. A culture of truth-telling is essential to creating social trust, and social trust is essential to creating a functional community. We can only have that kind of community if each of us commits fully to being honest in our statements, even when honesty is inconvenient or when it comes with unpleasant side effects. The alternative is a world in which we cannot fully trust anything that anyone says, in which everything is fake news. Kant thinks we could not rationally will to live in such a world. That's why we have to take a stand against it by committing ourselves to truth-telling.

Thus far, I have discussed truth-telling as a duty that we (usually) owe to others and that we (always) owe to the broader moral community. There is one more dimension to Kant's account of truth-telling, which is that it is something that we owe to ourselves. In fact, this is actually the primary way that Kant takes up lying in the *Metaphysics of Morals*. There he treats lying as a failure of self-respect insofar as it is a misuse of our own rationality. Using lies to achieve our ends is doing something that Kant thinks is incompatible with our dignity as rational agents.

This may seem like a stretch until you start thinking about how much we admire honesty in figures like George Washington, who supposedly would not lie about cutting down a cherry tree, even though he knew he would get in trouble. (That story, alas, appears to be false.) Or consider Abraham Lincoln's nickname, Honest Abe. We value honesty in people very much, and not just because of how it affects other people. Honest people seem to have a lot of integrity.

Kant would surely agree with this, but he adds something to this analysis, which is that when we lie, we are doing something unworthy of us as rational agents. At one point, Kant likens lying to poisoning, both of which are actions against which it is difficult to defend yourself. It is dishonorable, much as hitting your opponent in the back is regarded as dishonorable by traditional codes of fighting and, for that matter, football. When we use lies to achieve our ends, Kant thinks we are doing something that is beneath us. What makes it beneath us is that it is misusing the very thing that gives us our dignity. We're not simply allowing rationality to be overtaken by desires; we're twisting the aim of rationality, which for Kant is directed at truth. To use reason in the service of lies, Kant thinks, is to pervert its most important function. This is why he regards a propensity to lie as a vice, and also why he describes it as a failure of self-respect. In lying, we degrade ourselves by preventing our reason from operating properly and achieving what Kant takes to be its natural end. Reason should be used to uncover the truth, not to hide it.

In discussions of Kant on lying, the murderer-at-the-door case tends to take up all the oxygen in the room. This is understandable, but unfortunate, because the case is so peculiar. Most of the time when we tell lies, we're not lying to would-be murderers. Unlike murderers, most people do have a right to truthful answers from us. Kant seems to see even white lies, or lies we tell to spare people's feelings, as wrong on the grounds that such lies are paternalistic. We owe people the truth, and it's a disservice to them to assume they can't handle it. If you genuinely want to know what I think about your new haircut or your new romantic partner, and I don't tell you because I don't want to upset you or hurt your feelings, I'm not really treating you like the rational agent you are. I'm acting as though I know better than you do what's good for you. Kant would also say that it's more consistent with our own dignity to be truthful, even when it comes with costs. And then finally, the practice of truth-telling is essential to the stability of our entire community. We simply cannot function in a society in which we cannot trust what people say. The only way to avoid the tangled web that lies create is to build our lives around telling the truth.

19 | DRUNKENNESS
LOSING OUR GRIP ON REASON

Ever woken up one morning and cringed, remembering something you did the night before after a few beers? Kant can explain why you felt that need to cringe. He can probably also sympathize. Although this comes as a bit of a surprise to people who picture Kant as a dull, strait-laced old professor, he was known to be a bit of a partier in his younger days. Having attended his fair share of dinners and banquets, he apparently acquired some experience with alcohol and its effects. He also gave considerable thought to the moral implications of getting drunk and came up with some rather interesting ideas about it.

Kant describes drunkenness (along with opioid use and gluttony) as a vice. Crucially, he appears to draw a moral distinction between mild intoxication and being drunk. It's only drunkenness that troubles him. In fact, he acknowledges that a little bit of alcohol has the potential to liven up a party and loosen people's tongues, which in his eyes is not a bad thing. His view seems to be that drinking some alcohol here or there isn't a big deal so long as we are able to keep it properly contained. But if it gets out of control, whether in the moment or over the course of a lifetime, it can produce serious moral problems about self-respect and respect for others.

Alcohol comes up in a number of places in Kant's writings, although alas, he doesn't give us any details about his personal experience with it. His most extensive discussion of drunkenness occurs in the *Metaphysics of Morals*, where he characterizes it as a vice contrary to what we owe ourselves as animal beings. As with other vices we've discussed, avoiding this vice requires that we see ourselves as having duties to avoid getting drunk, as well as duties to avoid eating to the point of stupor and to avoid opioid addiction (a problem in his day as well as our own). In each case, what concerns him is the effects of certain bodily states on our ability to use our rational capacities effectively. This in turn is tied to his larger picture about the relationship we have with our bodies. Although Kant sometimes sounds as though he thinks of us as purely disembodied rational beings, this is not actually the case. He is well aware of the fact that our rationality is intertwined with our physical bodies and that our bodies affect our rational capacities, for better or for worse. Insofar as our ability to reason well or to carry out our duties depends on what we do to our bodies, it matters from a moral standpoint. Alcohol obviously affects our rational capacities and our bodies, as do certain drugs and—in Kant's experience, at least!—a great deal of food. If we are so stuffed, drunk, or drugged that we cannot function or even hold a rational conversation, something has gone wrong.[1]

For Kant, the morality of alcohol depends on why and how we're using it. If we are deep in the jungle and you have just suffered an accident that requires me to amputate your hand to save your life, there's no moral problem if I get you drunk first to ease the pain and help you hold still. In this case, our aim in getting you drunk is a perfectly justifiable one and indeed, might be necessary to preserve your ongoing rationality if your life depends on the amputation. It would be no different than undergoing anesthesia, and while anesthesia hadn't yet been invented when Kant was writing, presumably he wouldn't see a problem with it. We can have very good reasons for temporarily letting go of our rational capacities, particularly when our reasons have to do with the longer-term preservation of those capacities and the body that supports them.

What bothers Kant is using alcohol as a way of deliberately or at least carelessly interfering with our rational capacities for no particularly good reason, whether just for an evening or as a way of life. He has harsh words for alcohol and drug addicts, although in his defense, it is only relatively recently that alcoholism and drug addiction have come to be seen as diseases rather than vices. But let's set aside those circumstances and focus just on cases where a person who is not an alcoholic purposely sets out for an evening of drinking, with the expectation that he will be drunk at the end of it. Assuming that he's of legal age, not responsible for caring for small children, and not driving himself home, we may be inclined to think, "So what?" What's the big deal with an occasional night of letting go and having fun?

Kant does believe in having fun. In fact, he thinks that there's moral value in socializing with people. We'll return to this in Chapter 28, when we look at Kant's opinions about how to throw a good dinner party. A gathering in which we enjoy ourselves, meet new people, and learn things we did not know before is, for Kant, a place where moral communities can be built. (Granted, that's not what most of us are imagining when we invite friends over for pizza and beer, but that's what Kant would say is happening.) Socializing is good for us, and good socializing helps us interact with others as fellow members of the same moral community. Insofar as a six-pack of beer or a bottle of wine helps this process along, Kant does not seem to have major objections. But as anyone who has been around alcohol knows, things can and do go wrong.

It is evident that Kant thinks there is something undignified about being drunk, however a person got into that state and whatever the circumstances. Crucially, we don't *actually* lose our dignity when drunk. Drunk people are still people. But there's a sense in which we're not living up to our status as beings with dignity when we're drunk. In drinking to get drunk, we follow our inclinations, not our reason. We're not just ignoring reason, though. Getting drunk incapacitates reason, sometimes to the point of preventing us from using it at all. As Kant puts it in the *Lectures on Ethics*, "if I have drunk too much today, I am incapable of making use of my freedom and my powers . . . "[2] I am, in short, not in control of myself. For Kant, that is not a state I should deliberately be bringing on myself, at least not without an excellent reason, like the need to hold still for an emergency amputation. It's not even just about the time while I'm drunk. Kant says about opioids that "they are seductive because, under their influence, people dream for a while that they are happy and free from care, and even imagine that they are strong; but dejection and weakness follow."[3] As Kant sees it, there's a self-deceptiveness about using drugs or alcohol as a way of forgetting one's problems. Not only do the problems not go away, but the effects of overindulgence linger in ways that reduce our ability to solve them. (On this point, Kant sounds like a man who has experienced a bad hangover or two.)

Kant's insistence that it is undignified for us to sacrifice our rational capacities for the sake of a fun evening may just make him seem stuffy and boring. Possibly that's true, although Kant is not denying that drunk parties can be entertaining. His point, rather, is that the fun is not worth what it costs us. Consider what happens when parties go wrong. If everyone in the room is drunk and there's a medical emergency or a fire, it may be that no one is in a position to offer help or even call for it. Drunk people are not especially good at listening to reason; sometimes it's necessary to trick them, lie to them, or use physical force to keep them safe. This can be funny, but it can also be demeaning. (Indeed, it can be both funny and demeaning at the same time, as we know from our discussion of mockery.) When a sober person is dealing with a drunk friend, both of them are in a bad position by Kantian lights. The sober person cannot interact with the drunk person as a rational being, and the drunk person cannot respond as a rational being. Drunkenness thus interferes with our ability to engage in the kinds of relationships with others that Kant thinks are so important to the moral community.

This is probably evident to anyone who has ever lived with or been in a close relationship with someone who is an alcoholic or who has a drug problem. In such cases, the costs to the person and to those who love them are very high and very apparent. Drunkenness may seem much less costly when it is only occasional or when it happens only among friends. But we also know that drunk people do things that they would not do when they were sober. In some cases, that may seem like a good thing. Perhaps someone is too shy to talk to the person on whom they are crushing without the help of some beer or wine. Still, for every *New York Times* wedding story that began with a few drinks, there is another story that did not turn out so well. Drunk people, after all, also get into fights with people, harass them, and sexually assault them. They sometimes destroy property, vomit and urinate where they should not, and make life unpleasant for sober people in their vicinity. Let's assume that these are all actions that the drunk person who performs them would not perform when sober. We can frame the Kantian question this way: is the fun of a night of drinking worth the risk of becoming the kind of person who does such things, even if only temporarily?

Kant thinks that the answer to that question is no. On his view, it can never be a good idea to subordinate your rational capacities to your inclinations. That's like handing over the car keys to your ten-year-old. You might be lucky enough to have everything turn out all right, but that doesn't magically transform it into a harmless or rational choice. There is a sense in which for Kant, getting drunk is like abdicating your responsibility to be an adult. It is true that sometimes it is less fun to be an adult than a child, but if you are an adult, you had better act like one. Likewise, if you are a rational being with dignity, you had better act like one.

Let me stress this again because it's so important. Although it is true that drunk people cannot engage in reasoning, that does *not* mean that others can legitimately treat them as objects. A drunk person does not waive all his moral rights or forgo all his moral claims just because he is temporarily incapacitated. Drunk people need to be treated with dignity insofar as that is possible, even if they are not shouldering their part of the load. Importantly, this is something we owe not just to the drunk person, but to humanity itself. On Kant's view, drunkenness challenges our collective abilities to regard and treat each other with appropriate respect. This is something we already find difficult. We should not be making it more difficult on purpose.

Kant's discussion of drunkenness makes evident that he sees our bodies as playing a fundamental role in our efforts to cultivate rationality. We are only as capable as our bodies allow us to be, which is why he thinks we owe it to ourselves and to others to look after our bodies and make sure they are in a condition that will support our capacities for rationality and our ability to achieve our rational ends. We don't always have control over our bodies and what happens to them, but on Kant's view, we shouldn't relinquish whatever control we do have. That would be a form of enslavement to our inclinations, and as we know, Kant places great value on being able to act freely. On his view, you have to be sober in order to be free.

Part IV

Life Goals

20 | PERSONAL DEVELOPMENT
MAKING SOMETHING
OF OURSELVES

Did you know you're fulfilling a Kantian duty to yourself just by reading this book? The duty in question is the duty to develop your natural capacities, abilities, and talents. You may recall from way back in Chapter 9 that Kant thinks there are two ends that are also duties, or ends that we are required to take on as a matter of moral obligation. One of them is the duty to make the ends of others our own. The other is the duty to improve ourselves, to cultivate our moral and natural capacities. In many ways this entire book is about cultivating our moral capacities. In this chapter, however, we'll narrow our focus to the imperfect duty to cultivate our natural capacities and talents. For Kant, this duty, which I'll call a duty of self-development, is one of the central elements of self-respect.

Many of us have the sense, however vague, that we have a duty to make something of ourselves. On a day-to-day basis, this sometimes gets expressed as the thought that we should do something productive, instead of sitting on the couch binge-watching *The Office* all day. Not that there's anything wrong with the occasional television binge, but a life in which we did nothing else would not be a life of which we felt proud. We want to accomplish things, use our talents, and have a positive impact on the world. More generally, we want to lead lives that have purpose or meaning.

Some of the things we want to accomplish require specific skills, like learning a new language or mastering a particular software. Some of them require physical training, like improving endurance or muscle strength. If I want to hike the Appalachian Trail, I'll need to make sure I'm in decent shape and that I have the requisite practical skills. A couch potato who has no idea how to pitch a tent or build a fire in rainy weather should not just set out for the mountains on a whim. If we want to accomplish our goals, we need to figure out what capacities and skills we need for those goals, and then we need to develop them.

This may seem obvious but consider how often we fail to take the steps necessary to achieve the things we really want. It's irrational, to be sure, but for Kant, there's something more going on, at least when we're talking about goals that are important to our self-development. Not all our goals are especially important. Maybe I just want to get really good at this new video game I bought. But suppose that I'm working at a dead-end job and wondering whether I should pursue my dream of becoming a public defender. To make that dream a reality, I'd have to take the LSAT, apply to law school, figure out how to pay for it, and then of course spend three years in school and eventually pass the bar exam. That's a lot to take on! And yet it makes some sense to say that I owe it to myself to give it a shot, and that if I never bother to apply to law school from laziness or inertia, I'll be failing myself in some way.

Of course, it doesn't always make sense to pursue one's dreams. Sometimes other obligations get in the way, or sometimes those dreams are unrealistic or unattainable. Playing for the WNBA is not a dream I should be pursuing, given my height, age, and general lack of basketball talent. Still, Kant wants us to take seriously the idea that we owe it to ourselves to achieve what we are capable of achieving, both for ourselves and for the world as a whole.

Although Kant definitely thinks we should prioritize the cultivation of our rational abilities, he does intend us to think about our natural perfections broadly, including emotional, spiritual, and physical capacities. Some of this involves a kind of preparedness training. Let's return to the Appalachian Trail. If my dream is to hike the entire 2190 miles of it by myself, there's a lot I need to do to get ready. For my trip to be successful, I have to think broadly about what it will really take. Obviously, I should consider the physical demands of the hike and the practical skills I'll need to make sure that I'm not devoured by bears (or more likely, mosquitoes) along the way. But I also need to think about the possible emotional toll of spending months on my own in the wilderness. I have to prepare myself on all levels for what is bound to be an arduous, if rewarding experience.

Sometimes we focus on developing capacities needed for a particular end, like hiking the Appalachian Trail or playing in a band. People who don't have those ends will not necessarily have reason to develop those capacities. If I hate insects, the Appalachian Trail is probably not for me. And I can live a wonderfully fulfilling life without ever mastering a musical instrument. Now if I have a truly unusual talent for something, we might be inclined to think it's a shame if I never develop it. Had Sarah Chang or Joshua Bell chosen not to take up the violin, the world would be worse for it. Kant would say that there is also value to developing our capacities in a more general way, so that we will be ready for whatever we end up wanting to do in life, or for that matter, so that we will be ready for whatever life throws at us. (In the next chapter, we'll see how this plays out when it comes to our ability to do without the comforts and luxuries to which we may be accustomed.)

For Kant, developing our capacities in a way that leaves open a wide array of paths is an important part of treating ourselves respectfully, as rational beings capable of setting ends for ourselves and achieving them. The more I am ready to take on any challenge, the more possibilities are open to me. Although Kant thinks of the duty to cultivate our talents primarily as a duty we owe to ourselves, there are also ways in which we owe it to the larger community to put our talents to use in making the world better. A world without gifted musicians, artists, and athletes is an impoverished world. So is a world in which Rosa Parks never boarded a bus, or Jonas Salk never developed a polio vaccine, or Clara Barton never founded the Red Cross.

When we talk about a life that has purpose, our minds often travel first to people who devote themselves to important moral causes, like Malala Yousafzai or Mahatma Gandhi. But a life doesn't have to be that extraordinary to be meaningful or valuable. Recall that Kant's own parents led quiet, uneventful lives. They were not rich or famous. They just worked hard, raised their children well, and probably did a lot of good in their local community. In fact, much of the work that actually sustains communities happens on a very small scale. It's a casserole here or a ride to school there. If we become the kind of people who can identify problems, figure out effective solutions to them, and be creative about new ways to move forward, then we're already in a position to make important contributions to the world.

Kant deliberately leaves open the ways in which we can find purpose and direction in our lives. The duty to cultivate our talents is an imperfect one, requiring only that we commit ourselves to some form of self-development that makes the most of what we have. We might say that his advice boils down to this: whatever you are, be a good one. To be a good one is to use the full range of our human capacities and skills to take ourselves and the world a step forward. As Kant puts it, "a human being has a duty to himself to be a useful member of the world."[1] We get to decide how we're going to be useful, but not whether we'll be useful.

Before we leave this subject behind, let me take up a few considerations that may or may not be bothering you. I've suggested that this duty rules out spending your life sitting on the couch, but that leaves a lot of space open. Does just any pursuit or goal count as cultivating your talents? Can I cultivate my talents through a life of crime? What about dangerous pursuits that put my life at risk? Some people (although I am not one of them!) find great enjoyment in taking themselves to the very limits of human physical endurance, often at considerable risk to themselves and perhaps others.

The answer to these questions is that it matters that the duty to cultivate our talents is an imperfect duty. This has two key implications: (a) it is always overridden by the requirements of perfect duty and (b) it has to be balanced with the pursuit of our other imperfect duties. The fact that perfect duties override imperfect duties means that it's easy to rule out a life of crime as an acceptable way to cultivate your talents, even if you do manage to develop some mad skills at picking locks and evading the FBI along the way. If a project violates a perfect duty, I can't permissibly pursue it, regardless of whether it represents a lifetime dream.

Things become a little more complicated when it comes to other imperfect duties. Suppose that it's my goal to complete a very technically challenging and dangerous climb. It would certainly be a way of cultivating some of my talents, but it's expensive, time-consuming, and risky. All three of these could potentially pose problems for my pursuit of this goal. If it's money I need to be saving for my child's college education, or time that I should be spending taking care of my elderly parents, or a degree of physical risk that borders on recklessness, I may run up against competing demands from other duties. Whether a risk is reasonable or reckless is, to some extent, in the eye of the beholder, but we do tend to think that it's possible to exercise better or worse judgment in the course of taking risks. Firefighting is a risky job. On the other hand, not having firefighters is risky for the rest of us. Rock climbing is not firefighting, though, which changes the risk calculation. For Kant, failing to take my own safety seriously would be a violation of a duty I owe myself to take care of my body. Failing to take the safety of my fellow climbers seriously would be a violation of a duty to them. And if I am a single parent of seven dependent children, it may be that I would be violating a duty to them by risking my life to pursue an inessential activity, even if it's one I love.

This doesn't mean that Kant would rule out rock climbing, but it does mean that we have to look at the whole picture when we consider cultivating our talents in a way that might generate costs, whether for myself or for others. (Environmental harm is another such cost.) The mere fact that something would make me happy or give my life meaning or enable me to develop a skill doesn't automatically justify me in doing it. The duty to cultivate my talents is only one among many duties that I have. And because it's an imperfect duty, that means it must sometimes give way to other, more important things.

Let me close by pointing out some other implications of this duty of self-development. It almost certainly requires getting an education (and making education possible for others) because education is essential to cultivating our rational capacities. It might also require getting (and making available) treatment for depression or alcoholism, or any other mental health issue that impedes our capacity to function. It could require doing crossword puzzles and Sudoku to keep our minds active as we age. Perhaps more controversially, it could even require pharmaceutical interventions that enhance our cognitive function beyond what it would otherwise be.

As most people know, medication for attention-deficit disorder is a lifesaver for people with the disorder because it enables them to perform tasks and employ cognitive skills that would otherwise be out of reach. In Kantian terms, the duty to cultivate our rational capacities would seem to imply that people with ADHD should take medication, assuming they are able to do so safely and effectively. But when it comes to cognitive enhancement, as opposed to remedying existing cognitive impairments, things get more complicated. Some medications for ADHD seem to improve the cognitive performance of people who don't have the disorder. If that's true, should we all be taking medications to improve our cognitive functioning?

That would be a surprising and perhaps troubling implication, but it's not clear that Kant's account of this duty can avoid it. There are risks to taking medications of any sort, and those have to be considered. It may, however, be the case that the risks are worthwhile for the improved performance. Consider people who work in jobs that require them to be awake and attentive for many hours at a time (e.g., surgeons, pilots, truck drivers). If a neurosurgeon must perform an operation that is scheduled to last for twenty-six hours, it seems like it would be a good thing for her to take medication that would allow her to keep her focus for that length of time. Less controversially, many of us drink coffee to keep ourselves awake while driving long distances, attending boring but necessary meetings, and tending to energetic small children. If drinking three mocha lattes helps me write a better chapter, it seems like we're all winners.

Kant would undoubtedly say that if nothing else, we should do what we can to get enough sleep, stay hydrated, and get proper nutrition. Of course, even that much is impossible for many people. In cases where it isn't possible, maybe using artificial means to compensate is the best we can do. Maybe it's even a morally required thing to do. If so, then you'll might be fulfilling a duty to yourself if you get a cup of coffee before heading into the next chapter.

21 | STOIC CHEERFULNESS
LEARNING TO GRIN AND BEAR IT

I ended the last chapter by suggesting that you pour yourself a cup of coffee. In this chapter, we're going to talk about whether that was actually good advice. More generally, we're going to talk about our all-too-human tendencies to become dependent on things and what that might mean for how our lives go. As we'll see, Kant thinks that it's very important to cultivate a certain level of fortitude for those times when we can't get what we want. Alas, this has implications for those of us who happen to be pretty dependent on caffeine.

I don't know about you, but every morning, one of the first things I do is drink coffee. Sometimes more than one cup if I didn't sleep well or if I have a long day of meetings ahead of me. Probably I could get by without the coffee. Being caffeinated is hardly essential to my health. And yet, I am pretty sure that if I didn't have access to coffee in the morning, I would not be the world's most pleasant or effective parent, spouse, teacher, colleague, or neighbor. Caffeine is mildly addictive, after all, and humans are not at their best when we are deprived of substances to which our bodies have been accustomed.

As we saw in the last chapter, one could actually make a Kantian case for a moral duty to drink coffee, given that caffeine tends to enhance mental alertness. We have a duty to ourselves to cultivate our talents, as well as duties to others to help and protect them whenever we can. If caffeine enables me to drive to work more safely, teach my graduate seminar more effectively, and respond more nimbly to a reviewer's comments on my article, this is surely to my benefit and the benefit of people around me. In that case, my coffee habit might very well be defensible in Kantian terms insofar as it improves my cognitive functioning.

But there is a dark side to a caffeine addiction, and I'm not just talking about French roasted beans. Suppose that I'm under a quarantine order and can't get to the grocery store to replenish my coffee supply. Or suppose I'm out camping with my daughter's Girl Scout troop and someone forgot to pack the Starbucks Via. Or suppose I'm hunkering down in a hurricane with no way to heat water. These things happen. As the Rolling Stones have reminded us, you can't always get what you want. And if I start behaving badly to people just because I can't have my morning coffee, then I've got a bit of a problem. My caffeine dependence is interfering with other, more important things in my life. I'd be better off if I were more flexible in my morning routine, more able to roll with life's punches without a caffeine hit.

As we've seen, Kant places an enormous value on freedom. Freedom is at the very heart of our capacity to be moral and to lead a good life. To be a free being is to be capable of acting in accordance with reason, and we can't do that unless we are free *from* the things that get in the way of what reason tells us. I am not truly free when I am having a meltdown because I can't get a latte or because my WiFi connection is slow or because I have to wait in a long line to get my driver's license renewed.

Kant is very cognizant of the ways in which our mental and physical states affect our ability to think and act rationally. Sometimes this is not within our control, like when we're sleep-deprived or in a great deal of pain. More frequently, though, it *is* within our control. Kant thinks that insofar as I let my desires and feelings get the better of me, I'm undermining my own ability to live well and be a good person. This means that we have to be very careful about the things on which we become dependent.

To understand why Kant thinks this way, it helps to go back to an ancient philosophical tradition known as Stoicism, a tradition that had a significant influence on Kant. Stoicism traces its roots back to ancient Greece, although it is probably better known in its Roman form, exemplified in the work of Stoics like Seneca and Marcus Aurelius. Kant is clearly impressed by Stoicism, even if he is not entirely sold on it. Stoicism is a complex theory, but here's the basic idea: we will live well if we can reshape our desires so that they match the world as it is, not the way we want it to be. If I'm on a camping trip with no access to coffee, it's better if I no longer want coffee than if I spend the whole time wishing I had some. This isn't to say that Stoics think we should get rid of all our desires. If there's coffee available, there's no problem with my drinking it. But if I can't control whether coffee is always available, then a desire for unavailable coffee is going to make my life worse.

Kant doesn't really think we'll be able to get full control of our desires this way. (The Stoics didn't think it was a particularly easy task either.) There is, however, great benefit to us in trying. We might frame this in terms of acquiring self-control over what Kant describes as the "rabble" of inclinations and feelings that live within us. It's definitely in my self-interest to develop such control because doing things like exploding with anger at my boss will be bad for my career. For Kant, though, the deeper reasons we have for seeking self-control are moral ones. If we have control over our desires, we'll be less likely to perform immoral actions. Self-control also enables us to live according to our own principles, as opposed to being dragged around by our whims.

If we don't have self-control, the authority of reason in our lives will be seriously hindered. It's like a teacher who, despite technically having authority in his classroom, is unable to keep a room full of seventh graders in line. The authority still matters, but it won't be very useful if he doesn't also have control over the class. Likewise, when we have control over our desires and inclinations, we are better positioned to exercise the authority of reason that Kant thinks is expressive of our dignity as free beings. We might say that I am more myself when I have self-control.

If we're going to develop this self-control, Kant thinks, we should avoid luxuries, as they tend to make us soft and dissatisfied. (He is particularly concerned about the wearing of silk and riding horseback. Consider yourself warned.) Kant's fear is that when we become accustomed to such luxuries, we find it difficult to be happy in their absence: "The more dependent we are on such pseudonecessities, the more is our contentment at their mercy."[1] Anyone who has ever mislaid their cell phone for an extended period of time knows exactly what he means. Anyway, in the face of climate change, we'll all do well to learn to live without the pseudonecessities we've come to grow dependent on.

An excessive dependency on luxuries can make us more susceptible to vices like envy. The more I desire creature comforts, the more likely I am to be discontented with my own situation and resent those who can afford things that I cannot. Better for me to step away from Instagram and Pinterest entirely rather than let my heart be filled with desires for couches I can't afford and ugly thoughts about people who have money to burn on fancy vacations. As Kant puts it:

> The greatest source of happiness and unhappiness, of well-being and wretchedness, of satisfaction and dissatisfaction is to be found in comparison with other men. If every one in the town had nothing but bread and water for food and drink, I should be satisfied with so simple a diet and would submit to it with a cheerful mind; but if every one else were able to enjoy sumptuous repasts and I alone had to live in a wretched state, I should feel unhappy and regard it as a misfortune.[2]

Here we see yet another reason to take charge of our thinking and avoid comparing our situations with others. We may not be able to control whether we have a sumptuous repast in front of us, but we can control whether we're dwelling on what other people have in front of them. Channeling the Stoics, Kant reminds us that "good and ill-fortune depend on ourselves and upon the mental attitudes we adopt toward them."[3]

Besides, Kant clearly believes that a happy life is possible without luxuries: "I may find pleasure in living even though I live in poverty and yet have none of the comforts of life."[4] Because Kant did not grow up amidst wealth and splendor, he does have some personal experience on which to draw when he makes claims like this. And he does distinguish luxuries from necessities. Presumably he doesn't think that starvation is compatible with pleasure in living.

His key point is that we need to think hard about what we actually need, and then learn to detach ourselves from the things that we don't. As he says, "all comforts and pleasures should be enjoyed in such a way that we can dispense with them; we ought never make necessities of them."[5] So if I get to the point that coffee is a necessity for me, something has gone wrong. I've handed partial control of myself over to Starbucks and as a result, have made myself less capable of acting autonomously.

Now Kant does not think that the quest for self-control should take the form of extreme self-denial. He enjoyed a good dinner party himself and he also suggests that exposure to certain luxuries improves our capacity for taste and aesthetic appreciation. He's not telling us that we should aim to live like paupers. In fact, on multiple occasions he criticizes practices of penance that involve things like fasting and self-flagellation. Such "monkish virtues" do nothing but weaken the body and crush the spirit. (He even suggests that they might be motivated by self-conceit.) As he says, "it is true that the body must be kept under discipline, but it should not be shattered or have its strength broken."[6] We have a duty to care for ourselves, physically and mentally, and whatever virtue there is in self-control has to be compatible with this duty and with our more general duty of self-respect. This means, according to Kant, that we should not purposely impose discomforts or inconveniences on ourselves just for the heck of it. There's no virtue in that, despite what ascetics might think. What we need is to develop the habits of mind that will enable us to manage whatever discomforts and inconveniences come our way.

These habits of mind have two components. We need the ability to bear discomfort without complaining or shirking in our duties. We might call this the habit of equanimity in the face of inconvenience or discomfort. (Likely many of us have had the experience of traveling with someone who lacks this habit and cannot maintain equanimity in the face of long lines, cramped spaces, weather delays, and bad airplane food.) But there's another component which Kant also thinks important, which we might call the habit of cheerfulness. Kant thinks we can do better than simply avoiding being irritable and grumpy. He says (this time following one of his other muses, Epicurus) that we should aim to develop what he calls an "ever-cheerful heart."[7] More specifically, we need to develop habits of putting ourselves into a cheerful frame of mind.

Kant doesn't give us much specific guidance about how to develop this habit of cheerfulness. He mostly focuses on extolling its value. Insofar as contemporary psychologists agree with Kant about the importance of positive thinking, which many of them do, we can certainly get assistance in coming up with practices and strategies for maintaining cheerfulness in the face of adversity. It helps, of course, if we've cultivated the habit of equanimity because it's not easy to think cheerful thoughts when you're constantly focused on the vacations you're not taking and the furniture you can't afford to buy. But we can make an effort to redirect our thoughts away from what we don't have, with an eye toward appreciating what we do have. Kant would likely tell us not to dwell on the things that make us cranky and unable to maintain our composure. If there's no coffee to be had on the camping trip, I need to stop grumbling and complaining about it and instead turn my mind to something else. It's not easy, but it's a practical skill we can and should acquire.

Kant firmly believes that self-control is crucial for living happily. The more we are in the grip of our desires, the less freedom we have to set our own ends and achieve our goals. The person who can successfully contain their desires and dependencies will be better positioned to act on their own principles. They will also be able to handle difficulties and deprivations without losing their cool or treating other people badly. In Kant's words, "Let us then accept the benefits of life as we have received them, let us be satisfied with God's universal wisdom and care and not allow misery and misfortune to weigh upon us."[8]

22 | JUDICIOUS RESERVE
KNOWING WHEN TO SHUT UP

There are few skills in life as important as knowing when to keep your mouth shut. Although as we've seen, Kant is a huge believer in truthfulness, he is not actually a proponent of spilling your guts. In fact, in the *Lectures on Ethics*, he says that no one in their right mind is completely candid. Of course, we have self-interested reasons to keep some things to ourselves. It's not a good idea to let your chess opponent know what you're planning for your next move. Nor is it usually wise to tell your boss exactly what you think of his meeting management skills. Saying what you think can get you into trouble.

But Kant has other reasons for believing that we should be careful about what we say, and they aren't all about protecting ourselves from our own stupidity (though Kant does think that's important too). Knowing when to be candid and when to be reserved is actually a skill we need in conducting our moral lives. People do not always need to know what we're thinking. Very often, they don't *want* to know what we're thinking. Just as we owe it to other people and to the moral community as a whole to be truthful, so we also owe it to them to be reserved when the occasion demands it. Given what we human beings are like, some degree of reserve is essential to our ability to maintain the appropriate attitudes of respect and love for each other.

Have you ever watched a reality television show or a YouTube video that made you cringe on behalf of the person making the video or starring in the show? Some people don't seem to have any qualms about doing humiliating things in public or sharing extremely personal information on social media. Maybe you are such a person. If so, you may have trouble seeing the issue that Kant is trying to identify here. But if you are not such a person, and if you find it uncomfortable to watch other people let it all hang out on YouTube or cable television, then you already have a sense of what bothers Kant when no one seems to have any filters. Most people have a lot of dirty laundry. We don't necessarily want to see all of it. In fact, Kant worries that the constant parade of dirty laundry across our computer screens will make us worse as people and as a society.

Now of course Kant didn't say anything about computer screens and he didn't actually say anything about laundry either. But he did talk about toilets! In the *Lectures on Ethics*, he writes:

> If all men were good there would be no need for any of us to be reserved; but since they are not, we have to keep the shutters closed. Every house keeps its dustbin in a place of its own. We do not press our friends to come into our water-closet, although we have one just like themselves.[1]

It's possible that you have a fabulously decorated bathroom and that you do press your friends to come see it, but in general, Kant is strongly in favor of keeping those doors and shutters closed. He may well mean this literally in the sense that he does *not* want to see your toilet or the images from your most recent colonoscopy. (I mean, who does?) We're more concerned with the figurative meaning here. That figurative meaning has to do with our flaws and failings.

Most of us naturally want to hide our flaws from other people because we don't want them to think worse of us or lose their respect for us. Kant calls this a providential feature of our nature on the grounds that it's quite reasonable to worry about what might happen if we lay our souls bare to the wrong person. Not everyone can be trusted with our deep, dark secrets. Kant, however, is concerned with more than the prudential fallout of revealing our flaws. He's also worried about the moral implications of putting everything out in the open.

Let's go back to reality television shows. Some such shows seem harmless, insofar as they don't require people to do anything humiliating or expose deeply personal information. But other shows are set up in such a way that the characters will inevitably come off badly. Sure, we may feel sorry for them, but as most of us know from experience, pity sometimes comes with a heavy dose of condescension. "Oh, you poor thing!" can be an expression of true sympathy, but it can also express smug satisfaction at how low the person has sunk. As we know, Kant really worries about our tendencies toward self-conceit. Reality television shows are often designed to make us feel better about ourselves in comparison with the folks on the screen. Their failings are our successes because we would surely never do anything so stupid or fall into those ridiculous traps. A reality show contestant's bad taste, crass lifestyle, poor judgment, or lack of social skills all provide opportunities for us to scorn them and, as a result, feel smugly self-satisfied.

Now you might be thinking that not all reality shows are like this (true) and that feeling morally superior to awful people is not necessarily such a bad thing (iffy). There is little doubt that reality television is an effective showcase for some of the worst parts of human nature. Perhaps it can serve as an early warning system so that we know what *not* to do in public. Even if that were true, however, it wouldn't necessarily justify it in Kant's eyes. As we saw way back in Chapter 11, he is skeptical that bad examples are useful in making us morally better. If anything, they risk making us worse.

There's a difference between acknowledging a person's moral failings and taking pleasure in them. The first is an unavoidable part of living with other frail, flawed human beings. The second, Kant thinks, is corrupting. It's corrupting because reveling in someone else's downfall amounts to feeding my own self-conceit. If we would just limit ourselves to learning from other people's mistakes, rather than patting ourselves on the back for having avoided them or reassuring ourselves that we would never make them, things might be different. Kant just doubts that we will be so restrained. The problem, of course, is that we enjoy feeling superior to people. Insofar as reality television makes us feel superior, it's bad for us.

Would it be better if we *all* put our flaws on full display? That would seem to remedy the superiority problem. If I make my flaws public, I am hardly in a position to feel superior to others who are doing the same. In fact, it might even seem like it would inspire greater humility in all of us. If everyone's a sinner, no one's really a winner. We're all on the same footing again, and we know

Kant thinks that's a good thing. He also thinks humility is a good thing. So why can't we just all throw open the bathroom doors and accept that we're all flawed in more or less the same ways? Many of us often feel like we have to spend half our lives posturing and pretending to be someone we're not. It might even be a relief to be able to let go of that and be our very messy selves among people who won't judge us for that.

There's a lot to be said for this view, and Kant himself says things that might seem to favor it. We know he's not a fan of being judgmental. And as we'll see in Chapter 25, he values the intimacy and closeness that self-revelation in friendship can produce. But he's also skeptical that a world in which everyone's flaws are constantly on full display is a world in which we are going to be able to make any substantial moral progress (or for that matter, hang on to whatever progress we've managed to make). When everyone's flaws are visible to us, it is not necessarily going to inspire us to become better. Moral flaws may be perfectly normal, but we don't want to *normalize* them in the sense of condoning them or even regarding them as desirable.

Imagine that you have a friend who often behaves in very inconsiderate ways. Suppose that every time you try to make plans, they're slow to return your texts. When they do agree to do something together, they often show up late and sometimes not at all. But instead of apologizing and vowing to download a reminder app, they shrug their shoulders and say, "That's just the way I am." Probably you're not going to be very satisfied with this as a response. You're likely to be annoyed with your friend and feel as if they don't value you very much at all. You might also be put off by their apparent lack of interest in trying to do better.

In a way, this person is owning their flaw. They're not making excuses or trying to blame you or some third party for their constant lateness. You can give them credit for honesty. But there's another sense in which they're not owning it *as* a flaw. They just don't see it as an issue. If you're bothered by it, it's on you, not them. They're unwilling to change. And that's the real problem. This person has no interest in improving themselves, even though their flaw is getting in the way of your friendship. You'd be right to think they don't value you in the way that they should. If they did, they'd admit that you deserve better.

Kant sees hiding our flaws as a way of acknowledging them *as* flaws. Of course, we're also supposed to be trying to fix them, and not just sweeping them under the rug or shutting the door on them. Reserve is not supposed to be deceptive. (After all, everyone knows there's a toilet behind that door!) What being reserved about our flaws does is express the attitude that we're supposed to be trying to do better and that it's *worth* trying to do better. Your friend who can't be bothered to show up on time doesn't seem to acknowledge that there's a better way to conduct human relationships. There's no higher standard to which they are trying to aspire for themselves or for your friendship.

This belief in a higher standard is something Kant thinks we desperately need. It's why he thinks we should throw the veil of charity over the flaws of other people, and it's also why we need to keep our own flaws out of view as much as we can. If we're going to maintain any semblance of love and respect for each other, we need to be able to see that higher standard in action. That won't happen unless we put forward the appearance of adhering to it. Now this doesn't mean that Kant is promoting deception in our dealings with others. You shouldn't be lying about why you're late to lunch with your friend. But being reserved doesn't mean being deceptive. It's more of a way of shifting our focus to better things. When I close my bathroom door, I'm not pretending the toilet doesn't exist. Instead, I'm creating what is (let us suppose) a more aesthetically pleasing environment for us. For Kant, that kind of pleasing environment is important to our ability to sustain our commitment to morality. It's crucial that we not all drag each other down into the mud, or into each other's bathrooms.

Remember that Kant thinks that we find it hard to like each other, a problem that interferes with our ability to fulfill our duties of love. Those duties don't depend on our finding people likeable because I have a duty to help people I dislike as well as those I like. But let's face it—it's a heck of a lot easier to help people when you find them likeable. It's also a heck of a lot easier to respect people when you haven't just seen them do something completely humiliating on YouTube. Kant worries that these all-important attitudes of love and respect are fragile. They are hard to maintain in a world where everyone hangs their dirty laundry in public. That's why we have a duty to keep the worst parts of ourselves under wraps.

This may sound as though Kant wants evildoers to hide their dastardly deeds, and perhaps also wants us to hide those deeds from view. There are all kinds of problems with that view. Because Kant was a smart guy, it's reasonable to assume he did not mean that we should never admit our failings or call other people out on theirs. Not all flaws should remain hidden. Some dirty laundry has to be aired to keep people safe and allow wrongdoers to make amends and improve. Admitting a flaw is also not the same as endorsing it. Kant is definitely not suggesting that we pretend we're all perfect. What we need to avoid is both a sense of shame-lessness about our own flaws and a feeling of superiority when we witness flaws in others.

The upshot is that Kant thinks that candor is overrated. It's not that he doesn't appreciate the importance of being able to share our vulnerabilities with people we love and trust. He does, as we'll see when we get to his discussion of friendship. It's more that he strongly believes in the value of having a filter when it comes to what we say and do. Not everything on YouTube really belongs there. And some of the things that come out of our mouths would be better left unsaid.

23 | USEFUL BENEFICENCE
LENDING A GENUINELY HELPFUL HAND

Most people would agree that helping others in need is part of a good life. Put that way, it doesn't sound controversial, or even very difficult. Maybe we're picturing swooping in to save a life in an emergency or sending a donation to a relief organization after a natural disaster. These actions are good, of course, but notice that they could be actions that benefit the doer as much as the recipient. The first image might draw on our childhood fantasies of being a superhero. (Who doesn't want to jump in the Batmobile and rescue Gotham from evildoers?) The second allows us to regard ourselves as selfless philanthropists, albeit ones who save lives from the comfort of our couches instead of the trenches.

It probably won't surprise you to learn that Kant isn't convinced that helping actions done from motives like these provide much evidence for a person's good moral character, or good will. It's possible that they don't even fulfill the duty of beneficence as he describes it. Suppose you ask me to help out with the food drive you're organizing to help hungry children in our town. I agree, but only because I'm planning to run for office and I figure this will be a good look for my future campaign. It's true that I'm helping out, but I'm doing it for my sake, not theirs, which is why it may not even seem like beneficence at all.

As we saw back in Chapter 4, Kant thinks that our reasons matter. Of course it's good to do the right thing, but we should be doing the right thing for the right reasons. That's what is characteristic of a person with a good will. So, what are the right reasons for helping? In Kant's framework, our reasons have to be tied to our obligations to our fellow rational agents. Technically, Kant categorizes beneficence as a duty of love. Helping people is a way of showing that we care about them and their needs. But Kantian beneficence can just as easily be understood as a duty of respect. Helping someone out is also a way of respecting them as a setter of ends in his fancy language. To be a setter of ends is to be someone who has plans, projects, and goals. If I am going to fully respect you as a rational agent, I have to take into account the fact that you have ends of your own, things that you want and need to accomplish. What it means to take that into account is to regard your ends as something I have reason to help you promote, simply in virtue of the fact that they are the ends of a rational agent.

Now you have reason to help your friends and family members because you care about them and perhaps also because you know they'd do the same for you. This feeling of being able to rely on other people is a crucial aspect of relationships and Kant certainly isn't downplaying its importance. But beneficence, as Kant understands it, is actually something that we owe to all rational beings, not just our friends and relatives. He describes the duty of beneficence as a duty to "make the ends of others my own." By this he means that I have a duty to treat the ends that you have set for yourself as if they were my ends too. The fact that these things matter to you is itself a reason for me to help you with them, independently of whether they matter to me.

Let me make this more concrete. Suppose that we are friends and that you have asked me to help you paint your kitchen this weekend. This is the kind of favor that we think we should do for our friends when we can. I don't necessarily care whether your kitchen gets painted this weekend, but *you* care and that's enough to give me a reason to help you. It's something you want to accomplish, and you need my help. So far, so good. But now let's suppose that you plan to paint your kitchen canary yellow. I happen to think that the color you've picked out is ugly. Perhaps this is something friends should tell each other. For now, though, let's just suppose that you love the color and want to be surrounded by it every morning as you eat breakfast. Does the fact that I hate your paint choice give me a reason not to help you paint your kitchen? Does it give me a reason to secretly swap out your chosen paint with something a bit less awful?

Kant's answer here is a definite no. He is explicit about the fact that the duty of beneficence is a duty to help others achieve *their* ends in accordance with *their* ideas of happiness, not *my* idea of what would make them happy. The more I impose on you my own ideas about the color of your kitchen (or what kind of person you should be dating or the way you're raising your children), the further I get from the mindset necessary for genuine beneficence. It's supposed to be about you and what you want, not about what I want for you or think best for you. That's why beneficence is a matter of respect as well as love. Respecting you means accepting your choices as they are, not as I want them to be. This doesn't mean that I can't suggest that you consider other paint colors, but once you've made up your mind, your mind isn't mine to change.

One consequence is that fulfilling the duty of beneficence is sometimes going to be pretty frustrating because it means setting my own ideas aside and letting the other person's choices be the determining factor in my actions. We don't have to like what people are doing to be helpful to them and sometimes we should help people even when we don't like what they're doing. This applies to strangers as well as friends. Suppose that I am driving on a dark, isolated road and encounter someone with a flat tire. It turns out that they're on their way to a baseball game to cheer on their favorite team, which happens to be playing *my* favorite team. I still have reason to help them with their flat tire, even if I'm not keen on what they're going to do once their car is operational.

Crucially, Kant does not think that we have to help people with all their ends and projects. We definitely shouldn't be helping people with their immoral projects. If you ask me for a ride to the nearest bank branch because you're planning an armed robbery, I can and should say no. We also have some wiggle room when it comes to deciding what kinds of helping actions we'll perform. After all, we can't help everyone with everything they need. There simply aren't enough hours in the day. This is why beneficence has to be an imperfect duty. We're not acting wrongly if we don't take every single opportunity to help someone.

It's true for Kant that the mere fact that you have a (morally permissible) project generally implies that I have some reason to help you with it as a matter of beneficence. It does not, however, follow that you have a claim on my help with just *any* project that you happen to have. Suppose that after I help you change your tire, you ask me to clean the trash out of your car. It might be nice of me to agree, but if I said no and you complained about me to your friends, you'd come off as awfully petty and entitled. Cleaning the trash out of your car seems pretty different from helping you change your tire. Alternatively, your projects may conflict with mine. Suppose that I'm also on my way to that same baseball game and you ask me to swap out my team's jersey for one that supports your team. Because I want my own team to win, I don't have to wear your team's jersey just because you want them to win. I'm not necessarily disrespecting you as a setter of ends if I decline to help you pursue some of the particular ends that you happen to have.

Now things do change once we start talking about emergencies, or what Kant calls cases of "true need." The reason why intuitively it seems like I should stop and help you change your tire is because you're a fellow human being and you have a pretty significant problem happening in your life, one that I can help you solve. No one wants to be stranded on a dark, isolated road with an inoperable car. It might even be dangerous if it's especially cold or hot outside. We tend to think that there are cases where we should help people regardless of whether we like them or whether we agree with their politics or their taste in music. If someone's having a heart attack in front of you, you should do CPR. You shouldn't stop and ask for their voting history first.

Emergencies are, in many ways, a special case of helping actions. For one thing, helping in a true emergency is a very pressing moral obligation, not an optional extra nice thing, like cleaning out a stranger's car. I don't have to help every friend I have paint their kitchen or help one friend paint every room in his house. But when a person's life is at stake, it seems like I need an extremely good reason to refuse to help them. There could be such reasons. Maybe I'm busy saving someone else's life. Or maybe helping that person would put my own life in danger. In general, though, the more desperately the person needs my help and the easier it is for me to provide it, the less latitude I have when it comes to deciding whether to help. If it's a matter of wading into a shallow pond to pull a toddler to safety, it's obvious that I have to do it. If it's a matter of trying to rescue you from a rip tide when I'm not a good swimmer, it's a very different story. Not only will I probably fail to save you, there's a good chance that I'll drown in the process. There's a balancing act of sorts between your genuine needs and my own.

Kant doesn't try to spell out all the details of this balancing act. He thinks there will have to be some space for judgment. We may disagree about what counts as an emergency. (A cat stuck in a tree? A child's toy left behind on an airplane?) And there are times when we should drop what we're doing to help friends with lesser emergencies, even though we wouldn't have to do the same thing for strangers. Maybe I should cancel my plans for the afternoon to come fix your clogged sink if you're my good friend. If you're a stranger who just approached me outside of the hardware store, however, it seems like enough if I just suggest that you find yourself a good plumber.

Some critics of Kant have claimed that he lets us off the hook too easily when it comes to beneficence. If there's so much space for choosing which helping actions I perform, it seems quite likely that most of us will end up doing too little for other people. We've seen how good we are at rationalizing our choices, especially when those choices serve our self-interest. (Remember my decision to stay in bed and nurse a hangover rather than work at the homeless shelter?) How do we know when we're doing enough? Or in more technical language, how do we know when we've succeeded in adopting the end of beneficence and truly made the needs of others our own?

The duty to commit ourselves to the ends of others can be understood in part as a duty to try to see others in the right light, as fellow rational beings worthy of our help. To really make this commitment part of our deepest moral self, it helps to try to cultivate that attitude of love, the one that disposes us to feel sympathy for people and concern for their fate. In the section of the *Doctrine of Virtue* where Kant explains the duty of beneficence, he also says that sympathy is a duty. As we know, Kant doesn't think that we can have duties to have particular feelings. The duty of sympathy is a duty to make ourselves into the kind of people that pay attention to others and that take seriously the harms that befall them.

You may recall that Kant tells us not to avoid sickrooms and other places where we'd have to confront the suffering of other people. We have to be reminded of how much our help is needed, even if we prefer not to think about it, as we so often do in the case of desperate strangers on the other side of the world. Most of the time, most of us are pretty responsive to people in dire need when they're right in front of us and we can readily help them. The trick is getting ourselves to extend that responsiveness to other, less visible cases where the need is just as great and the ability to help just as simple.

Kant sees the cultivation of sympathy as a remedy to our tendency to be insufficiently concerned with the needs of others, or even just our tendency to get distracted by the everyday stuff in our own lives. Truly fulfilling the duty of beneficence requires an effort to become sympathetic and caring people, the kind of people who will pull over and help someone change a flat tire on a dark road because that's just how they are. Cultivating sympathy is how we make beneficence part of our character. With any luck, the imaginative capacities we cultivate in the sickroom will enable us to extend that sympathy to people whose plights we never witness firsthand. We have duties of beneficence to people regardless of whether we feel sorry for them. Sympathy, however, is a really useful tool in getting us to do what we already know we should be doing.

There's another dimension of Kantian beneficence that's worth our attention, and that has to do with its dark side. Yes, there's a dark side to beneficence, at least when help is delivered with a side of superiority or experienced with a dash of inferiority. One of Kant's more interesting insights about beneficence is that it can generate problems about self-respect. As we've seen, Kant thinks that arrogance and servility are two sides of the same self-respect coin. The arrogant person overinflates their own worth and the servile person underinflates theirs. Kant sees that beneficence can disrupt our feelings of being the moral equals of others. The benefactor, having provided some essential service, can feel smugly self-satisfied. The beneficiary, having been in the position of needing help, can feel as though they are lesser than others in virtue of their dependency. It threatens their self-respect. Kant isn't saying that either of these responses is rational or defensible. It's just that he knows that in real life, beneficence can have the unwelcome side effect of undermining mutual respect.

Fortunately, Kant doesn't just leave us hanging when it comes to resolving this problem. He suggests that whenever possible, we do beneficent actions in secret, thereby ridding ourselves of the temptation to bask in our philanthropic glory. Secret beneficence also makes it impossible for the beneficiary to feel in the debt of a particular person. Kant further suggests playing down the burdens of what we're doing when we're helping others, as we often do when we say things like, "It's not a big deal" or "I was already going that direction" or "I had extras on hand." If we're really tactful, we might even turn it around so that we treat the favor we're doing someone else as a favor they're doing for us. These are minor social maneuvers that can have a big effect on how people feel about being the recipient of help. Whether Kant actually practiced them, we'll never know, but he is certainly aware of their importance.

One last point. Kant does say that wealthy people sometimes consider as charity actions that are actually obligations of justice. Kant's political philosophy, with its emphasis on property rights, can seem libertarian, but that's not necessarily accurate. He is keenly aware of the ways in which poverty affects a person's ability to pursue their own ends and the negative implications of that for self-respect. He warns us not to be too complacent in thinking that we've succeeded in fulfilling the demands of beneficence. Maybe what we think of as charity is simply giving to people what they were already due. Even when it's genuine beneficence, we should try very hard to avoid patting ourselves on the back for our generosity. There's a lot of luck involved when it comes to being on the giving or the receiving end of beneficence. We all need help from time to time. Giving help to those who need it is a duty, but it's a duty that, if we're not careful, we can really get wrong.

Kant's account of beneficence is driven by his commitment to moral equality, combined with the facts about our mutual vulnerability. We are all susceptible to the whims of fate. The mere fact that we have bodies puts us at risk of disease, injury, and death. Our ability to pursue our ends is constantly under threat. Even if we think of ourselves as invulnerable, or at least strong enough to bear what life throws at us without help, we're wrong. Like it or not, we need other people. Because of that, we have to be prepared to help each other out. We deserve no less from each other. If we can remember that much, we're on our way to getting beneficence right.

24 | HEARTFELT GRATITUDE
ACKNOWLEDGING OUR DEBTS

Do you have any unfinished thank you notes, perhaps ones that have been sitting on your dining room table since your last birthday? Any unsent emails thanking people for writing you a letter of recommendation or helping you out with a project? Most of us are in that same boat. Just to warn you, this chapter might make you feel a bit guilty about it because as far as Kant is concerned, gratitude is an important moral obligation. He even calls it a sacred duty. He also thinks that ingratitude is a vice. (Not just an ordinary vice, but a *satanic* vice!) Clearly Kant thinks something important is going on with those thank you notes. Let's see what he means by gratitude and why he thinks it has such moral significance.

Kant describes gratitude as a duty that we owe to people who have benefited us. Gratitude is a way of honoring them. He immediately rules out the idea, perhaps widely held, that the main point of doing things like writing thank you notes is to encourage the givers to keep on giving to you. Thank you notes written out of that kind of motivation are simply acts of self-interest, not an expression of moral commitment. But he does think that the importance of gratitude is tied to the importance of beneficence. It's because beneficence is such a valuable thing that it deserves honor in the form of gratitude. This means that the person who is ungrateful fails to value beneficence properly. Suppose the person who gave you that gift spent a lot of time picking out something that they thought you'd really enjoy. Maybe they even went a little over budget just to get you just the right present. Now they are wondering whether you like the gift as much as they had hoped (or maybe even if you got the gift in the first place).

Kant would say that if I don't express my gratitude, then I'm not really valuing your act of beneficence properly. I'm not acknowledging the trouble you went to on my behalf and the good will that your efforts showed. Failing to thank you is, on Kant's view, a failure to respect you. But ingratitude is not merely disrespectful. It also shows that I'm deficient when it comes to love. Sometimes we're just being forgetful or lazy when we don't express gratitude for what people have done for us. Sometimes, however, the explanation runs a bit deeper, in which case it might hint at a more serious moral problem.

It's certainly true that we don't always feel grateful for what others have done for us. There are all kinds of reasons for this. Maybe they did something that we didn't really want them to do, or that we wanted to do for ourselves. This is pretty irritating, even when the person means well. And sometimes people take selfish (or at least self-centered) pleasure in helping, because they enjoy the subsequent accolades about their generosity. As we've seen, Kant is reluctant to call these acts of beneficence at all. For a helping action to count as fulfilling the duty of beneficence, it must be aimed at promoting the beneficiary's own ends, not the benefactor's ends.

Do we owe gratitude to a would-be benefactor who isn't actually benefiting us? It's an interesting question, and one that Kant doesn't answer directly. But we can draw some inferences from what he does say. Much depends on whether they are genuinely *trying* to benefit us and whether their subsequent failure to pull off the beneficent action is their fault. Suppose your computer is acting up one Sunday afternoon and I offer to fix it for you. This seems like a good candidate for a beneficent action because I probably have other, more pleasant things to do with my day. It may very well be beneficence if you indeed want your computer fixed and I'm doing it so that you have a fixed computer (as opposed to doing it because I want a chance to steal all the loose change in your apartment). But suppose that I'm not very good at what I'm doing and I accidentally wipe your hard drive, which, like most of us, you have not properly backed up. Not only is your computer still broken, but you've also lost your data. Are you supposed to be grateful to me?

The Kantian answer here is probably yes, with the caveat that Kant likely wouldn't blame you if you have to express your thanks through gritted teeth. After all, I was genuinely trying to help you, even if I ended up making things way worse. You could at least be grateful for my good intentions, despite the fact that the actual outcome wasn't exactly what you were imagining. Gratitude seems warranted for major efforts made on behalf of others. This is consistent with Kant's picture, as gratitude is aimed at honoring beneficence, and my good intentions do show that I'm really making the effort.

Gratitude, however, doesn't always track effort. We sometimes feel massive gratitude to people who solve a major problem for us, even if it didn't involve much effort on their part, like when a customer service representative clicks a few buttons and magically fixes a byzantine problem that has taken us weeks of phone calls. I doubt Kant would object to thanking the customer service representative effusively. The world could always use a bit more gratitude and anyway, customer service can be a very thankless job. Maybe my over-the-top gratitude will make up for someone else's angry rant. In general, though, gratitude's proper target is beneficence shown toward us by another person. As such, it should be responsive to the aims and intentions of the person to whom we owe gratitude.

But here's the thing about actual human beings. Sometimes we are not grateful for well-meant beneficence that genuinely helps us. And it's not because we're lazy or forgetful, but because we're actually feeling a bit resentful. Why would we feel resentful when someone does something nice for us? Probably we have to dig more deeply into our psyches to answer that question. It may not seem to make a whole lot of sense, but it does happen. It may have even happened to Kant himself, which is perhaps why he notices it.

Kant had to depend on the help of his uncle to finance his education. No doubt he also needed the help of others at various other points during his life. And although this is a bit speculative on my part, reading Kant's remarks on gratitude gives the impression that he really hates being indebted to others. He clearly values independence and freedom. Having to rely on other people doesn't seem to sit well with him, even as he recognizes both its necessity and its value. Sacrificing yourself for someone else is genuinely admirable and we definitely should be grateful to those who sacrifice for us. Beneficence is a beautiful thing. But in general, it's more pleasant to be the one doing the admirable actions than the one doing the grateful honoring of those actions.

In the last chapter, we discussed Kant's important insight that beneficence can throw off our basic relationships of moral equality. If you're always the one who needs help, you can begin to feel a bit low in comparison with those who are helping you. This is why Kant thinks we should try to do our beneficent actions anonymously if possible, or at least minimize the sacrifices we're making. Otherwise, our intended beneficiary may have trouble maintaining their self-respect, and this is not something we want to wish on people. (The benefactor who does wish that on his beneficiary is not a nice person.)

That insight about moral equality is also at work in Kant's account of gratitude. When someone does me a favor, I should be grateful. I should also try to return the favor if I can (or pay it forward if I cannot), but Kant thinks that this will never really be enough to rebalance the scales. If someone does something nice for me and I try to pay it back, there are two not-so-great things that happen. First, I turn the act of beneficence into something that's more transactional. This doesn't mean I shouldn't attempt to pay the person back, but it does explain why, when we're trying to do something nice for someone, we might be offended if they offer us money. There's a difference between helping someone from beneficence and providing a paid service. If my beneficiary tries to pay me for my efforts, they turn my efforts into something much less noble. So, we have to be careful about how we return favors. It's important that they don't start to feel like quid pro quo exchanges. The reciprocity will work only if it remains beneficence on each side. You help me because you want to help me. And then when you next need help, I help you because I want to help you, not simply so that I can even the score.

This takes us to the second not-so-great thing about trying to pay back a favor. It doesn't actually work. By that I mean there is some sense in which the score can never be evened. Kant thinks that when it comes to beneficence, the person who does the first beneficent action permanently occupies the top moral position in virtue of having been the first one to do a good deed. If that's not me, then I am always coming in second from a moral standpoint. This may just make us all sound like whiny children. ("*I* wanted to have the first bite! *I* wanted to sit in the front seat!") But Kant seems to think that it's a pretty natural reaction to never being able to ride shotgun, so to speak. We're not wrong to think that the backseat is a lesser place to be. The initial act of beneficence has a moral quality to it that can't be duplicated, no matter how hard the recipient tries to do something even more generous in return. It will still feel like returning a favor, not doing a favor, and Kant thinks there's a difference.

This explains why we might feel resentful of people who benefit us. It's not that we can't use the help; it's that we don't always like the fact that we need help. We often feel uncomfortable when we are dependent on others and unhappy to be obligated to them. It puts us in an inferior position with respect to them and hence, threatens our self-conceit. It is no surprise that beneficence, rather than generating gratitude, can sometimes generate negative attitudes instead. The vice of ingratitude is what happens when we give into these feelings and allow ourselves to resent or even hate the people who are helping us. To avoid the vice, Kant thinks, we need to make an effort to appreciate beneficence when it comes our way.

Insofar as gratitude is a duty, it's a duty to engage in particular acts of expressing gratitude. It's not a duty to have a grateful feeling. Sometimes we just can't summon up the grateful feeling itself. We can say the words or write the note, but it won't be heartfelt. If this is all we can manage, then we're fulfilling the duty. Still, Kant wants something more from us. He wants us to develop a grateful heart. To really embody the spirit of gratitude, we have to work to cultivate what we might call a grateful orientation or disposition. I should aim to be the kind of person who is prone to feeling grateful when someone does something nice for me, just as I should aim to be the kind of person who feels sympathy when other people are suffering.

Recall that Kant thinks we can develop sympathy by doing things like visiting sick rooms. When it comes to developing gratitude, the parallel just might be things like keeping a gratitude journal or writing thank you notes. When I sit down and describe how much I enjoy the gift you so thoughtfully chose for me, it should remind me of what a loving and generous person you are and perhaps also how lucky I am that you think highly enough of me to take the trouble on my behalf. Like reflecting on the moral law, reflecting on beneficence can help elevate our feelings and make us really appreciate just how wonderful people can be. Maybe it will even inspire us to be more beneficent ourselves.

I'll close this chapter with some comments on one of Kant's more interesting points about gratitude, which is that it is something we can still owe to people who are long dead. This may sound a little strange. Are we supposed to write thank you notes to Jonas Salk for his work on developing the polio vaccine? Likely Kant would say that's not a good use of our time, but that doesn't mean that it's not a good thing to be appreciative of Salk once in a while. Some of the most important contributions to our present world have been made by people essentially lost to history, but sometimes we can identify past figures whose efforts still benefit us today. And when we can, Kant thinks we ought to feel properly grateful.

What would this look like in practice if it doesn't involve writing notes? Kant focuses on figures from the past (specifically the ancient past) from whom he takes himself to have learned important things. Even if he ends up disagreeing with those ancient authors, he might not have been able to arrive at his own insights had it not been for their work. They have benefited him in a very important way. He can't exactly repay them in kind, but he can repay them by defending them against "all attacks, accusations, and disdain," as he puts it.[1] Presumably he also means that he should not attack, accuse, and disdain them himself. Crucially, this doesn't mean that he can't criticize them. In fact, Kant warns us not to just assume that everything was better in the past and that it's all been going downhill since the Athenian golden age. But when we do end up criticizing people from whom we have learned, we need to do so with respectful and grateful hearts. Maybe Kant knew that someday we'd be writing about what we'd learned from him.

Part V

Socializing

25 | FRIENDS AND FRENEMIES

Friends. We can't live without them, but it's not always easy to live with them either. Kant's theory is well suited to explaining just what makes friendships so very important to our lives, and also what makes them so very complicated. What makes them important is that friends fulfill a fundamental human need and contribute to our moral development. What makes them complicated is that the participants in a friendship are human, with our associated natural propensities toward self-love and self-conceit. Kant thinks that if we can pull it off, a successful friendship both improves our lives and improves us as individuals. For a friendship to be truly successful, it has to exemplify a mutual commitment to an intimate relationship that is both deeply loving and deeply respectful. We might put Kant's view this way: good friends should love each other without smothering each other.

Kant's remarks on friendship are not very long, but they are full of interesting insights. There are two main discussions of friendship in his writings, one in the *Lectures on Ethics* and one at the very end of the *Metaphysics of Morals*. Despite the obvious importance that Kant places on friendship, his account of it is, sadly, often ignored. When philosophers think about friendship, they tend to reach for Aristotle first, as Aristotle has a lengthy and well-known discussion of it. Kant's ideas about friendship are largely compatible with Aristotle's, but he adds some interesting twists. Like Aristotle, Kant thinks that friendships are one of the greatest goods in human life and that they contribute to our moral development. But Kant also sees the potential for problems in close relationships, particularly when it comes to mutual respect. Friendship comes with risks, and while Kant thinks friendship is worth those risks, we need to be attentive to the forces that threaten friendships, as well as those that sustain them.

Kant divides friendship into three categories, as Aristotle does. There are friendships based on mutual need, friendships based on taste or pleasure, and friendships based on disposition or character. We'll focus on the third form of friendship because that's where we find what Kant calls moral friendship. It's not that he thinks the other forms of friendship are bad or that it's a mistake to have them. Rather, it's that friendships that aim at mutual advantage or pleasure aren't able to provide us with the kind of deep connection with other people that gives friendship the moral value that Kant thinks it has. It's only within moral friendships that we can really achieve the goods that friendship can offer. Kant goes so far as to say that we have a duty to cultivate moral friendships. We'll come back to that, but let's first see what Kant thinks such friendships are like and what they do for us.

As he often does, Kant starts by describing a very idealized form of friendship, which he calls perfect friendship. He says it is the "union of two persons through equal mutual love and respect."[1] That does sound perfect, but it is also rather hard to achieve, which is why Kant thinks this is really only an ideal. It is, however, well worth striving for, even if we can't actually pull it off. This is because such a union makes possible certain forms of morally valuable self-disclosure and intellectual exploration that we can't otherwise access. Of course, there's more to friendship than intellectual conversation, but it's this part of friendship that, for Kant, provides it with its special moral role. Moral friendships are friendships that aim at this ideal of perfection, even though they will never quite get there.

As we've seen, Kant thinks that we have duties of love and respect toward everyone, not just our friends. We are supposed to wish everyone well, along with respecting their rationality. These duties do sometimes require positive action from us. If someone is drowning in a river, it's not enough for me to wish him well from my picnic spot on the bank. I have a duty of love (specifically a duty of beneficence) to try to help him. In that sense, my relationship with everyone is a relationship characterized by love. But when Kant talks about love in friendship, he certainly means something beyond jumping in a river to save someone from drowning. In a moral friendship, love for a friend means sharing in that person's ends and caring about their well-being as we care for our own. Crucially, it is a reciprocal form of care: "I, from generosity, look after his happiness and he similarly looks after mine; I do not throw away my happiness, but surrender it to his keeping, and he in turn surrenders it to mine."[2] Reciprocal love of this kind forms part of the ideal of moral friendship.

But Kant is also adamant that friendship requires respect, not just love. Good friendships have boundaries, and good friends respect those boundaries. The boundaries are certainly different between friends than they are between strangers. (Thus, it might be okay to enter my very good friend's unlocked house to borrow a pair of shoes for a crucial job interview. It is obviously not okay to enter a stranger's unlocked house to borrow a pair of shoes, no matter how important the interview.) That does not, however, mean that boundaries don't matter in close friendships. If anything, boundaries in friendships might matter more. Consider that we often feel more betrayed by a breach of confidence by a friend than by a stranger, or more hurt by a cutting remark made by a friend than a similar one made by a stranger. We have higher expectations from our friends when it comes to things like respecting our privacy and being considerate of our feelings. We place our trust in them that they will care for our well-being and not disregard it for a few Instagram likes.

In fact, trust is very much at the center of a good Kantian friendship. It is absolutely essential for our ability to achieve what Kant takes to be one of the most important goals of friendship, which we might describe as creating a space in which we can be ourselves. Here's how Kant describes our situation:

> The human being is a being meant for society (though he is also an unsociable one), and in cultivating the social state he feels strongly the need to reveal himself to others. But on the other hand, hemmed in and cautioned by fear of the misuse others may make of his disclosing his thoughts, he finds himself constrained to lock up in himself a good part of his judgments. He would like to discuss with someone what he thinks about his associates, the government, religion, and so forth, but he cannot risk it.[3]

This might seem a little paranoid on Kant's part, but his larger point is one we can readily appreciate. We need people whom we can really trust with our deepest, darkest secrets, secure in the knowledge that they won't mock, scorn, or betray us. This is what friends do for us. They fill in that gap by providing us with an intimate, secure context in which to be ourselves. What is so valuable about a good friend is that they are someone with whom we can let down our guard. In a really good friendship, we can reveal our true feelings without fear of being judged and try out new thoughts or ideas with no danger of being called stupid or naïve.

We've seen that Kant thinks that it is through interacting with people, especially in conversation, that we learn more about the world and about ourselves. Friends can help us clarify our thoughts, expand our horizons, and keep us from veering off in the wrong direction when needed. This last part is especially important. He puts it this way: "to have a friend whom we know to be frank and loving, neither false nor spiteful, is to have one who will help us correct our judgment when it is mistaken." This includes our moral mistakes. Kant says that friends have a duty to point out each other's flaws. The duty as he characterizes it is a duty of love. If you care about your friend's well-being, you care about their moral character. You can't magically transform them into a better person, but if you see a friend heading down a path to ruin, you'd certainly want to intervene. Such interventions, when they're coming from friends, are probably more likely to be successful, but for Kant, they're also very much the natural expression of our love for our friends.

But there's a catch, and the catch comes from the respect part. As we probably all know from personal experience, it's not always easy to hear your friend telling you what's wrong with you. Actually, it's often worse than having a stranger tell you what's wrong with you, mostly because it's easier to brush off a stranger's opinion. We care what our friends think, and if my friend thinks I'm rude or uncaring or snobbish, it will impact my self-respect. I'll worry that my friend will find me less worthy of our friendship. Kant recognizes this, which is why he says that the duty to point out our friend's flaws is a duty that we undertake at some risk to the friendship. Friendships can't survive constant fault-finding, particularly when it's not reciprocal. (Not that reciprocal fault-finding is so great either!) This means we have to tread very carefully when we carry out the duty to point out flaws in our friends. Whatever we say or do, it must be done in a way that doesn't threaten the other person's self-respect and doesn't imply that we've lost our respect for them.

Our friendships are fragile, Kant thinks, even when they are built on strong foundations. The fragility comes from human nature. We care deeply about what others think, and we hate it when people don't think highly of us. We also have that nagging tendency to want to think ourselves better than others. This is why, in that initial definition of a perfect friendship, Kant emphasized the equality of the love and respect. Friendships need to be reciprocal if they are to maintain equality.

Friendships are threatened when one person bears more of the burdens of the friendship than others. As we saw in Chapter 23, Kant worries about the imbalance that beneficence creates, even when it's well-meant. If you do me a favor, I am always in your debt. This may not bother you as much as it bothers Kant, but we are all aware of how friendships can become lopsided, whether we're talking about love or respect. If I'm constantly criticizing you, you're eventually going to feel disrespected. If I'm constantly asking you for favors, you're eventually going to feel like I'm taking advantage of you. This doesn't mean that we should be walking around with a mental calculator or an iPhone app that tracks the number of critical remarks or favors that each of us is racking up. But it does mean that we have to attend to the importance of equality in our friendships because without it the union that Kant describes won't really be possible. What threatens that equality of love and respect threatens the relationship.

It's not surprising that friendships are so complicated, given what human beings are like. The fact that Kant clearly thinks they are still so worth pursuing shows how much he values friendship, and also how optimistic he is about the possibility of approximating this kind of friendship in our actual lives. No friendship is ever going to be perfect, but there's a lot we can do to make our existing friendships better. And we have good reason to try to build such friendships.

In fact, Kant thinks we have a duty to pursue moral friendships so far as we can. He's not very clear on what kind of duty it is. Perhaps it's a duty to ourselves because friends promote our moral and intellectual capacities. Perhaps it's a duty to our friends because we can also promote *their* moral and intellectual capacities. Or perhaps it's a different kind of duty, one that's linked to the kind of world Kant believes we should be creating. Kant clearly thinks that there is something beautiful and admirable about moral friendship. These kinds of friendships model for us an ideal of human relationships. The ideal isn't necessarily one that we can put into universal practice. From a practical standpoint, we can't be friends with everyone. We'd also lose a lot of the value of friendship in the process of attempting to extend it too broadly.

Still, moral friendships illuminate what it would be like if all our relationships were characterized by mutual love and respect. That is more or less the world that Kant has in mind when he talks about the kingdom of ends. As you know by now, Kant definitely does not recommend revealing the deepest and darkest parts of our soul to every stranger we meet. But wouldn't it be a marvelous thing to live in a world in which we could actually trust those strangers in the same way we trust our friends, in which we could count on other people to respect and care for us in the way that our friends respect and care for us? In this sense, we might describe Kant's lofty kingdom of ends as a kingdom of friends.

26 | A KANTIAN LOVE LIFE

You may find this hard to believe, but Kant is a bit of a romantic. Actually, you may not find that so hard to believe, based on his account of friendship in the previous chapter. Much of what he says about friendships would apply to romantic relationships as well. But there are going to be some twists. In the classic 1980s movie, *When Harry Met Sally*, one character insists that men and women can't be friends because "the sex part" always gets in the way. Kant, as we'll see, agrees that sex complicates everything.

Not that Kant necessarily has a lot of experience on which to draw. He was a lifelong bachelor, although he did apparently have one or two serious relationships. Likely Kant himself would have regarded his romantic life (or lack thereof) as no one's business but his own, and perhaps you have some sympathy for that view. Still, that does make it a bit strange that he has well-thought-out views about romantic relationships, especially the sexual dimensions of them. Or maybe it's not really that strange, given that he was a human being with the same sexual desires and feelings as any other human being. As is often the case with Kant, some of what he says seems dated, implausible, and perhaps downright repressed, while other parts seem insightful and still useful to us today.

Kant is, like many people of his day, in the grip of a picture of human sexuality that largely follows the particular form of Christianity in which he was raised. It is a fairly negative picture. One can easily get the impression that Kant sees sexual desire as little more than as a dangerous and destabilizing force in our lives, despite its obvious importance for continuing the species. This is partly correct. Kant *does* think that sexual desire brings with it a host of problems. But it's not entirely correct. Kant also paints some rosy visions of romantic relationships, even if they proved not to be his thing. In many ways, he is an idealist about love and marriage. Here, however, we will focus on Kant's insights into the ways in which sexual desire complicates the moral requirement to treat other people as ends in themselves and not merely as objects. Those insights are as relevant now as they were when he wrote them. They provide us with a framework for thinking about the moral complexities of romantic relationships. And so, while Kant may not have known how to use Tinder, it's still possible that he can teach us a few things about romance.

Let's start with the dark side. Kant holds that the only natural purpose of sexual desire is procreation. This leaves a lot of space for sexual desire to go awry on his view. Any employment of sexual desire that is not aimed at procreation is going to raise moral problems for him. Needless to say, he is not exactly a progressive when it comes to anything other than highly traditional heterosexual relationships. But let's set that aside and instead focus on why he thinks sexual desire, in whatever context, raises challenges for the moral requirement to treat others as rational beings who deserve respect in virtue of our rational nature. This point applies to any kind of sexual relationship, regardless of the gender or sexual orientation of the people engaging in it. It's just a claim about human beings acting in very human ways.

In the *Lectures on Ethics*, Kant argues that sexual desire is different from other desires that we have. What makes it different is that it is a desire that is aimed at another person: "Amongst our inclinations there is one which is directed towards other human beings. They themselves, and not their work and services, are its objects of enjoyment."[1] To desire a person is to see them as an object that can potentially fulfill your desire. As Kant sees it, this desire is fundamentally objectifying in ways that other desires related to persons are not. By contrast, when we enjoy a dance performance, our enjoyment of the dancers does not mean that we are seeing them as things that can fulfill our desire to enjoy dance. In admiring dancers, we are admiring their skill and artistry in ways that incorporate their agency. But sexual desire, at least when it takes the form we might now call lust, has nothing to do with rational agency. By itself, it's just a desire for someone's body. Kant finds this troubling because "as soon as a person becomes an object of appetite for another, all motives of moral relationship cease to function, because as an object of appetite for another a person becomes a thing."[2] If Kant is right, then sexual desire always involves treating its target like a "thing" rather than a being with dignity. And that seems like a bit of a problem from a moral standpoint.

Kant definitely sees it as a problem. He also points us in the direction of a solution. Before we talk about his solution, however, it's worth pausing to note that his picture is extremely useful when we are trying to articulate why sexual objectification and degradation are especially awful things to do to other people. Rape and other forms of sexual assault, of course, often involve desires that are not simply sexual desires. Sexual assault is frequently used as an instrument of power, as we see all too often in war zones and prisons. Kant's account of sexual desire can help make sense of that. Employing a person purely as a sexual object is, on Kant's view, an extraordinarily effective way of degrading and dehumanizing them. It reduces them to a mere thing, not a human being with dignity. When dehumanization is the aim, then it is no surprise that sexual objectification would be the method of choice. The effectiveness of sexual assault and domination as a form of objectification is part of what makes it such a heinous assault on the dignity of its target.

Kant's account of the badness of sexual objectification provides a straightforward explanation of why consent is so important in sexual relationships. Consent is a way of expressing one's rational agency. Making sexual activity contingent on consent ensures that the people involved are not treating each other as objects, or as mere means in Kant's language. Consent itself is a complicated and highly charged issue, something that Kant's theory can both acknowledge and accommodate. It's not always easy to tell when we're using someone as a mere means. Manipulating someone into sex might technically count as consensual, at least in the legal sense, but it would certainly not meet the test for treating them respectfully. Remember that anytime we aim to bypass, control, or thwart a person's reasoning, we're treating them as a mere means. Clearly there are lots of areas in relationships where this kind of subversion of rationality can occur, but sexual contexts will, for Kant, always be particularly risky ones because of the ever-present danger of objectification.

I've been focusing on what I've called the dark side of sexual relationships because Kant's humanity formulation is helpful in articulating the ways in which such relationships can go badly wrong. The bright side is that Kant does not think that sexual relationships are inevitably doomed. There is more to a relationship than sexual desire. We do, however, have to ask ourselves what counts as a mutually respectful sexual relationship. In asking this question, we are asking not just about what it takes not to treat a sexual partner as a mere means. That is of course central to Kant's humanity formulation, but remember that there is a second part to it as well. To fully respect another person as an end, we must see them as a setter of ends. This is to see them as an end in the positive sense. So, when we ask what counts as a mutually respectful sexual relationship, we are asking about what it means to respect one's partner as an end in both senses.

Kant has his own answer to this. He thinks that sexual relationships can only meet this standard in the context of marriage. His reasons for this reflect both a certain kind of idealism and also a hard-headed realism. The realism comes from his recognition that women in his society had very few rights against men outside of marriage. (Mind you, he does not criticize this fact about his society. He largely takes women's subordinated status as a given.) The idealism comes from his vision of marriage as a form of reciprocal self-giving. What he says about this in the *Metaphysics of Morals* is a bit confusing: "the one who is acquired acquires the other in turn; for in this way each reclaims itself and restores its personality."[3] The idea, presumably, is in marriage, one acquires rights not just to the other person's body, but to their whole person. But this is reciprocal; each spouse acquires the same rights over the other. So, there's some sense in which you get yourself back when you give your whole self away.

This is the more romantic picture. The less romantic picture is that marriage contracts essentially force spouses to treat each other as ends by requiring them to be responsible for the other's good. In Kant's time, this meant that in practice, a woman acquired rights over her husband that she would not have had over a lover. This means that marriage would have been especially protective for women. Of course, Kant didn't consider the fact that sexual objectification is possible within marriage as well as outside of it. He did, however, take seriously the importance of ensuring that sexual partners treat each other as ends, and not merely as objects of sexual fulfillment. And this, presumably, matters as much as ever.

Regardless of what you think about Kant's ideas about marriage, it certainly does make sense to ask what conditions must be in place for sexual relationships to be fully respectful. Much of this will depend on an individual's view of how sexual relationships fit into a larger picture of a good life. For instance, people disagree on whether one-night stands are fully respectful, and the terms on which they would be so. But there are also areas where we might see fairly widespread agreement about the conditions necessary for respect, such as clear communication and full transparency about one's commitments and plans. It's one thing for both people to agree to a casual fling. It's something else if one person is viewing the relationship as a casual fling while the other is hoping it will turn into something more serious.

As we've already learned, Kant sees trust as essential to respectful human relationships. Many people see betrayals of trust as especially harmful and hurtful when they involve sexual betrayals. Here again, we can use Kant's views about objectification and sexual desire to explain why sexual betrayals tend to cut as deeply as they do. Kant's view is that there is always greater danger of being treated as an object in a sexual relationship than in other kinds of relationships. If so, then it's reasonable to feel especially "used" by one's partner if it turns out that they have been cheating with a neighbor or engaging in some other form of sexual betrayal.

Kant is hardly a romance columnist, and that's probably just as well. His views about sexual relationships are somewhat overly idealistic and certainly narrow-minded. Yet his theory provides us with surprisingly useful ways of talking about what can go wrong in sexual relationships, as well as what is needed to make them go better. His idea that sexual relationships should involve mutual respect between the partners, with strict prohibitions against treating each other as a mere means and a compelling moral obligation to take seriously each other's ends? That idea is surely as important now as it was in Kant's day.

27 | GOOD MANNERS

Kant may not have been all that well suited to dispensing romantic advice, but he might have had a decent career as an etiquette advisor. This is, for many people, yet another unexpected side of Kant. He thinks we have a moral duty to cultivate good manners, or social graces as he calls them. These days, very few people associate a person's manners with their moral character. We also probably all know people who have great social skills but who are complete jerks underneath. In fact, such people can be especially aggravating because other people are often fooled by their good manners. *Seeming* like a good person is very different from *being* a good person.

Kant would not deny this. But he also believes that seeming like a good person is more important than we might think. We've already seen that Kant believes we have good reason to keep our flaws under wraps so as to help us all maintain our attitudes of love and respect for humanity. In Kant's mind, the social graces serve the same function. They create an environment in which we act like better versions of ourselves. This environment, which Kant calls a "beautiful illusion resembling virtue," is essential to our ability to cultivate actual virtue.[1] In other words, seeming like a good person actually helps make me a better person.

It's worth noting that Kant sometimes appears to be of two minds about the moral effects of social life. We've discussed the ways in which bad social environments, like ones characterized by contempt and ridicule, can make us worse. Our natural propensity to self-conceit can become an entrenched way of thinking when we're surrounded by people who normalize and reinforce the attitude that some of us are superior to others. Kant does not think that our established social practices are always good for us. In this respect, his view is similar to that of his Swiss contemporary, Jean-Jacques Rousseau. Rousseau took the view that human beings would be much better off without social conventions, which serve only to corrupt and warp our fundamentally good natures. As we know, Kant is not convinced that human nature is all that good, and certainly not as good as Rousseau portrays it. But he would agree with the idea that social conventions and practices can corrupt us further and make us worse. Where Kant parts from company from Rousseau is in his apparent confidence that *good* social conventions and practices can have the opposite effect. The right social conventions can instill in us good habits and also help us imagine what it would be like if we actually lived in a kingdom of ends.

One thing that Kant does not explicitly mention, but which seems true, is that good manners are a crucial way in which we express respect and concern for others. We know we all have Kantian duties of respect and love. Many of our duties of respect are fulfilled by what we don't do to others. We don't lie to them, steal from them, manipulate them, and so forth. But it would be a mistake to think that this is the only way in which our respect or lack of respect for others gets expressed in our interactions with them.

The arrogant person, after all, violates duties of respect toward others by treating them like his inferiors. That tends to manifest itself in behaviors like demanding immediate service when others are waiting, diminishing the accomplishments of others in conversation, and so forth. We'd be likely to call these behaviors rude, but rudeness and disrespectfulness in Kant's sense are not really that far apart. In fact, sometimes they amount to the same thing.

Consider the category of actions that are usually referred to as microaggressions. An awful lot of sexism, racism, and ableism occurs in these seemingly small encounters—repeatedly mispronouncing someone's name, interrupting them in meetings, talking to their companions rather than to them. Sometimes these behaviors are deliberate, sometimes they aren't. And if they just happened once in a while, they might not be a big deal. Unfortunately, they happen quite frequently to many people. Over the course of a day or a lifetime, those little digs really add up. Insofar as microaggressions affect a person's ability to feel like a full member of the moral community, with the same dignity as anyone else, they pose a major problem for respect.

As we've seen, Kant thinks that how we present ourselves in public makes a big difference to the overall social climate. This can work both ways, but presumably he wants us to develop social habits and manners that improve the moral environment in which we operate. That would seem to involve manners that reflect the respect and consideration that people actually deserve. We owe it to other individuals not to treat them rudely or perpetuate microaggressions against them. We also owe it to the moral community more generally to create an environment conducive to moral progress. This suggests that if good manners make our social world morally better, then we need to get working on our social skills.

Now Kant is fully aware that the good manners we display in public do not always reflect reality. There's a sense in which good manners merely create an illusion. When we behave politely, we are very often simply acting a part. In the *Anthropology*, he says:

> On the whole, the more civilized human beings are, the more they are actors. They adopt the illusion of affection, of respect for others, of modesty, and of unselfishness without deceiving anyone at all, because it is understood that nothing is meant sincerely by this.[2]

It would definitely be a bad thing if good manners were deceptive because we know that Kant thinks that deception is a major moral problem. He does seem to have a lot of confidence in our ability to see through each other's portrayals of affection and respect, in the sense that we don't interpret them as sincere. Perhaps he has too much confidence. Humans may be better actors than he gives us credit for being.

But let's just grant for the moment that he's right that we can all see through this illusion. We're aware that what we're creating is mostly a network of surface appearances. Why should we think that it's morally important to create such surface appearances? Kant goes on to tell us:

> And it is also very good that this happens in the world. For when human beings play these roles, eventually the virtues, whose illusion they have merely affected for a considerable

length of time, will gradually really be aroused and merge into the disposition.[3]

The idea here seems to be that if we act as though we have the attitudes we're expressing in our polite behavior, we'll eventually come to have those attitudes for real. (Just to make sure we get the point, Kant repeats it twice a few paragraphs later in that section of the *Anthropology*, comparing social graces to pocket change that can be traded for the real gold of virtue.)

Kant's claim is that developing habits of treating people respectfully and considerately, even when we're not sincere, makes us more likely to develop actual attitudes of respect and love. We know how important Kant thinks those attitudes are. Recall that he says that when we do nice things for people, we come to like those people better. It's a positive feedback loop of sorts. I have duties of love toward people regardless of whether I like them. But fulfilling those duties of love makes me like them more, and when I like them more, it becomes easier to fulfill my duties of love toward them. It's just plain easier to help people when we like them, which is why we should try to like them to the extent we can manage. The duties are duties regardless, but the more our helping actions flow from the attitude of love, the more Kant thinks they approximate the ideal of human relationships. Kant seems to think something similar will happen when we behave politely toward people. We will come to like them better and eventually the appearance we are putting on will reflect an internal reality.

It is, of course, worth asking whether Kant is right that putting on the appearance of loving and respecting people will actually make us love and respect them more. Although "fake it till you make it" has a nice ring, that doesn't make it true. Does faking respect for people by being polite to them really make it more likely that you will come to respect them? There's always the possibility that it will make us cynical instead, treating good manners as nothing more than an act that gets us social rewards. Besides, even if good manners do have a positive effect on my character, it might come at a cost. There's moral value to sincerity and frankness, after all, and if good manners get in the way of those goals, it may not be worth it.

Suppose that I feel social pressure to be respectful to my political opponent, whom I despise, while we're debating. I bite my tongue when I feel like hurling insults, I try to wipe the contemptuous expression off my face, and I shake hands at the conclusion of our exchange. Let's also suppose that I still feel contempt and I still want to insult him, but that I manage to behave politely anyway. Let's also suppose, as Kant does, that neither my opponent nor the debate audience is deceived by my act. They know, or at least can guess, my true feelings.

Some people would just say that I'm being inauthentic or insincere, and that by hiding my real attitudes, I'm doing everyone a disservice, including myself. (This may be especially the case if my opponent is someone who deserves the contempt I'm feeling. But Kant doesn't say whether we have to be polite to truly vicious people, so let's assume that my rival is not a menace to society.) Certainly, Rousseau would argue on behalf of sincerity in such situations. What would be the point of faking it, beyond improving my own self-control?

The key to understanding Kant's position on this is to recognize that we're not entirely faking it. There's a sense in which my debate performance is an act, but there's another sense in which it is not, at least not if I endorse the ideals of interaction that I'm pretending to uphold. I'm playing a part, but the part I'm playing is myself, only better. In other words, I'm acting like the kind of person that on Kant's view, I have reason to want to be.

Let me make this a little more concrete. We often find ourselves in situations where we know how we should behave, but we have trouble actually getting ourselves to behave that way sincerely. Suppose that I'm having a rough day and my friend calls me with news about her major promotion at work. I should be happy for my friend, but at this particular moment, it's pretty hard for me to muster any kind of happy feelings. So, I fake it instead. I say all the happy, excited things without actually feeling the happy excitement that I'm conveying through my words.

In this situation, there's a sense in which I'm not being sincere, but also a sense in which I am. I might genuinely be happy for her even if I'm not feeling happy right this very second. Maybe I wish that I could let go of my own problems enough to feel happy right now. It might even be a flaw in me that I can't look past my problems long enough to feel some genuine enthusiasm for her. In acting more excited than I feel, however, I'm able to live up to my own beliefs and attitudes, at least on the surface. The better version of me would be feeling happy for her. Alas, that better version of me is out of my reach at the moment. All I can do is pretend to be that better self. But this kind of pretending isn't like pretending to be what I'm not so that I can sell you a car or get you to do what I want. I'm pretending to be the self that I think I should be. I am putting on the appearance of a morally better self.

It's this kind of pretending, or acting, that Kant thinks is morally valuable. Pretense of this form is what helps me in my efforts to become that better version of myself, the kind who can be genuinely happy for my friend. In the *Doctrine of Virtue*, Kant says that "affability, sociability, courtesy, hospitality, and gentleness (in disagreeing without quarreling) are indeed only tokens, yet they promote the feeling for virtue itself by a striving to bring this illusion as near as possible to the truth."[4] The value of the social graces lies in their ability to create an illusion of virtue, one that resembles a world in which we actually have the virtues that we are pretending to have.

Kant calls this illusion beautiful. It is an illusion that appeals to our aesthetic sensibilities, as well as our moral ones. Kant thinks that we would rationally will to live in a world where the courtesy, hospitality, and gentleness are not merely affectations, but reality. Creating this world through our social behavior helps us imagine what such a world would be like. And through living in that illusory world, we can envision a social world that is *really* like that, where the appearance of virtue is not simply an appearance and where respectful treatment of each other is not simply for show. Kant thinks that this is the world we should be aiming to have. In fact, as we'll see in Chapter 29, it's essential that we believe in the possibility of such a world. By creating this collective illusion of virtue, we give ourselves hope that it might someday come to reflect reality.

28 | DINNER PARTIES WITHOUT DRAMA

To many people, Kant does not seem like the kind of guy who would have had any opinions about how to host a good party. In fact, he may not seem like the kind of guy who even *went* to parties. But by now you know that there's far more to Kant than meets the eye and that he had things to say about a wide range of topics. Including, as it turns out, dinner parties.

No doubt you've been to a bad party or two. It's not always easy to know what makes the difference between a good party and a bad one, although sometimes it's pretty clear when you're in the middle of a bad one. If someone gets injured, or if the food is inedible, or if a fistfight breaks out, it's probably a bad party. (It's also probably time to leave.) Sometimes a party goes wrong because a guest has had a bit too much to drink and is starting to get obnoxious, or because the host is engaged in passive-aggressive behavior toward their partner, or because someone's ex has unexpectedly shown up and there's a lot of tension in the air, or because the partygoers are splitting themselves into cliques. There are a lot of ways for a fun party to turn ugly. How do we make sure our parties stay on the right side of the line?

Kant's opinions about dinner parties are driven by his underlying interest in the moral contours of social life. As we saw in the last chapter, he takes good manners quite seriously because they help us envision and enact a world in which people actually treat each other with respect and consideration. He also takes social events like dinner parties seriously. For Kant, dinner parties have moral aims—two, in particular. The first is the aim of cultivating our understanding, which is part of our duty of self-improvement. The conversation at a good dinner party will expand our horizons and make us feel as though we've learned something new, or at least thought about something differently. It keeps our brains active and livens up our thinking. (Kant makes a point of saying how dangerous it is to the life of the mind for people to eat alone.) The second is the aim of cultivating fellow-feeling among other members of our community. At a good dinner party, we'll make new friends and deepen the relationships we already have with people. We'll leave feeling good about other people and maybe even more hopeful about the world.[1]

This may seem like a tall order, but Kant thinks that we can pull off this kind of party by paying close attention to the details, including the food, the conversation, the number of guests, and the after-dinner entertainment. Done right, all these elements of a party combine to create an environment in which the two aims can be realized. So, let's see what Kant thinks should be on our checklist when we're hosting friends for dinner.

We'll start with the question of how many people to invite. Following tradition, Kant says that the number of guests should be more than the Graces and fewer than the Muses. (That's four to eight for those of us not deeply immersed in Greek mythology.) Why that number? Kant thinks we need enough people around the table to keep things lively and interesting, but not so many that the party breaks into a bunch of smaller conversations. If you've ever been at a dinner where people run out of things to say, or where the people on either side of you start talking to others and leave you in the lurch, you might be able to see his point. A dinner party, as Kant sees it, is a unified event, involving everyone in the same activity. This doesn't necessarily mean that he has anything against big cocktail parties or cozy romantic dinners. It's just that he's describing a very specific kind of gathering, one in which everyone participates together. (He does, however, speak disparagingly of banquets.)

So now that you have your four to eight guests assembled, you obviously have to feed them. Kant lived in a world with cooks and servants, with the result that he doesn't pay much attention to the work that goes into providing and serving the actual dinner. But he does care about the ways in which food and drink affect the behavior of the guests, in both positive and negative ways. Remember that Kant thinks the state of our bodies has a big effect on the operations of our minds. He certainly thinks dinner parties should involve good food and he takes for granted that there will be wine. But hosts and guests alike should be mindful of the physical effects of food and wine, whether we're talking about too little of it or too much of it. Hungry people are often cranky; drunk people are often obnoxious. At a good party, people will feel satisfied, but not so full that they can't move from their chair. They will have had enough wine to loosen up a bit, but not so much that they start to misbehave. It's all a matter of striking the right balance and of course, inviting the right people.

Now that we have the menu sorted out, what about the conversation? Here Kant becomes really specific. In a multi-course dinner (again, easier if you have servants!), the conversation should go through three stages. It begins with narration, or a reporting of the news of the day. It then moves to amiable argument before concluding with a round of jesting. Why this particular structure? In part, it's tied to the physical states of the guests. At the beginning of a meal, there's some risk that people will be cranky from hunger. In Kant's day (though alas, not in ours), reporting on the news you'd read and heard was a low-key, uncontroversial activity, one that could be managed even by "hangry" people. But once the food starts coming out and everyone is in a better state of mind, the group can move on to what Kant calls the reasoning stage. He's not imagining that everyone will start doing logic puzzles over the roast beef, but he does think that at this stage, guests should be throwing out ideas and batting those ideas around with each other. Crucially, though, it's not a total free-for-all. We still have to tread carefully lest people get bored or angry. This means that the topics should be ones that interest everyone and about which everyone might have an opinion. They should also be ones that won't lead to fistfights or duels in the alleyway.

Kant thinks that for the dinner party conversation to go well, we have to be attentive to conversational flow. We should aim to avoid those dreaded long silences, and we should try not to jump around from topic to topic. Remember, the goal is for everyone to leave the party feeling like we've learned something, and disjointed conversations aren't really conducive to that. We should avoid becoming dogmatic or irritated, and we should do our best to redirect anyone who is falling into that trap. (Kant suggests using humor to turn the conversation away from dangerous terrain.) Although he does think that it matters what topics we choose to discuss, the tone of the conversation matters more. We're supposed to enjoy dinner parties, and while a good-natured argument can be fun, it's more important to make sure things don't go off the rails.

As the meal draws to a close, we should be leaving our arguments behind and turning to jesting. There are multiple Kantian reasons for thinking this is a good idea. For one thing, all that spirited argument is exhausting and we likely need a break. Also, guests might have been drinking lots of wine along the way, making it more difficult to sustain a serious but good-natured rational conversation. Less plausibly, Kant also suggests that jesting pleases the ladies in company and that it aids in the digestion of the meal. (The latter may seem a little weird, but there were definitely weirder medical practices around at the time. At least laughing is harmless.)

Because we're supposed to leave the party with warm fuzzy feelings about our fellow guests, Kant is adamant that dinner not be followed by any sort of competitive games. This may seem a bit harsh for people accustomed to rousing games of Scrabble or Pictionary after Thanksgiving turkey, but as usual, Kant has his reasons. Competitive games, he thinks, stir up our emotions and, moreover, they do so in the service of our self-interest. The dinner conversation is a joint endeavor, one in which we all have the same aim that we're working to achieve. But competitive games put us at odds with our fellow guests. At least some of us are going to be in it to win, especially if money or pride is at stake. Given what Kant thinks about our natural propensities (especially when much wine has been drunk), he just doesn't think this going to go well. So, no games. No music either, although that's because he sees it as an unnecessary distraction from conversation, not because it will make us hate each other.

There's one more element of a Kantian dinner party that contributes to its moral value, and that has to do with the kind of social compact we form around a table. We know that Kant thinks that trust is the foundation of moral community. As he sees it, sharing a meal with someone creates special obligations of discretion and loyalty. He reminds his readers of the widespread view across history and cultures that it's bad form to kill the people you invite to dinner, or the people who have issued the invitation. Offering or accepting hospitality implies mutual agreement not to engage in violence, at least not until after dessert. When we gather around a table with others, we are taking on certain associated obligations. For Kant, the most important of these (apart from the obligation not to kill your fellow guests) is the obligation to keep the confidence of everyone present. He thinks that for a dinner party to achieve its moral aims, we have to be able to feel free to express ourselves without fear of retribution or exposure. That can happen only if there is a general rule that people do not gossip about (or instantly post on social media) the absurd, foolish, or idiotic thing that their fellow guest said. In other words, what happens at the dinner table stays at the dinner table.

Hosting a Kant-approved dinner party may seem like a lot of work, and perhaps not how you want to spend your free time. Plus, Kant wasn't trying to orchestrate a perfect party conversation while also grilling steaks, putting together appetizers, and keeping dogs and toddlers from getting into those steaks and appetizers. But that doesn't mean that we can't take some of Kant's lessons and apply them to our own gatherings. Consider Thanksgiving again. We probably already know that bad things will happen if we bring up politics with Uncle Fred, or if we pull out the Scrabble board when Cousin Marcia is around. We also know that people aren't at their best when they're hungry or drunk. And when we have people over for dinner, we probably want our guests to leave our houses happy and relaxed, after an energizing and entertaining evening. We can make this happen with delivery pizza and cheap beer, so long as everyone does their part to keep things fun. The only knives that should be out at a Kantian dinner party are the ones used for cutting your food.

Part VI

Looking Forward

29 | STAYING HOPEFUL

As you've now come to realize, Kant thinks that becoming a better person is a lot of hard work. Cultivating a good will is a long process, and it encompasses a lot of different areas of our lives. Does that mean we can expect it to pay off in the end? Alas, Kant's answer is "no," at least not if what you mean by a payoff is that you will be happier and more successful at achieving your goals. A good will is not a golden ticket to the Land of Happiness. Plenty of really good people have terrible things happen to them. And plenty of very bad people manage to do quite well for themselves. You might very well be wondering, "What's the point, then?"

Kant wonders that too. He also wonders what would happen if we came to believe that there's no point to trying to become better, that the whole enterprise of moral improvement is doomed to fail from the start. We've seen in previous chapters that Kant issues warnings about the dangers of misanthropy and cynicism. These are dangers he takes seriously. Because he lived during politically tumultuous times, it's possible that he saw the negative effects of conflict and distrust in the world around him and was responding to his own experiences. No doubt if you look around your own social circle, you too will see people succumbing to disillusionment or maybe even despair. This can manifest itself in the form of a negative attitude toward pretty much everyone and everything. Cynicism sometimes even disguises itself as keen insight into the pathetic state of the world and the people who are running it. Indeed, cynics often see the more hopeful or optimistic people around them as naïve or foolish. If they knew the world better, they would see how wrong they are.

Kant does not believe that the hopeful people are wrong. In fact, it's the cynics who are wrong. This is not because the world is actually better than the cynics think it is. It's because the cynics reject the possibility of moral progress, and Kant thinks that believing in the possibility of moral progress, both in ourselves and in our communities, is the rational thing to do. We have reason to be hopeful about humanity, even when things look grim. In this chapter, we'll explore why Kant thinks this is true and what that would mean for how we live.

In his *Critique of Practical Reason*, Kant claims that there are three great questions in philosophy: "What can I know? What must I do? For what may I hope?" (Kant's answers are roughly: "not as much as I might want," "many things I won't like," and "quite a lot.") In this book, we've mostly been talking about the second question, but the third question is actually linked to the second one. This is because Kant thinks that a commitment to morality requires hope for it to make sense. It requires hope because we need morality to have a point if we're going to build our lives around it, and hope is what gives it a point.

To understand why morality itself requires hope, we have to return to Kant's basic ethical framework. You probably remember that Kant thinks that there are two obligatory ends: our own improvement and the happiness of others. If your memory is really good, you may recall that I said in Chapter 9 that the first of those two ends is actually a duty to perfect ourselves. I am required to have my own moral and natural perfection as my end. Here's why that matters. Kant thinks that we can set things as ends and have duties to pursue them only if they are possible. We cannot will what it is impossible. How can I will my moral perfection, as it's obvious that I will not manage perfect virtue in my lifetime? Kant recognizes the problem here. His solution is to argue that we are rationally required to hope in the possibility of immortality, as moral perfection cannot be accomplished in a finite lifetime. We can only have moral perfection as our end if it's a real possibility. And it's a real possibility only if we are immortal. This means that it's rational to hope for immortality.

There's more. Kant believes that rationality requires believing in the possibility of what he calls the highest good, or if you prefer Latin, the *summum bonum*. The highest good, he says, is perfect virtue combined with perfect happiness. After all, virtue without happiness is not as good as virtue with happiness (or virtue crowned with happiness, as Kant likes to say.) Kant argues it is a rational necessity for us to believe that the highest good is a real possibility, that virtue will be crowned with happiness. We need to believe this to be able to commit ourselves to morality. Alas, we are not capable of bringing about the highest good ourselves. All we are capable of doing is making ourselves worthy of happiness. The only one who can bring it about that moral worth is rewarded with happiness is God. We thus have reason to hope that God exists. Actually, Kant says something a bit stronger. This hope is rationally required of us. We *must* hope in the existence of God as well as our own immortality.

The idea that we *have* to hope for anything at all, much less something as significant as God's existence or our own immortality, may seem strange. Kant's argument has generated a lot of discussion, some enthusiastic and some skeptical. It's also part of the reason why it is so hard to pin Kant down as a theist, atheist, agnostic, or none of the above. Is hoping that God exists, as Kant presumably does, sufficient to make him a believer? Maybe not in the usual sense. But Kant's conception of hope is not merely wishful thinking, as happens when, say, we're hoping that it won't rain on the day we plan to go to the beach. Kantian hope is more of a practical orientation toward a goal or an end that we are unable to bring about, but that we have compelling reason to want to become real.

If we are to believe in the possibility of the highest good, we must have some kind of practical faith in God's existence because only God can bring it about. We can have this practical faith even if, as Kant thinks is the case, we have—and can have—no compelling theoretical arguments for God's existence. Hope in the existence of God and the possibility of immortality is necessary for committing ourselves to morality. And because we're rationally required to commit ourselves to morality, we're rationally required to be hopeful about God's existence and everything that it entails.

Let's set aside the question of the Kantian case for God's existence, which could take up an entire book of its own. Instead, let's turn to what contemporary Kantian philosopher Allen Wood calls "this-worldly" hopes, in contrast to the "other-worldly" hopes in God and immortality. Although Kant does focus on other-worldly hopes, he also thinks we can have reasonable this-worldly hopes. Kantian hopes for this world are focused on the possibility of moral progress. For Kant, this means progress for ourselves as individuals, and also progress for political and moral communities.

Martin Luther King Jr. famously said that the arc of the moral universe is long, but that it bends toward justice. We are (however slowly!) making progress. King's claim can be understood as an expression of his faith, both his religious faith and his faith in his fellow human beings. Kant's view on moral progress is rather like King's. Despite plenty of evidence to the contrary, we have reason to hope that the arc of the moral universe is bending toward justice. We have reason to believe that the crooked timber of humanity can get straighter over time. Indeed, we must see things that way if we are to make sense of our aspirations for moral progress, aspirations that Kant thinks that we can't help but have. Even if the world around us seems grim, as it so often does, we are, in effect, rationally required to be optimists.

This view is downright countercultural in many respects. It may also seem hopelessly naïve to modern readers who look around at a rapidly warming world, endless conflict and war, countless refugees, people stuck in seemingly intractable poverty, and the widespread inability of the international community to cooperate to solve even the most basic problems. But Kant was not naïve. He is not suggesting that we ignore the world's problems or treat them as merely illusory. They're real, all right. Climate change is not going to fix itself. What he's hopeful about is the possibility for human beings to get our act together and do something about it. Indeed, if we don't believe in this possibility, it won't happen. Moral progress will take place if we choose it, but only if we choose it. The silver lining, for Kant, is that we're capable of choosing it. But we have to constantly remind ourselves of this fact.

Recall from our discussion of contempt that Kant thinks we must continue to regard everyone, even the most heinous criminals, as capable of moral reform. No human being is a lost cause. Every single one of us is able to know and choose what's right. We couldn't have a duty to cultivate a good will if it weren't possible. This view about our potential is central to Kant's thinking about hope. Even when it seems very unlikely that a heinous criminal will change their ways, we can still hope that it will happen. This doesn't mean that we have to hand over our car keys to a known thief. We can, however, set our expectations high. Perhaps most importantly, we can work to build a community in which it's more likely that we'll each be able to live up to our moral potential.

There's a lot of research out there on the value of optimism, particularly when it comes to achieving goals. It stands to reason that if you don't think you can do something, you won't be motivated to try. In some cases, merely believing that something is possible seems to have a positive effect on the likelihood of our actually achieving it. Kant appears to have something like this in mind when it comes to moral progress. Believing in the possibility of moral progress is a self-fulfilling prophecy of sorts. If we want to see moral improvement in ourselves and our communities, we have to believe we can pull it off. And when we do believe that we can pull it off, it's far more likely to happen.

How do we go about making ourselves believe in the possibility of moral progress? After all, things don't look so great, either out there in the world or in our own hearts. Human nature, as we know, is not exactly our ally when it comes to doing what we should, and history may not seem encouraging. But Kant holds fast to the idea that it always comes down to our choices. Although radical evil is a constant threat, he also believes that we each have a predisposition to the good in us. We are free to choose whether it's good or evil that becomes the principle of our will. And just as importantly, regardless of what principles we have acted on in the past, we can choose differently for the future. Radical evil need not be a permanent affliction. No one is fated to be a supervillain.

In his essay, *On the Common Saying: That May Be Correct in Theory But It Is of No Use in Practice* (yet another catchy title!), Kant suggests that our belief in that predisposition toward the good, and the possibility of people following it, is what makes it rational to love humanity and work toward its fullest development:

> Are there in human nature predispositions from which one can gather that the [human] race will progress toward what is better and that the evil of present and past times will disappear in the good of future times? For in that case we could still love the race, at least in its constant approach to the good; otherwise, we should have to hate or despise it.[1]

We can interpret Kant as saying that the only way we can love humanity enough to fulfill our duties to each other and to the moral community is if we believe in the possibility of progress. Because the love is required of us, so is the belief.

It helps to keep in mind that the alternative, where we stop seeing each other as worthy of love and respect, seems like a pretty awful one. Cynicism about other people is a short step away from despair about humanity and its future. In Fyodor Dostoevsky's epic novel, *The Brothers Karamazov*, it is this kind of despair that leads Ivan Karamazov to contemplate suicide as the only way to escape the horrific moral ugliness he sees around him. In the novel, the sole remedy for this despair is love. This is why another character, Father Zossima, describes hell as the terrible state of being unable to love.

Kant doesn't put it in quite those terms, but it's clear that he thinks maintaining our capacity for love is crucial to staving off the hatred of humanity that constantly threatens us. When we focus only on the terrible things that human beings have done, it becomes hard not to despise them. It is only by seeing people as capable of moral progress that we are able to love them. And in taking up the attitude of love toward people, we express the view that they are *worth* loving and that humanity is *worth* preserving and sustaining, which is what Ivan Karamazov doubts. Each of us is capable of choosing the good and so of being more than our worst selves.

Now, of course there is an important difference between believing that human beings *can* choose the good and being optimistic that human beings *will* choose the good. But as we've seen in our discussions of various vices, Kant thinks that we can set ourselves up for success (or at least a greater likelihood of success) if we create communities that discourage vice and encourage virtue. Indeed, it's not really possible for us to bring about the highest moral good by ourselves. A community in which people are both moving toward perfect virtue and toward earthly happiness is something that we can only build together. Kant puts it this way in the *Religion*:

> This highest moral good will not be brought about solely through the striving of one individual person for his own

moral perfection but requires rather a union of such persons
into a whole toward that very end, [i.e.] toward a system of
well-disposed human beings in which, and through the unity
of which alone, the highest good can come to pass.[2]

A society of "well-disposed human beings" is exactly what we are
supposed to be trying to bring about. It is a kingdom of ends, insofar as that is possible for a community of flawed and frail human
beings. Kant sees our task as one of making our actual world as
much like this ideal world as we possibly can.

Kant's ideal vision for community extends to political communities. In an essay called *Toward Perpetual Peace*, Kant sets out his
vision for a kind of international federation of states, living peace-
fully together. Because Kant lived during a period of considerable
political turmoil in Europe, it's not surprising that he would be
so concerned with the conditions under which peace could be
achieved. Nor is he naïve about the challenges of achieving perpetual peace. But at the end of the essay he says of perpetual peace
that it is "no empty idea but a task that, gradually solved, comes
steadily closer to its goal."[3] Striving for peace is, after all, the only
way to achieve it. And even though we're unlikely to succeed in
achieving it (people and nations being what they are), our efforts
will bring it closer to the goal. In that sense, whatever progress we
make will count as a success. This is why, as Kant sees it, it is a duty
for nations to work toward peace.

Likewise, we have a duty to work toward a better form of ethical community than we see around us. Our hope that the world
will improve can't simply be an idle one, or a mere wish. We have
to put in effort to make it happen. In a very modern spirit, Kant

recommends that we start by building local communities. He has church communities in mind, but other forms of community would also serve the purpose, so long as they are places where we can work with others to bring about both virtue and happiness to the extent that it is within our power. As with perpetual peace, we're unlikely to reach the goal. But the striving for it will necessarily bring us closer than we were before.

Many of us have the hope that we will leave the world a better place than we found it. This kind of hope has a natural home in Kant's ethical framework. It's a long-term vision that asks us to look beyond our particular interests and needs and toward the bigger human picture. Kant thinks that this vision is just as important as our individual moral progress. Maybe even more important, because our individual moral progress isn't possible without it. To sustain this kind of hope, we have to believe that humanity is worth the trouble.

Michael, everyone's favorite reformed *Good Place* demon, explains the grounds for hope this way, "What matters isn't if people are good or bad. What matters is if they're trying to be better than they were yesterday. You asked me where my hope comes from? That's my answer.[4]" That's more or less Kant's take on hope as well. The rationality of hope stems from the rationality of believing that each of us can choose to be better than we were yesterday. In making this choice, we'll be moving ourselves and our communities closer to the Good Place.

30 | KANT AS A GUIDE TO LIFE

I have not always been so keen on Kant. In fact, when I started studying his works, I was pretty skeptical about his ethical system. Like many other people, I found it abstract, hard to understand, and not very compelling. What happened was that through many years of studying Kant's works, teaching those works to undergraduate and graduate students, writing about his ideas, and trying to put them into practice, I've come to see that there's a lot of value in a Kantian way of life. That value is what I've tried to share with you in this book.

Given Kant's fame, it's hard to argue that he is unappreciated. But he is very often misunderstood. My aim in writing this book was to lessen some of those misunderstandings, in part by approaching him through ideas and texts that are not as widely known as his famous and perhaps off-putting *Groundwork*. Kant, like all of us, was trying (and sometimes failing) to be a good person in the face of a lot of challenges. For all his fancy language, his ideas are easy enough to understand and share. Some of them, I hope, have resonated with you, although I'm sure some of them have not. But as you know by now, Kant wouldn't approve of your adopting his way of life just because he's a famous moral philosopher. Your moral voice has to be your own.

One of the things I most admire about Kant is the fact that while he takes a pretty despondent view about the state of humanity, he also has really high hopes for us. Although he's ready to acknowledge that the world is a mess in many ways (as are the people who populate it), he reminds us that it doesn't have to be that way and that we can be optimistic about the future. Things can get better. *We* can get better. There's hope for us, despite what we read in the news or observe around us. This isn't to say that we can just sit back and let things happen. Nothing will get better without quite a lot of elbow grease. And it's possible that we won't see all our hard work pay off in our lifetimes. Improving ourselves and our community is a long process. Kant doesn't promise us that it will be easy. But he does think it's the path to true freedom.

Kant is buried in Konigsberg (now Kalingrad, Russia), not far from where he was born. His tombstone is inscribed with this quote from his masterpiece, the *Critique of Pure Reason*:

> Two things fill the mind with ever new and increasing admiration and awe, the more often and steadily we reflect upon them: the starry heavens above me and the moral law within me.

Our rational capacity is what enables us to choose what's right, no matter how strong the temptations to do otherwise. In choosing what's right, we choose freedom. We also demonstrate to ourselves and the world just why each of us is worthy of admiration and awe. A Kantian life is a challenging one, but it has at its core a fundamental hopefulness about humanity and our future. It's a theory that may seem overly optimistic in dark times like these. But for Kant, dark times are when we most need a dash of optimism. Hope in humanity is always rational and sometimes absolutely necessary.

NOTES

CHAPTER I

1. It is also not exactly the same. For Kant, mathematical truths and moral truths are both known through reason, but the way we come to know them is different. That difference, while very important to Kant, is not very important for our purposes, so we'll leave it to the side.

CHAPTER 3

1. *Anthropology, History, and Education*, p. 113.
2. *Practical Philosophy*, p. 199.
3. *Practical Philosophy*, p. 199.
4. *Anthropology, History, and Education*, p. 111.
5. *Practical Philosophy*, pp. 533–534.
6. *Religion*, pp. 53–54.

CHAPTER 5

1. *Groundwork*, p. 222.

CHAPTER 6

1. *Groundwork*, p. 230.
2. *Lectures on Ethics*, p. 118.
3. *Groundwork*, p. 231.

CHAPTER 7

1. *Groundwork*, p. 239.
2. *Religion*, p. 105.
3. *Religion*, p. 106.

CHAPTER 8

1. *Practical Philosophy*, p. 569.
2. *Lectures on Ethics*, p. 199.
3. *Practical Philosophy*, p. 569.

CHAPTER 9

1. This example is loosely based on the classic movie, *High Noon*, which is so good that if you've never seen it, you should stop reading this book and go watch it right now.
2. Some scholars think that Kant's theory rules out only moral dilemmas that we didn't cause, meaning that it's possible for us to paint ourselves into a moral corner in which all our options are bad ones.

CHAPTER 10

1. *Practical Philosophy*, p. 562.
2. *Practical Philosophy*, p. 567.

CHAPTER 11

1. *Lectures on Ethics*, p. 128.
2. *Lectures on Ethics*, p. 215. This particular translation refers to the child as John, although other translations refer to him as Fritz. I like Fritz better, but feel free to call him John if you prefer.

CHAPTER 12

1. *Practical Philosophy*, p. 582.

CHAPTER 13

1. Having briefly worked as an executive secretary, I can personally attest to the fact that it's an intellectually demanding job.
2. *Practical Philosophy*, p. 558

CHAPTER 14

1. I first heard this expression from a New Zealand native. I gather it's common in both New Zealand and Australia although alas, not in the United States.

CHAPTER 15

1. *Practical Philosophy*, p. 580.

CHAPTER 16

1. Just to be clear, my husband doesn't have a brother. But if he did, I'm sure I'd like him.
2. *Practical Philosophy*, p. 582.
3. *Practical Philosophy*, p. 582.
4. *Practical Philosophy*, p. 582.
5. *Practical Philosophy*, p. 582.

CHAPTER 17

1. *Practical Philosophy*, p. 583.
2. *Practical Philosophy*, p. 583.

CHAPTER 18

1. *Lectures on Ethics*, p. 224.

CHAPTER 19

1. If you're wondering what kind of parties Kant attended and just how much food was consumed at them, you're not alone.
2. *Lectures on Ethics*, p. 123.
3. *Practical Philosophy*, p. 551.

CHAPTER 20

1. *Practical Philosophy*, p. 566.

CHAPTER 21

1. *Lectures on Ethics*, p. 173.
2. *Lectures on Ethics*, p. 145.
3. *Lectures on Ethics*, p. 145.
4. *Lectures on Ethics*, p. 172.
5. *Lectures on Ethics*, p. 172.
6. *Lectures on Ethics*, p. 158.
7. *Practical Philosophy*, p. 597.
8. *Lectures on Ethics*, pp. 145–146.

CHAPTER 22

1. *Lectures on Ethics*, p. 225.

CHAPTER 24

1. *Practical Philosophy*, p. 574.

CHAPTER 25

1. *Practical Philosophy*, p. 584.
2. *Lectures on Ethics*, p. 203.
3. *Practical Philosophy*, p. 586.

CHAPTER 26

1. *Lectures on Ethics*, p. 163.
2. *Lectures on Ethics*, p. 163.
3. *Practical Philosophy*, p. 427.

CHAPTER 27

1. *Practical Philosophy*, p. 588.
2. *Anthropology, History, and Education*, p. 263.
3. *Anthropology, History, and Education*, p. 263.
4. *Practical Philosophy*, 588.

CHAPTER 28

1. This aspect of a Kantian dinner party is really well exemplified in the film, *Babette's Feast*, based on the novel by Isak Dineson.

CHAPTER 29

1. *Practical Philosophy*, p. 307.
2. *Religion*, p. 109.
3. *Practical Philosophy*, p. 351.
4. For fans of *The Good Place*, he says this during Season 4, Episode 6, "A Chip Driver Mystery" (October 31, 2019).

BIBLIOGRAPHY

This book has sought to give you what we might call the flavor of Kant's ethical thought. It will probably not surprise you to know that there are controversies about how best to interpret his difficult texts and what shape a Kantian ethical theory might have. Perhaps you've now become interested enough in Kant to want to keep reading more. Where should you start?

You can't go wrong by reading Kant's own work, although you might consider brewing some strong coffee in advance. (Remember, Kant would probably approve of using caffeine to enhance your cognitive skills!) It's not easy going, but it's well worth the trouble. Of Kant's main ethical works, the *Lectures on Ethics* is the most accessible, followed by the *Metaphysics of Morals* and then the *Groundwork*. The *Anthropology* is also useful, and sometimes even entertaining. (That's where you'll find his discussion of dinner parties.) Listed below you'll find the translations that I've used in this book.

As you might expect, there are also countless books and articles about Kant and his ethical thought. I've included some of my favorites below. Here you'll find work by the contemporary Kantian ethicists mentioned in this book, along with additional suggestions. And of course, you'll be fulfilling a Kantian duty of self-improvement while you're reading!

WORKS BY KANT

Kant wrote a lot of things—books, essays, letters, reviews of other works. He also gave a lot of lectures, notes from which were often published under his name. This makes it a little difficult to cite him in a way that makes sense to people new to his work. In this book, I've chosen to forgo the usual scholarly way of citing him (known as the Prussian Academy citation method) in favor of something a bit more straightforward. Below you'll find specific translations and compilations of Kant's main ethical works. The page numbers that follow the Kant quotations in this book correspond to page numbers in the books below.

Kant, Immanuel. *Groundwork for the Metaphysics of Morals*. Translated by Arnulf Zweig and edited by Thomas E. Hill, Jr. Oxford: Oxford University Press, 2002. This volume contains an extremely helpful introduction, argument analysis, and set of notes on Kant's most famous text.

Kant, Immanuel. *Practical Philosophy*. Translated and edited by Mary Gregor. Cambridge: Cambridge University Press, 1996. This volume contains the following works:

   Groundwork of the Metaphysics of Morals

   Critique of Practical Reason

   On the Common Saying: That May Be Correct in Theory, But It Is of No Use in Practice

   Toward Perpetual Peace

   The Metaphysics of Morals

   On a Supposed Right to Lie from Philanthrophy

Kant, Immanuel. *Anthropology, History, and Education*. Edited by Gunter Zoller and Robert Louden. Cambridge: Cambridge University Press, 2007. This volume contains the following works:

   Idea for a Universal History with a Cosmopolitan Aim. Trans. Allen Wood.

   Anthropology from a Pragmatic Point of View. Trans. Robert Louden.

Kant, Immanuel. *Religion within the Boundaries of Mere Reason*. Edited by Allen Wood and George DiGiovanni. Cambridge: Cambridge University Press, 1998.

Kant, Immanuel. *Lectures on Ethics*. Translated by Louis Infield. Indianapolis: Hackett Publishing, 1963.

WORKS ABOUT KANT

Stanford Encyclopedia of Philosophy (online and free!)

   "Immanuel Kant" by Michael Rohlf

   "Kant's Moral Philosophy" by Robert Johnson and Adam Cureton

   "Kant's Social and Political Philosophy" by Frederick Rauscher

Anderson-Gold, Sharon. Unnecessary *Evil: History and Moral Progress in the Philosophy of Immanuel Kant*. Albany: SUNY Press, 2000.

Allais, Lucy. "Kant's Racism." *Philosophical Papers* 45, no. 1–2 (2016): 1–36.

Baron, Marcia. *Kantian Ethics (almost) without Apology*. Ithaca: Cornell University Press, 1995.

Baxley, Anne Margaret. *Kant's Theory of Virtue: The Value of Autocracy*. Cambridge: Cambridge University Press, 2010.

Biss, Mavis, "Avoiding Vice and Pursuing Virtue: Kant on Perfect Duties and 'Prudential Latitude'." *Pacific Philosophical Quarterly* 98, no. 4 (December 2017): 618–635.

Bell, Macalester. *Hard Feelings: The Moral Psychology of Contempt*. Oxford: Oxford University Press, 2013.

Callanan, John, and Lucy Allais. *Kant on Animals*. Oxford: Oxford University Press, 2020.

Cohen, Alix. "The Ultimate Kantian Experience: Kant on Dinner Parties." *History of Philosophy Quarterly* 25, no. 4 (October 2008): 315–336.

Cureton, Adam. "Reasonable Hope in Kant's Ethics." *Kantian Review* 23, no. 2 (June 2018): 181–203.

Darwall, Stephen. "Two Kinds of Respect." *Ethics* 88, no. 1 (October 1977): 36–49.

Dean, Richard. "Humanity as an Idea, as an Ideal, and as an End in Itself." *Kantian Review* 18, no. 2 (July 2013): 171–195.

Denis, Lara. *Moral Self-Regard*. New York: Garland Publishing, 2001.

Ebels-Duggan, Kyla. "Moral Community: Escaping the Ethical State of Nature." *Philosophers' Imprint* 9, no. 8 (August 2009): 1–19.

Frierson, Patrick. *Kant's Empirical Psychology*. Cambridge: Cambridge University Press, 2014.

Grenberg, Jeanine. *Kant and the Ethics of Humility*. Cambridge: Cambridge University Press, 2010.

Herman, Barbara. *The Practice of Moral Judgment*. Cambridge: Harvard University Press, 1993.

Hill, Thomas. *Autonomy and Self-Respect*. Cambridge: Cambridge University Press, 1991.

Hill, Thomas. *Virtue, Rules, and Justice: Kantian Aspirations*. Oxford: Oxford University Press, 2012.

Holtman, Sarah. "Kantian Justice and Poverty Relief." *Kant-Studien* 95, no. 1 (2004): 86–106.

Johnson, Robert. *Self-Improvement: An Essay in Kantian Ethics*. Oxford: Oxford University Press, 2011.

Kerstein, Samuel. *How to Treat Persons*. Oxford: Oxford University Press, 2013.

Kleingeld, Pauline. "Kant's Second Thoughts on Race." *Philosophical Quarterly* 57 (2007): 573–592.

Korsgaard, Christine. *Creating the Kingdom of Ends*. Cambridge: Cambridge University Press, 1996.

Korsgaard, Christine. *Fellow Creatures: Our Obligations to the Other Animals*. Oxford: Oxford University Press, 2018.

Langton, Rae. "Duty and Desolation." *Philosophy* 67, no. 262 (1992): 481–505.

Lu-Adler, Huaping. "Kant on Lazy Savagery, Racialized." *Journal of the History of Philosophy* (forthcoming).

Martin, Adrienne. "Love, Incorporated." *Ethical Theory and Moral Practice* 18, no. 4 (August 2015): 691–702.

Moran, Kate. *Community and Moral Progress in Kant's Moral Philosophy*. Washington DC: Catholic University Press, 2012.

Papish, Laura. *Kant on Evil, Self-Deception, and Moral Reform*. New York: Oxford University Press, 2018.

Preston-Roedder, Ryan. "Faith in Humanity." *Philosophy and Phenomenological Research* 87, no. 3 (2013): 664–687.

Rawls, John. *A Theory of Justice*. Cambridge: Harvard University Press, 1971.

Schapiro, Tamar. "What is a Child?" *Ethics* 109 (July 1999): 715–738.

Stohr, Karen. "Keeping the Shutters Closed: The Moral Value of Reserve." *Philosophers' Imprint* 14, no. 23 (July 2014): 1–25.

Stohr, Karen. "Kantian Beneficence and the Problem of Obligatory Aid." *Journal of Moral Philosophy* 8, no. 1 (Jan 2011): 45–67.

Thomason, Krista. "Shame and Contempt in Kant's Moral Theory" *Kantian Review* 18, no. 2 (2013): 221–240.

Varden, Helga. "Kant and Women." *Pacific Philosophical Quarterly* 98, no. 4 (2017): 653–694.

Varden, Helga. "Kant on Sex. Reconsidered—A Kantian Account of Sexuality: Sexual Love, Sexual Identity, and Sexual Orientation." *Feminist Philosophy Quarterly* 4, no. 1 (2018): 1–33.

Velleman, David. "Love as a Moral Emotion." *Ethics* 109, no. 2 (January 1999): 338–374.

Veltman, Andrea. "Aristotle and Kant on Self-Disclosure in Friendship." *Journal of Value Inquiry* 38 (2004): 225–239.

Wood, Allen. *Kant's Ethical Thought*. Cambridge: Cambridge University Press, 1999.

Wood, Allen. *Kantian Ethics*. Cambridge: Cambridge University Press, 2008.

INDEX

For the benefit of digital users, indexed terms that span two pages (e.g., 52–53) may, on occasion, appear on only one of those pages.